Kathryn Howarth is a barrister at Temple Garden Chambers. She practices in international law, including international criminal law, public law, including public inquiries and extradition. Over the last two decades her work in the field of international criminal law has taken her to The Hague, as well as countries including Sierra Leone, Tanzania and Bosnia-Herzegovina. Her expertise in international criminal law and extradition is consistently recognised in the Legal 500.

Kathryn's most notable cases include the case against Charles Taylor, the former President of Liberia, in relation to which Kathryn was prosecuting counsel during the trial and appellate proceedings before the Special Court for Sierra Leone, sitting in The Hague. She appeared in cases before the United Kingdom Supreme Court (*R v TRA* [2019] UKSC) (concerning Agnes Taylor) and Court of Appeal (*R v KL* [2014] EWCA 1729) (concerning Kumar Lama), examining torture as an international crime. Kathryn also acts in extradition proceedings involving requests in relation to international crimes and advises Government departments and NGOs in relation to potential prosecutions of international crimes in the United Kingdom.

A Practical Guide to International Crimes in Proceedings Before the Courts of England and Wales

A Practical Guide to International Crimes in Proceedings Before the Courts of England and Wales

Kathryn Howarth

Barrister, Lincoln's Inn

MA (Hons)(Cantab) LLM (Toronto)

Law Brief Publishing

Published 2023 by Law Brief Publishing, an imprint of Law Brief Publishing Ltd
30 The Parks
Minehead
Somerset
TA24 8BT

www.lawbriefpublishing.com

Paperback: 978-1-914608-34-6

To Dan, Axel and Raife

FOREWORD

By Karim A. A. Khan KC,
Chief Prosecutor of the International Criminal Court

In our work to ensure accountability for international crimes, it is essential that we adopt a holistic approach, with effective and connected actions taken across the national and international levels. Our common efforts towards justice must also view and define success in a collective sense. Progress in domestic courts form a crucial, indeed foundational, basis for the realization of the goals of the Rome Statute.

'A Practical Guide to International Crimes in Proceedings before the Courts of England and Wales' presents an overview of the developments and initiatives taken domestically in the United Kingdom to the furtherance of this shared endeavour: meeting the legitimate expectations of victims and survivors. With the adoption of the International Criminal Court Act 2001 in England & Wales and the corresponding legislation in Scotland, the United Kingdom took an active step in the fight against impunity, taking its place in the international accountability landscape. Codifying war crimes, crimes against humanity, and genocide into domestic law enables domestic authorities to investigate and prosecute any ICC crimes committed in the United Kingdom or overseas by a United Kingdom national, a United Kingdom resident or a person subject to the United Kingdom Service jurisdiction.

While to date no prosecution has taken place under the Act, there have been a number of cases resulting in the prosecution of individuals for international crimes at the Central Criminal Court. These include cases under the War Crimes Act 1991, which is concerned with individuals who committed war crimes under the Nazi regime, and under section 134 of the Criminal Justice Act 1991, which implements certain United Kingdom obligations under the United Nations Convention against Torture and Other Cruel, Inhuman or Degrading Treatment or

Punishment. These prosecutions have led to some internationally significant case law – take for example *R. v Reeves Taylor Agnes* [2018] EWCA 2843 in relation to the Convention against Torture in the United Kingdom Supreme Court.

'A Practical Guide to International Crimes in Proceedings before the Courts of England and Wales' is the first significant work to set out and examine the domestic legislation which allows for the prosecution of international crimes in the courts of England and Wales, focusing on torture, war crimes, crimes against humanity and genocide. By providing an overview of the jurisdiction of English and Welsh courts with regard to these crimes, the author guides the reader on a journey that bridges case law from the ICC, the *ad hoc* international criminal tribunals, and domestic case law from the courts of England and Wales.

This publication challenges the reader to appreciate the UK's legal ecosystem holistically by pulling together the relevant UK domestic case law in relation to international crimes – together with criminal, extradition and immigration law cases – and traversing the Supreme Court, Court of Appeal, Administrative Court, Upper Tier Immigration and Asylum Chamber, and the Crown Court.

This book is a practical guide that I am confident will be hugely valuable to a range of individuals and organizations with an interest in contributing to the referral, investigation, or prosecution of cases involving the commission of international crimes in the United Kingdom. Taking a dual approach, the author highlights guidelines and provides practical suggestions with regard to what information or material to provide when referring cases to the domestic authorities. At the same time this work will be a useful resource to those involved in investigating, prosecuting, defending and adjudicating international crimes in the courts of England and Wales, enabling the reader to navigate both the substantive law as well as the practical issues which are likely to arise in these cases.

Drawing on the author's practical experience, this publication is timely given the renewed focus on international crimes in national jurisdictions.

As Prosecutor of the International Criminal Court and a criminal law practitioner, the lessons that can be drawn from the UK's experience and practice to date will be helpful indeed. To this end, this new publication is to be commended and its author thanked.

Karim A. A. Khan KC
January 2023

PREFACE

As far as I am aware, this is the first publication to set out in one place the relevant legislation, practice and procedure in relation to international crimes under the law of England and Wales.

I decided to write this book following my involvement in two cases at the Central Criminal Court, which concerned allegations of torture under section 134 of the Criminal Justice Act 1988. First, the case against Kumar Lama, a Colonel in the Nepalese army, who the prosecution alleged tortured two civilians at the Gorusinghe army barracks during the civil war in Nepal in 2005. Secondly, the case against Agnes Taylor, a member of the National Patriotic Front of Liberia, whom the prosecution alleged was responsible for the torture of civilians at the beginning of the first Liberian civil war in 1991. Agnes Taylor had been married to Charles Taylor, the former rebel leader, turned President of Liberia, whose prosecution, coincidentally, I had been involved with in The Hague several years earlier. During the years that spanned these cases, I had conducted training sessions and delivered lectures to various audiences in relation to the jurisdiction of the courts of England and Wales to try international crimes – genocide, crimes against humanity, war crimes and torture. These sessions and lectures focussed in particular on the International Criminal Court Act 2001, which incorporated genocide, crimes against humanity and war crimes, as set out in the Rome Statute of the International Criminal Court, into the domestic law of England of Wales, and gave rise to the possibility of persons responsible for these crimes being tried in this jurisdiction.

Despite the advent of the International Criminal Court Act 2001, there are yet to be any prosecutions in the Crown Court under this legislation. There have been just three cases under section 134 of the Criminal Justice Act 1988. In this regard, the United Kingdom is lagging far behind its European neighbours, such as France and Germany, where there have been many more prosecutions of international crimes in domestic courts, arising from conflicts in various countries across the globe. This book does not seek to explore why this is the case. However, it is hoped that future cases in this jurisdiction may be assisted, and perhaps even encouraged by this publication, by bringing together the relevant substantive law, practice and procedure.

This book also aims to draw on some of the learning from the cases heard thus far in the courts in this jurisdiction. This includes the cases of Faryadi Sarwar Zardad, who was an Afghan war law convicted of torture at the Central Criminal Court, as well as the case of Anthony Sawoniuk, who was convicted, also at the Central Criminal Court, of war crimes arising from the Nazi regime, under the War Crimes Act 1991. It is important to acknowledge that cases involving international crimes are difficult. To see this, one need only to consider the history of the proceedings at the international criminal tribunals, including the International Criminal Court, which took some time before conducting its first trial and which registered both acquittals and convictions amongst its initial cases. The most recent international criminal law cases heard in this jurisdiction bear testament to the difficulties that are involved. Both the cases of Kumar Lama and Agnes Taylor resulted in litigation before the appellate courts in relation to jurisdictional issues and although the prosecution succeeded before the appellate courts, neither case ultimately resulted in convictions. No doubt initial cases under the International Criminal Court Act 2001 will likewise give rise to fresh challenges and appellate litigation, as new legal territory is entered for the first time.

This book has been written in a year from January 2022 to January 2023 and the contents of the book are believed to be up to date and accurate as at 14 December 2022. The jurisprudence in relation to international criminal law is, of course, evolving all the time. Indeed, just as I finished drafting the manuscript a judgement was handed down by the Appeals Chamber of the International Criminal Court in the case of Dominic Ongwen, upholding his conviction for war crimes and crimes against humanity. This book does not attempt to document all of the relevant case law from the International Criminal Court and other international criminal courts and tribunals. Such a feat is far beyond the scope of this publication. However, it is hoped that this book will provide a helpful starting point, by pointing the reader towards relevant cases, judgments and decisions, which are available on the websites of the international courts and tribunals. In particular, I have sought to flag up the relevant appeal, trial and pre-trial decisions from the International Criminal Court, which the Crown Court has a duty to take into account under the International Criminal Court Act 2001. Owing to the size of this book, the analysis of these different decisions and judgment varies, but the reader will at least know where to go and look in relation to the different war crimes and crimes against humanity that have been examined by the International Criminal Court to date.

Finally, I would like to thank Tim Kevan and Garry Wright of Law Brief Publishing for publishing this book and for their support and enthusiasm throughout the process. I would like to express my gratitude to Declan O'Callaghan who very kindly read over the draft manuscript in a short window of time before the Christmas holidays and whose advice and support has been invaluable. I would also like to thank all those who offered words of support and encouragement whilst I was writing the book. There are a few too many people to name but your words were really very much appreciated. I would like to thank the clerks at Temple Garden Chambers for their support and understanding, in particular during December 2022 when I hunkered down at home to finish the book. Finally, I would like to thank my family for their unwavering support. Mum and Dad, for always encouraging and never discouraging me from working overseas. My husband and sons, who have seen a little less of me this year than they might, had I not taken on this project.

Kathryn Howarth
January 2023

GLOSSARY

CAH – Crimes Against Humanity

IHL – International Humanitarian Law

ICL – International Criminal Law

IL – International Law

ICCA – International Criminal Court Act 2001

ICCA (Elements of Crimes) Regulations (or "Regulations") – International Criminal Court Act 2001 (Elements of Crimes) Regulations 2001

GCA – Geneva Conventions Act 1957

WCA – War Crimes Act 1991

UNCAT – United Nations Convention against Torture and Other Cruel, Inhuman or Degrading Treatment or Punishment 1984

ICC – International Criminal Court

Rome Statute – Statute of the International Criminal Court

ICJ – International Court of Justice

ICTY – International Criminal Tribunal for the former Yugoslavia

ICTR – International Criminal Tribunal for Rwanda

SCSL – Special Court for Sierra Leone

IMT – Nuremberg International Military Tribunal

Geneva law – law arising from the Geneva Conventions 1949 and Additional Protocols 1977

Hague law – law arising from the Hague Conventions 1899 and 1907

IAC – International Armed Conflict

NIAC – Non-international Armed Conflict

Persons *hors de combat* – A person who has laid down their arms, or is 'out of combat'

ECHR – European Convention on Human Rights

ECtHR – European Court of Human Rights

CPS – Crown Prosecution Service

CTD – Counter Terrorism Division of the CPS

SO15 – Branch of the Metropolitan police which includes the war crimes team

CPIA – Criminal Procedure and Investigations Act 1996

DMD – Disclosure Management Document

DPP – Director of Public Prosecutions

YJCEA – Youth Justice and Criminal Evidence Act 1999

CPR – Criminal Procedure Rules

CONTENTS

CHAPTER ONE

JURISDICTION TO TRY INTERNATIONAL CRIMES

This chapter will consider the jurisdiction of the Crown Court in England and Wales over war crimes, crimes against humanity ("CAH"), genocide and torture. There are four principal pieces of legislation which criminalise these international crimes and which provide a legal basis for a prosecution, namely:

- The Geneva Conventions Act 1957 ("GCA");
- Section 134 of the Criminal Justice Act 1988 ("CJA");
- The War Crimes Act 1991 ("WCA");
- The International Criminal Court Act 2001 ("ICCA"), as amended by the Coroners and Justice Act 2009.

In practice, it is most likely that a prosecution for international crimes before the Crown Court will involve charges under the ICCA, or section 134 CJA. Therefore, this chapter will begin by setting out the jurisdiction to try international crimes under the ICCA, followed by section 134 CJA, then the GCA and finally the WCA. There have been three cases in relation to section 134 CJA.[1] There is yet to be a case before the Crown Court in relation to the ICCA. There have not been any cases before the

1 Prosecutions were brought in relation to: Faryadi Zardad, Kumar Lama and Agnes Taylor. Only the case against Faryadi Zardad (*R. v Faryadi Sarwar Zardad* [2007] EWCA Crim 279) resulted in a conviction.

Crown Court in relation to the GCA.[2] There have been two cases including one conviction under the WCA.[3]

The International Criminal Court Act 2001 ("ICCA")[4]

The ICCA entered into force on 1 September 2001.[5] In summary, the ICCA:

- Sets out the law governing the United Kingdom's interrelationship with the International Criminal Court (the "ICC").[6] This is detailed primarily in Parts 2[7], 3[8] and 4[9] of the ICCA.

- Incorporates the relevant parts of the Rome Statute of the ICC into domestic law, enabling courts in England, Wales and Northern Ireland to prosecute war crimes, CAH and genocide.[10]

---

2 Robert Cryer and Olympia Bekou, *"International Crimes and ICC Cooperation in England and Wales"*, J.I.C.J. 5 (2007) 441-459 at p.442.

3 Anthony Sawoniuk was convicted on 1 April 1999 at the Central Criminal Court (*R v. Sawoniuk* [2000] 2 Cr.App.R 220). Szymon Serafinowicz was found unfit to stand trial at the Central Criminal Court in January 1997.

4 The ICCA can be found at: https://www.legislation.gov.uk/ukpga/2001/17/contents

5 In England, Wales and Northern Ireland. See the International Criminal Court Act 2001 (Commencement Order) 2001: 2001 No.2161 (C.69) and The International Criminal Court Act 2001 (Commencement) (Amendment) Order 2001: 2001 No.2304 (C.77).

6 These parts of the ICCA give effect to the UK's obligations under Article 88 of the Rome Statute to ensure that there are procedures under domestic law to enable cooperation with the ICC in relation to the arrest of suspects and the investigation of crimes under the ICC's jurisdiction.

7 Part 2 is titled *"Arrest and delivery up of persons"*.

8 Part 3 is titled *"Other forms of assistance"*.

9 Part 4 is titled *"Enforcement of sentences and orders"*.

10 The Explanatory Note to the ICCA, para 6, states that one of the principal aims of the ICCA is to incorporate the offences into domestic law *"so that the UK will*

This is addressed in Part 5 of the ICCA titled *"Offences under domestic law"* and Schedule 8 to the ICCA.

- Sets out the jurisdiction of the Crown Court in relation to the prosecution of these crimes that is territorial, personal and temporal jurisdiction, as well as some preconditions to prosecution under the ICCA (also Part 5, ICCA). Notably, the ICCA does not establish universal jurisdiction in relation to these international crimes.

ICCA offences

Section 51 of the ICCA creates the following offences under the domestic law of England and Wales:

- Genocide,
- Crimes against humanity,
- War crimes.

Rather than three offences, the ICCA in fact creates over 90 substantive offences when the different war crimes, acts which constitute CAH and forms of genocide are considered separately.[11] It is worth noting that prior to the ICCA, genocide was already an offence in this jurisdiction under the Genocide Act 1969,[12] although that Act did not provide for extra-territorial jurisdiction.[13] Certain war crimes were also already

always be in a position to investigate and prosecute any ICC crimes committed in this country, or committed overseas by a UK national, a UK resident or a person subject to UK service jurisdiction".

11 This includes five genocide offences, 16 acts which constitute CAH and more than 70 war crimes.

12 See the Genocide Act 1969 (repealed by Schedule 10 ICCA).

13 *Archbold Criminal Pleading, Evidence and Practice* 1999 ed. 19-352 at 1660, which described it as *"doubtful"* that genocide committed by a British subject abroad was an offence under the Act.

offences in the UK prior to the ICCA, under the GCA, which is still in force and is discussed below.

Section 52 of the ICCA explicitly makes conduct ancillary to genocide, CAH and war crimes an offence.[14] Section 55 sets out that ancillary offences refer to:

- Aiding, abetting, counselling or procuring the commission of an offence;
- Inciting a person to commit an offence;
- Attempting or conspiring to commit an offence;
- Assisting an offender or concealing the commission of an offence.[15]

Section 65 of the ICCA also establishes for the first time in domestic law,[16] the criminal liability of military commanders[17] and other superiors[18] for the failure to prevent the commission of the substantive international crimes and ancillary offences by their subordinates.

Section 50 of the ICCA, titled *"Meaning of "genocide", "crimes against humanity" and "war crime""*, explains that the definitions of these crimes under domestic law, are the same as those definitions found in the Rome Statute of the ICC. Article 6 of the Rome Statute, defines genocide,

14 Section 52 ICCA. Note that section 52(3) ICCA explains that that the reference to ancillary conduct is *"to conduct that would constitute an ancillary offence in relation to that act if it were committed in England and Wales"*.

15 The Explanatory Notes to the ICCA explain that section 55 includes the forms of secondary liability in Article 25.3 of the Statute but are defined in terms of the principles of secondary liability under the law of England and Wales.

16 See S. Powles and R. May, *"Command Responsibility – A New Basis of Criminal Liability in English Law?"* [2002] Crim.L.R. 363 at 377.

17 Section 65(2) ICCA.

18 Section 65(3) ICCA.

Article 7 of the Rome Statute defines CAH and Article 8.2 of the Rome Statute, defines war crimes.[19] These provisions are replicated at the end of the ICCA in Schedule 8.[20] Thus, the meaning of genocide, CAH and war crimes as a matter of domestic law is directly lifted from the Rome Statute.

The ICCA states that in *"interpreting and applying"* Articles 6, 7 and 8.2, the courts *"shall take into account"* the ICC Elements of Crimes document[21] and any relevant jurisprudence or decision of the ICC and that *"account may also be taken of any other relevant international jurisprudence"*.[22] Additionally, domestic courts must interpret Articles 6, 7 and 8.2 *"subject to and in accordance with any relevant reservation or declaration made by the United Kingdom when ratifying any treaty or agreement relevant to the interpretation of those articles"*.[23] Otherwise, with two exceptions, the ICCA provides that in determining whether an offence has been committed, the court shall apply the principles of the law of England and Wales; meaning that the ordinary principles of criminal law will apply in relation to causation, participation, ancillary liability and defences.[24]

---

19 Section 50(1) ICCA.

20 Note that Article 8.1 of the Rome Statute, which indicates that the ICC has jurisdiction in respect of war crimes in particular when they are committed as part of a plan or policy or as part of a large-scale commission of crimes, is not incorporated into the ICCA and therefore is not a jurisdictional requirement in relation to an ICCA case.

21 Section 50(2) ICCA. Emphasis added.

22 Section 50(5) ICCA. Emphasis added.

23 Section 50(4) ICCA. For a discussion of the potential implications of this provision see Robert Cryer and Olympia Bekou, *"International Crimes and ICC Cooperation in England and Wales"*, J.I.C.J. 5 (2007) 441-459 at 444-445, noting in particular the reservations or declarations made by the UK alongside the ratification of the 1977 Additional Protocol I to the four Geneva Conventions of 1949 and the UK's statement on ratification of the Rome Statute.

24 Section 56(1) ICCA. The two exceptions are the incorporation of the definition of *"intent"* and *"knowledge"* from Article 30 the Rome Statute, as set out in section 66 ICCA, and the introduction of the concept of command or superior responsibility

Territorial Jurisdiction

The ICCA gives the courts of England and Wales jurisdiction over genocide, CAH and war crimes, committed both inside and outside the UK. For offences committed inside England and Wales the court has jurisdiction over all persons. For offences committed outside the UK jurisdiction is limited. The court only has jurisdiction when these crimes are committed by a: (i) UK national, (ii) a UK resident, or (iii) a person subject to UK service jurisdiction (see below in relation to personal jurisdiction).[25]

Temporal Jurisdiction

In relation to temporal jurisdiction there are two important dates under the ICCA:

- 1 September 2001,
- 1 January 1991.[26]

The ICCA was enacted on 1 September 2001 and it applies to all ICCA offences committed after that date.[27] Section 65A (inserted by the Coroners and Justice Act 2009) subsequently extended jurisdiction back to crimes committed after 1 January 1991 but,[28] there are very important

---

from Article 28 of the Rome Statute, as set out in section 65 ICCA. See also *"Implementation of the International Criminal Court Statute in England and Wales"*, Robert Cryer, I.C.L.Q., 733-747 at 740.

25 Section 51 ICCA and section 52 ICCA with respect to conduct ancillary to genocide, CAH and war crimes.

26 Section 65A ICCA.

27 See footnote 4. This coincides with the jurisdiction of the ICC under the Rome Statute Article 11(1), although note the caveat on temporal jurisdiction contained in Article 11(2).

28 Notably, the date of 1 January 1991 meant that crimes committed during the conflicts in the former Yugoslavia and Rwanda could be caught but the date of 1 January is not without controversy and some commentators have argued that jurisdiction under the ICCA could be extended back further than 1991 – see for

caveats to the 1 January 1991 date, as it does not automatically apply to all ICCA crimes.[29] First, the backdating provisions do not apply to either: (a) CAH, or (b) war crimes within either Article 8.2(b)[30] or (e)[31] committed before 1 September 2001, *"unless, at the time the act constituting the crime was committed the act amounted in the circumstances to a criminal offences under international law"*.[32] Secondly, the backdating provisions do not apply to accessorial liability under section 52 ICCA, *"unless, at the time the person engaged in the conduct, it amounted in the circumstances to a criminal offence under international law"*.[33] Thirdly, the backdating provisions do not automatically apply to command and superior responsibility under section 65 ICCA. Section 65A(8) states that the date of 1 January 1991 *"does not apply to a failure to exercise control"* as a military commander (as described in section 65(2) ICCA), or as a superior (as described in section 65(3) ICCA) *"unless, at the time the*

---

example: Cryer and Mora, *"The Coroners and Justice Act 2009 and International Criminal Law: Backing into the Future?"* (2010) 59 I.C.L.Q, 803 at 805.

29 The rationale for caveating the backdating provisions is to ensure compliance with the general principle against non-retroactivity under the law of England and Wales as well as Article 7 ECHR. See the Explanatory Note to the Coroners and Justice Act at paras. 399- 400. Para. 400 notes that the backdating provisions do not apply *"to genocide and certain categories of war crimes because it is beyond dispute that those offences were fully recognised in international law in 1991"*. However, in relation to the other ICCA offences, it is noted that, *"whilst the vast majority of them were recognised in international law during the relevant period, a small number may have been recognised in a narrower form than that provided for in the 2001 Act and a very small number of offences may not have been sufficiently recognised at all"*.

30 Schedule 8, Article 8(2)(b) refers to *"Other serious violations of the laws and customs applicable in international armed conflict, within the established framework of international law"*.

31 Schedule 8, Article 8(2)(e) refers to *"Other serious violations of the laws and customs applicable in armed conflicts not of an international character, within the established framework of international law"*.

32 Section 65A(2) ICCA.

33 Section 65A(6), which should be read in conjunction with section 65A(3) and 65A(5).

failure occurred, it amounted in the circumstances to a criminal offence under international law".[34]

Thus, where the alleged conduct occurs between 1 January 1991 and 1 September 2001, and where a domestic court is dealing with: (1) CAH, (2) war crimes involving *"other serious violations of the laws and customs of war"*, (3) accessorial liability, or (4) command responsibility, the court will have to examine whether the alleged conduct amounted to a crime under international law at the time it was committed. This will involve domestic courts considering evidence about whether the alleged conduct was a crime contrary to customary international law at the time. In relation to some crimes and conduct, the domestic courts will be able to refer to jurisprudence from international tribunals who have conducted such exercises previously; although such jurisprudence is, of course, not binding. In relation to other crimes and conduct the domestic courts may have to perform this exercise for the first time. Whilst such an exercise is not unfamiliar to our domestic courts, it can be challenging and time-consuming.

Personal Jurisdiction

As noted already above, the ICCA applies to anyone if the crime is committed in England and Wales.[35] Where the crime is committed outside of the UK, the Crown Court has jurisdiction over:

- A UK national,
- A UK resident,

[34] Section 65A(8) read in conjunction with section 65A(7) and section 65A(9) which confirms that command and superior responsibility under section 65, can include responsibility for ancillary offences committed by a subordinate.

[35] Section 52(4)(a) ICCA.

- A person subject to UK service jurisdiction.[36]

The ICCA does not provide for jurisdiction over mere transitory visitors. This is a significant limitation, which notably does not apply to section 134 CJA, or the GCA. In practice, it means that whereas SO15 may commence an investigation into an individual who it is anticipated will come to the UK and who is suspected of torture, or grave breaches of the Geneva Conventions,[37] an investigation will not be undertaken in relation to a potential visitor to the UK who is suspected of genocide, CAH, or war crimes (other than grave breaches). In other words, a suspected genocidaire, or person suspected of CAH or war crimes (other than grave breaches) can travel to the UK without fear of being arrested in relation to their prosecution in the Crown Court for ICCA crimes.[38]

Section 67(1) ICCA sets out the meaning of an *"United Kingdom national"* as follows:

> *(1) In this Part a "United Kingdom national" means an individual who is –*
>
> *(a) A British citizen, a British Dependent Territories citizen, a British National (Overseas) or a British Overseas Citizen,*
>
> *(b) A person who under the British Nationality Act 1981 (c.61) is a British subject, or*

---

[36] Section 52(4)(b) ICCA. Note that there is no jurisdiction over a person subject to UK service jurisdiction in Northern Ireland, where the relevant crimes are committed outside of Northern Ireland (section 58(2)(b)).

[37] CPS War Crimes / Crimes Against Humanity Referral Guidelines, under the sub-heading *"Scoping Exercise"* at para. 2.8. See: https://www.cps.gov.uk/publication/war-crimescrimes-against-humanity-referral-guidelines. The Referral Guidelines were last updated on 30 September 2019. See further chapter 6, *Investigation, Referral and Pre-Trial.*

[38] Of course, if there is an extradition request from a third country with whom the UK has extradition arrangements then such a person would be liable to arrest and extradition proceedings.

(c) A British protected person within the meaning of that Act.

Section 67(2) ICCA provides that a *"United Kingdom resident"* means *"a person who is resident in the United Kingdom"*. An ostensibly simple definition but see section 67A below. Section 67(3) ICCA explains that a *"person subject to UK service jurisdiction"* means *"a person subject to service law, or a civilian subject to service discipline, within the meaning of the Armed Forces Act 2006"*.

Significantly through section 68 ICCA, jurisdiction extends to a person who becomes a UK resident, even though they were not a UK national, UK resident or person subject to UK service jurisdiction, at the time an offence was committed.[39] This jurisdiction includes both the substantive and ancillary offences.[40] The jurisdiction bites once two conditions are fulfilled:

(i) The person is a resident at the time that the proceedings are brought, and

(ii) The acts would have constituted an offence in the UK at the time they were committed.[41]

The definition of a UK *"resident"* was further articulated in the Coroners and Justice Act 2009, which introduced a new section 67A into the ICCA. Section 67A(1) explains that *"UK resident"* includes the following ten different categories of person:

- A person who has indefinite leave to remain;[42]

39 Section 68(1) ICCA.

40 Section 68(3) ICCA.

41 Section 68(2) ICCA.

42 Section 67A(1)(a) ICCA.

- A person who has made an application for indefinite leave to remain (whether or not the application had been determined) and who is in the UK;[43]

- A person who has leave to enter the UK for the purpose of work or study and who is in the UK;[44]

- A person who has made an asylum claim, or a human rights claim, which has been granted;[45]

- A person who has made an asylum claim, or a human rights claim (whether or not the claim has been determined) and who is in the UK;[46]

- A person named as a dependent in an application for indefinite leave to remain, an asylum claim or a human rights claim, where either: (i) the application or claim has been granted, or (ii) the named dependent is in the UK (whether or not the application or claim has been granted);[47]

- A person who is liable for removal or deportation from the UK but who cannot be removed for human rights reasons or practical reasons;[48]

---

43 Section 67A(1)(b) ICCA.

44 Section 67A(1)(c) ICCA.

45 Section 67A(1)(d) ICCA.

46 Section 67A(1)(e) ICCA.

47 Section 67A(1)(f) ICCA.

48 Section 67A(1)(g) ICCA. Regarding human rights reasons see section 6 of the Human Rights Act 1998.

- A person who is in the UK and who has appealed against a deportation order on made on *"conducive to the public good"* grounds;[49]

- An illegal entrant who is liable to removal;[50]

- A person detained in lawful custody.[51]

Additionally, section 67A(2) sets out that in determining whether *"any other individual"* is to be regarded as resident in the UK *"regard is to be had to all relevant circumstances"* including:[52]

- Periods of time during which the person has or intends to be resident in the UK;[53]

- The purpose of the person being in the UK, or the purpose for which they intend to be in the UK;[54]

- The persons family or other connections in the UK;[55]

- Whether the person has a residential property in the UK.[56]

---

49 Section 67A(1)(h) ICCA. See section 5(1) Immigration Act 1971 and section 3(5)(a) in relation to *"deportation conducive to public good"* grounds.

50 Section 67A(1)(i) ICCA, which refers to an illegal entrant within the meaning of section 33(1) of the Immigration Act 1971, or who is liable to removal under section 10 of the Immigration and Asylum Act 1999.

51 Section 67A(1)(j) ICCA.

52 Notably paragraph 402 of the Explanatory Note to the Coroner's and Justice Act states that section 67A provides a *"non-exhaustive list of considerations a court must take into account in determining whether a person is resident in the UK"*.

53 Section 67(A)(2)(a) ICCA.

54 Section 67(A)(2)(b) ICCA.

55 Section 67(A)(2)(c) ICCA.

56 Section 67(A)(2)(d) ICCA.

The ICCA (as amended) defines *"UK resident"* by referring to the detailed provisions of immigration law. Any practitioners dealing with litigation involving a *"UK resident"* will therefore need to be alive to the legislation and authorities applicable in immigration law because the Crown Court will not have jurisdiction unless it can be established that the defendant is a UK resident.

Pre-conditions to Prosecution

ICCA crimes are triable only on indictment[57] and proceedings for ICCA crimes cannot be instituted without the consent of the Attorney General.[58]

Section 134 of the Criminal Justice Act 1988 ("CJA")[59]

Section 134 of the Criminal Justice Act 1988 ("CJA") implements in domestic law certain UK obligations under the United Nations Convention against Torture and Other Cruel, Inhuman or Degrading Treatment or Punishment of 1984 ("UNCAT").[60] This includes the obligation of States Parties to enact legislation to make torture an offence under their domestic criminal law.[61] The UK's obligations under UNCAT mean that where a person alleged to have committed torture is present within the UK, and is not extradited to face a trial elsewhere, the UK is required to submit the case to its authorities for the purpose of

57 Section 53(2) ICCA.

58 Section 53(3) ICCA.

59 The CJA 1988 can be found at: https://www.legislation.gov.uk/ukpga/1988/33/contents

60 United Nations, Convention against Torture and Other Cruel, Inhuman or Degrading Treatment or Punishment, New York, 10 December 1984, (1990) (Cm 1775), 1465 UNTS 85 ("UNCAT"). UNCAT was adopted and opened for signature, ratification and accession by General Assembly resolution 39/46 of 10 December 1984 and entered into force, 26 June 1987, in accordance with article 27(1).

61 See UNCAT, Article 4, regarding the obligation of each state party to make torture an offence under their criminal law.

prosecution.[62] Thus, there is an obligation pursuant to UNCAT to either prosecute or extradite torturers who are present in the UK.[63]

Section 134 makes torture an offence of universal jurisdiction i.e. anyone who commits torture anywhere in the world can be prosecuted for this offence in the Crown Courts of England and Wales.[64] Jurisdiction is limited only temporally, by the requirement that the offence took place after 29 September 1988, which is the date when section 134 entered into force.[65] By virtue of section 135 CJA 1988, prosecutions under section 134 in England and Wales, require the consent of the Attorney General. The consent of the DPP is needed before an arrest warrant can be issued for allegations under section 134.[66] There is no UK nationality or residency requirement (unlike the ICCA). Thus, section 134 CJA can apply to individuals merely visiting the UK. Further, there is no requirement that the torture took place in an armed conflict.[67] This reflects the fact that torture under the CJA has its origins in UNCAT and international human rights law, rather than international humanitarian law. In summary:

- Temporal jurisdiction is from 29 September 1988,
- Territorial jurisdiction is anywhere in the world,

---

62 UNCAT, Article 7(1).

63 This is known as the principle *"aut dedere aut punier"* - see Lord Browne-Wilkinson at pp.200F-H and 201A, in *R. v Bow Street Metropolitan Stipendiary Magistrate, ex parte Pinochet Ugarte* (No.3) [2000] 1 AC 147 ("*Pinochet (No.3))*".

64 This gives effect to the UK's obligations under Article 5 of UNCAT.

65 Section 171(6) CJA 1988 i.e. two months after the CJA 1988 entered into force on 29 July 1988.

66 Magistrates Court Act 1980, section 1, as amended by the Police, Reform and Social Responsibility Act 2011, section 153(1).

67 Although the three cases under section 134 to date did in fact relate to armed conflicts: *Faryadi Zardad* related to the conflict in Afghanistan, *Kumar Lamar* related to the civil war in Nepal and *Agnes Taylor* related to the first Liberian civil war.

- Personal jurisdiction is anyone, there is no residency or citizenship requirement.

R v Kumar Lama

An example of a visitor to the UK being arrested in relation to allegations under section 134 CJA is Kumar Lamar. Kumar Lama was a Colonel in the Nepalese army, who was arrested when visiting relatives in England during a break from duties with the Nepalese army in South Sudan. He was accused of torturing two Nepalese citizens, Janak Raut and Karam Hussein, who had been detained as suspected Maoists at the Gorusinghe Army Barracks in Nepal in 2005.[68] His trial took place at the Central Criminal Court in September 2016. He was acquitted of a charge in relation to Karam Hussein and the prosecution did not seek another trial after the jury were unable to reach a verdict in relation to the charges in respect to Janak Raut.[69]

The Geneva Conventions Act 1957 ("GCA")[70]

The Geneva Conventions Act 1957 ("GCA") creates as a matter of domestic law, an offence of committing a *"grave breach"* of the Geneva Conventions. The Geneva Conventions are the four principal legal documents of international humanitarian law ("IHL"). IHL is part of international law ("IL") and refers to a set of rules which seek to limit the ill effects of armed conflict for humanitarian reasons. IHL is derived from

68 Reports of the appellate proceedings in this case, which outline the allegations made by Janak Raut and Karam Hussein can be found at: *R. v Lama* (Kumar) [2014] EWCA Crim 1729, [2017] Q.B. 1171, [2017] 3 W.L.R. 469.

69 An initial trial had begun in 2015 but had to be aborted owing to problems with interpretation. This is discussed in the final chapter.

70 The GCA 1957 is available at: https://www.legislation.gov.uk/ukpga/Eliz2/5-6/52/contents

international conventions and customary rules of IL. [71] The Geneva Conventions have been signed by almost every nation in the world. [72] They were agreed as a result of an international conference held in Geneva in 1949 in the shadows of the Second World War.[73] Although, the development of the Conventions can be attributed to a process that progressed in stages between 1864 and 1949.[74] In 1977 each of the Geneva Conventions were supplemented by Additional Protocols.[75] The Conventions provide specific rules to safeguard:

- Combatants (members of the armed forces) who are wounded or sick, or shipwrecked,
- Prisoners of war,
- Civilians,
- Medical personnel, military chaplains and civilian support workers of the military.[76]

---

71 For a summary about IHL and the place of the Geneva Conventions in IHL, see for example, the ICRC Advisory Service Note, *"What is International Humanitarian Law?"*, July 2004, at: https://www.icrc.org/en/doc/assets/files/other/what_is_ihl.pdf

72 For a summary of the historical development of the Geneva Conventions see the American Red Cross, *"Summary of the Geneva Conventions of 1949 and Their Additional Protocols"*, April 2011 (https://www.redcross.org/content/dam/redcross/atg/PDF_s/International_Services/International_Humanitarian_Law/IHL_SummaryGenevaConv.pdf).

73 *Ibid.*

74 *Ibid.* See also, *International Law,* Malcolm N. Shaw, ninth ed., Cambridge University Press, p.1031 and 1031-1033 in relation to the development of the Geneva Conventions and Additional Protocols.

75 *Ibid.*

76 See the *War Crimes under the ICCA* chapter under the sub-heading *"The Geneva Conventions of 1949"*, for the full citations in relation to the four Geneva Conventions and their Additional Protocols, as well as further discussion of the same.

The Geneva Conventions will be considered in greater detail in the chapter on *War Crimes under the ICCA.*

The GCA gives effect to the UK's international law obligations under the Geneva Conventions, specifically the obligation to criminalise *"grave breaches"* of the Geneva Conventions under domestic criminal law.[77] *"Grave breaches"* are defined in similar terms in each of the Geneva Conventions.[78] For example, Article 50 of the first Geneva Conventions states:

> *"Grave breaches to which the preceding Article relates shall be those involving any of the following acts, if committed against persons or property protected by the Convention: wilful killing, torture or inhuman treatment, including biological experiments, wilfully causing great suffering or serious injury to body or health, and extensive destruction and appropriation of property, not justified by military necessity and carried out unlawfully and wantonly".*[79]

The grave breach regime only relates to international armed conflict and not to non-international armed conflict. Grave breaches under the 1949 Conventions therefore refer to the following specific war crimes when committed in international armed conflict:

- wilful killing,

---

[77] See for example, Article 49 in relation to the *"Geneva Convention for the Amelioration of the Condition of the Wounded and Sick in Armed Forces in the Field"*, which is set out along with the rest of the text of the Convention in the first schedule to the GCA.

[78] See GCA, section 1A, which indicates that the grave breach provisions are contained in Article 50 to the First Schedule to the GCA, Article 51 to the Second Schedule, Article 130 of the Third Schedule, Article 147 of the Fourth Schedule and in paras. 1-4 of Article 11, or para. 2, 3 or 4 of Article 85 of the first protocol. The schedules to the GCA contain the text of the Geneva Conventions and relevant protocols.

[79] Article 50, *ibid.*

- torture or inhuman treatment, including biological experiments,
- wilfully causing great suffering or serious injury to body or health, and
- extensive destruction, and appropriation of property, not justified by military necessity and carried out unlawfully and wantonly.

Additionally, the grave breaches regime and jurisdiction under the GCA extends to grave breaches of Additional Protocol I and III of the Geneva Conventions.[80] Specifically, those grave breaches listed in paragraphs 1-4 of Article 11 and paragraphs 2, 3 and 4 of Article 85 of Additional Protocol I, as well as the misuse of the distinctive emblems referred to in Article 6 to Additional Protocol III. The list of grave breaches added by these provisions is lengthy, so will not be set out here, but can be found in the schedules to the GCA.[81] Some examples of conduct in international armed conflict which became part of the grave breach regime through Additional Protocol I include: *"practices of apartheid"*[82], *"making the civilian population or individual civilians the object of attack"*,[83] and *"launching an attack against works or installations containing dangerous forces in the knowledge that such attack will cause excessive loss of life, injury to civilians or damage to civilian objects"*.[84]

In relation to temporal jurisdiction, the GCA applies to:

---

80 Geneva Conventions (Amendment) Act 1995, extended the GCA to include grave breaches under Additional Protocol I of the Geneva Conventions and the Geneva Conventions and United Nations Personnel (Protocols) Act 2009, extended the GCA to include grave breaches under Additional Protocol III.

81 GCA, Fifth Schedule Protocol I and Schedule 7 in relation to Protocol III.

82 Article 85(4)(c) Additional Protocol I, Fifth Schedule to the GCA.

83 Article 85(3)(a) Additional Protocol I, Fifth Schedule to the GCA.

84 Article 85(3)(c) Additional Protocol I, Fifth Schedule to the GCA.

- grave breaches of the Geneva Conventions of 1949 from 31 July 1957,[85]
- grave breaches of Additional Protocol I committed from 20 July 1998,[86]
- grave breaches of Additional Protocol III committed from 5 April 2010.[87]

Like section 134 CJA, the GCA is based upon the principle of universal jurisdiction, so can apply to anyone, anywhere. Thus, territorial jurisdiction is both inside and outside of the UK,[88] and personal jurisdiction is *"any person"*;[89] there is no requirement of nationality or residence. As with the other international crimes, proceedings under the GCA cannot be instituted without the consent of the Attorney General.[90] Additionally, the consent of the DPP is needed before an arrest warrant can be issued for allegations under the GCA.[91]

Notably, the ICCA created concurrent jurisdiction in relation to grave breaches of the Geneva Conventions.[92] However, jurisdiction under the

85 The date of entry into force of the GCA. The GCA entered into force on the day it received Royal Assent.

86 The date of entry into force of the Geneva Conventions (Amendment) Act 1995. See the Geneva Conventions (Amendment) Act 1995 (Commencement) Order 1998, S.I. No. 1505 (C.30), section 2.

87 The date of entry into force of the Geneva Conventions and United Nations Personnel (Protocols) Act 2009. See the Geneva Conventions and United Nations Personnel (Protocols) Act 2009 (Commencement No.1) Order 2009, S.I. No. 2892 (C.128), section 2.

88 Section 1(1) GCA 1957.

89 Section 1(1) GCA 1957.

90 Section 1A(3) GCA 1957.

91 Magistrates Court Act 1980, section 1, as amended by the Police, Reform and Social Responsibility Act 2011, section 153(1).

92 Grave breaches are discussed further in relation to the chapter on *War Crimes under the ICCA.*

GCA is more expansive. Temporal jurisdiction under the GCA stretches back to 1957, rather than 1991 under the ICCA. Personal jurisdiction is wider under the GCA because there is no requirement of nationality or residency, unlike the ICCA. Additionally, the GCA also covers grave breaches of Additional Protocols which are not covered by the ICCA.[93] Thus, despite the advent of the ICCA, the GCA may still be utilised in a Crown Court case.

The War Crimes Act 1991 ("WCA")

The War Crimes Act 1991 ("WCA") is a concise piece of legislation which is limited in scope. It is concerned with individuals who committed war crimes under the Nazi regime and who reside in the UK.[94] The WCA entered into force on 9 May 1991. It applies to England, Wales and Northern Ireland.[95] It permits proceedings to be brought for murder, manslaughter or culpable homicide, which violate the laws and customs of war between 1st September 1939 and ending 5th June 1945, in a place which at the time was part of Germany, or under German occupation.[96] Personal jurisdiction is limited to any person who *"was on 8th March 1990, or subsequently became a British citizen, or resident*

93 See the Explanatory Notes to the ICCA at para. 92, which explains that the GCA takes a wider jurisdiction than the ICCA and by virtue of the Geneva Conventions (Amendment) Act 1995 and covers grave breaches of Additional Protocol I of the Geneva Conventions. See also, for example, *"Implementation of the International Criminal Court Statute in England and Wales"*, Robert Cryer, I.C.L.Q., pp.733-747 at p.740, which gives the example of the war crime of launching attacks that cause excessive collateral civilian damage, which has a "*higher threshold for conviction*" under the ICCA than the GCA Additional Protocol I, and noting that a prosecutor may seek to charge this offence under the GCA rather than the ICCA.

94 See the preamble to the WCA.

95 Section 3(5) WCA.

96 Section 1(1) WCA.

in the UK".[97] The consent of the Attorney General is required in order to bring proceedings under the WCA.[98]

The WCA has its genesis in revelations in the 1980s that individuals who had committed war crimes under the Nazi regime were living in the UK. These revelations resulted in an Inquiry, which recommended the enactment of legislation to enable domestic courts to try acts of murder and manslaughter committed as war crimes.[99] The Inquiry looked at hundreds of potential cases. However, only two of those cases ultimately proceeded to trial, resulting in a single conviction against Anthony Sawoniuk.[100] Anthony Sawoniuk, was a senior member of the local police force in Domachevo, Belarus, a town that had been under German occupation. He was convicted of two counts relating to the murders in 1942 of two civilian members of the Jewish population of the town.[101] In practice, there will not be any further prosecutions under the WCA, owing to the limited jurisdiction and given that any potential defendant would now be well into their 90's. Consequently, the consideration of the WCA in this chapter has been kept correspondingly concise.

---

97 Section 1(2) WCA.

98 Section 1(3) WCA.

99 See *"International crimes in the courts of England and Wales"*, Dr. Kate Grady, C.L.R., 2014 693 at p.704, referring to Richardson, *"War Crimes Act 1991"* (1992) 55 M.L.R. 73, at p.75 citing the Report of the War Crimes Inquiry (1989), Cm 744 and noting that the legislation was very controversial at the time. See further, Rosalyn Higgins (Baroness Higgins, GBE, KC), *"Time and the Law: International perspectives on an Old Problem"* (1997) I.C.L.Q.501-520 at p.509, who observes that the WCA 1991 was drafted in *"the narrowest possible terms"*.

100 The other case concerned Szymon Serafinowicz, who was found unfit to stand trial at the Central Criminal Court.

101 See *R. v Sawoniuk (Anthony)* [2002] 2 Cr.App.R. 220 (2000). For further discussion of this case see the final chapter, *The Trial.*

CHAPTER TWO

TORTURE

Torture as an international crime

Torture is an international crime in the *"highest sense"*, which is prohibited as a *"peremptory norm"* or *"jus cogens"* customary rule of international law.[102] A *"peremptory norm"* or *"jus cogens"* is a *"norm that enjoys a higher rank in the international hierarchy"* than treaty law and *"ordinary"* customary international law rules, and cannot be derogated from by states, either through international treaties, or as a result of customary international law rules which do not hold the same status.[103] In *R v. Bow Street Magistrate, Ex p. Pinochet (No.3) [1999] 1. A.C. 147* (hereinafter, *"Pinochet No. 3")* Lord Browne-Wilkinson, quoting from a judgment of the International Criminal Tribunal for the former Yugoslavia ("ICTY") referred to it as *"one of the most fundamental standards of the international community"* and as an *"absolute value from which nobody must deviate"*.[104] Lord Browne-Wilkinson explained that:

> *"The jus cogens nature of the international crime of torture justifies states in taking universal jurisdiction over torture wherever committed. International law provides that offences jus cogens may be punished by any state because the offenders are "common enemies of all mankind*

102 *R v. Bow Street Magistrate, Ex p. Pinochet (No.3) [1999] 1. A.C. 147 (Pinochet (No. 3))*, per Lord Browne-Wilkinson at p.198B and p.198G; Lord Hope at p.247C-G; Lord Hutton at p.261B; Lord Saville at p.266B; and Lord Millet at pp.272H-275E, 276E. See also, *R v RTA* [2018] EWCA 2843, paras. 14-22.

103 Lord Browne-Wilkinson at p.198A-F.

104 Lord Browne-Wilkinson at p.198A-F, referring to the ICTY Trial Judgment in *Prosecutor v. Furundžija* (IT-95-17/1-T 10), 10 December 1998.

> *and all nations have an equal interest in their apprehension and prosecution"".*[105]

The Convention against Torture and Other Cruel, Inhuman or Degrading Treatment or Punishment ("UNCAT")

The Convention against Torture and Other Cruel, Inhuman or Degrading Treatment or Punishment ("UNCAT") was adopted on 10 December 1984 by resolution 39/46 of the United Nations General Assembly and it entered into force on 26 June 1987. UNCAT is widely ratified by states across the globe and there are currently 173 state parties to the Convention.[106] It is important to note that UNCAT did not create, but rather recognised the pre-existing international crime of torture.[107] The purpose of the Convention was to provide an international system to punish persons guilty of torture and to ensure that torturers could find *"no safe haven"* by escaping the consequences of their actions by going to another country.[108] Thus, the Convention requires all state parties to make *"all"* acts of torture within their own territory a criminal offence under their domestic law,[109] as well as acts of torture where the alleged offender is a national of their state and in certain circumstances when the victim is a national of their state.[110] Further, UNCAT requires a state party to take jurisdiction over any alleged

---

105 Lord Browne-Wilkinson at p.198F.

106 See: https://indicators.ochr.org for the status of ratification.

107 *Pinochet* (No. 3), Lord Browne-Wilkinson at p.199C. See also Lord Lloyd-Jones *R v RTA* [2019] UKSC 51 para. 27.

108 *Pinochet* (No. 3), Lord Browne-Wilkinson at p.199C-D, referring to Burgers and Danelius, *Handbook on the Convention against Torture and Other Cruel, Inhuman or Degrading Treatment or Punishment* (1998), p.131 (Burgers was the chairman of the UN Working Group on the 1984 Torture Convention and Danelius, the draftsman of its first draft). See also Lord Goff at p.212B. See also Lord Lloyd-Jones *R v RTA* [2019] UKSC 51 para. 27.

109 UNCAT, Article 2(1).

110 UNCAT, Article 5(1).

torturer who is found within its territory.[111] Thus, there is an obligation pursuant to UNCAT to either prosecute or extradite torturers who are present in the territory of a state party.[112] As explained by Lord Lloyd-Jones in *R v RTA* [2019] UKSC 51:

> *"the object of UNCAT has been to make torture [...] a criminal offence of universal jurisdiction enforceable by domestic courts and, by virtue of very extensive State participation in the Convention, to establish a machinery capable of reducing the likelihood of perpetrators of "official torture" escaping justice before national courts".*

Article 1(1) of the Convention *"defines torture as the intentional infliction of severe pain and of suffering with a view to achieving a wide range of purposes "when such pain or suffering is inflicted by or at the instigation of or with the consent or acquiescence of a public official or other person acting in an official capacity""*.[113] Article 1(2), acknowledges that national legislation may contain provisions of wider application. Thus, Article 1(1) sets a minimum requirement, with Article 1(2) leaving it open to state parties to define torture in wider terms in their own domestic criminal legislation. It is important to note that a single incident of torture under the Convention constitutes a discrete international crime.[114] This was emphasised by Lord Hutton in *Pinochet* (No. 3) who stated that *"a single act of torture carried out or instigated by a public official or other person acting in an official capacity constitutes a crime against international law, and that torture does not become an international crime only when committed or instigated on a large scale"*.[115] Further, there is no

---

[111] UNCAT, Article 5(2).

[112] This is known as the principle *"aut dedere aut punier"* - see Lord Browne-Wilkinson at pp.200F-H and 201A, in *Pinochet (No.3)*. See also Lord Goff at p.212F, referring to Article 7(1) UNCAT.

[113] *Pinochet* (No. 3), as per, Lord Browne-Wilkinson at p.199E.

[114] *Pinochet* (No. 3), Lord Browne-Wilkinson, p.201B, Lord Goff ay p.219H; see also *R v Reeves Taylor* [2018] EWCA Crim 2843 para. 20.

[115] *Pinochet* (No. 3), Lord Hutton at p.264B.

requirement that torture occur as part of an armed conflict, which reflects the international human rights law genesis of the Convention.[116]

Section 134 CJA

The statutory basis to try the *"international crime of torture"* in the Crown Court is section 134 of the Criminal Justice Act 1988 ("CJA") which implements in domestic law certain UK obligations under UNCAT.[117] This chapter will look at the terms in which section 134 is drafted and consider the elements of the offence.[118] The definition of torture under domestic law is not identical to the definition of torture in Article 1 of UNCAT. Most significantly, the definition in section 134 CJA is wider in the important respect that it does not include a purposive requirement i.e. a requirement that the torture was carried out for a specific purpose, such as obtaining a confession, or punishing the victim for an act they or a third party are suspected of having committed.[119]

Section 134 CJA sets out that:

> *Section 134 Torture.*
>
> *(1) A public official or person acting in an official capacity, whatever his nationality, commits the offence of torture if in the United Kingdom or elsewhere he intentionally inflicts severe pain or suffering on another in the performance or purported performance of his official duties.*

---

116 Pinochet (No. 3), Lord Browne-Wilkinson, p.197G-198B.

117 The relevant jurisdictional provisions have been set out in the first chapter. In short, torture under section 134 CJA is a crime of *"universal jurisdiction"* limited only by the requirement that the alleged conduct must have taken place after 29 September 1988.

118 Torture as a war crime and torture as a CAH are distinct offences and the elements of these offences are set out in chapters three and four.

119 See the list of purposes in Article 1(1) of UNCAT.

(2) A person not falling within subsection (1) above commits the offence of torture, whatever his nationality, if—

(a) in the United Kingdom or elsewhere he intentionally inflicts severe pain or suffering on another at the instigation or with the consent or acquiescence—

(i) of a public official; or

(ii) of a person acting in an official capacity; and

(b) the official or other person is performing or purporting to perform his official duties when he instigates the commission of the offence or consents to or acquiesces in it.

(3) It is immaterial whether the pain or suffering is physical or mental and whether it is caused by an act or an omission.

(4) It shall be a defence for a person charged with an offence under this section in respect of any conduct of his to prove that he had lawful authority, justification or excuse for that conduct.

(5) For the purposes of this section "lawful authority, justification or excuse" means—

(a) in relation to pain or suffering inflicted in the United Kingdom, lawful authority, justification or excuse under the law of the part of the United Kingdom where it was inflicted;

(b) in relation to pain or suffering inflicted outside the United Kingdom—

(i) if it was inflicted by a United Kingdom official acting under the law of the United Kingdom or by a person acting in an official capacity under that law, lawful authority, justification or excuse under that law;

> *(ii) if it was inflicted by a United Kingdom official acting under the law of any part of the United Kingdom or by a person acting in an official capacity under such law, lawful authority, justification or excuse under the law of the part of the United Kingdom under whose law he was acting; and*
>
> *(iii) in any other case, lawful authority, justification or excuse under the law of the place where it was inflicted.*
>
> *(6) A person who commits the offence of torture shall be liable on conviction on indictment to imprisonment for life.*

Section 134 is comprised of six paragraphs. The first and second paragraphs concern how and by whom the offence is committed; it can either be committed by: (i) a public official, or person acting in an official capacity, or (ii) by an individual at the behest of such a public official or person acting in an official capacity. The third paragraph concerns the nature and threshold of the offence. The fourth and fifth paragraphs concern a potential defence of *"lawful authority, justification or excuse"*. The sixth and final paragraph concerns the penalty. The statutory provision is fairly succinct, which means that judicial decision making has an important role to play in examining the contours of liability under section 134 and articulating the elements of the offence.

The elements of the offence

The elements of the offence under section 134 can be simply stated as follows:

Actus reus:

- The infliction of severe pain of suffering, whether physical or mental, on a person;

- By, or at the instigation or with the consent or acquiescence of a public official, or person acting in an official capacity, in the performance of, or purported performance of their official duties.

Mens rea:

- The infliction of the pain or suffering must be intentional.

Notably, section 134 expressly states that torture can be committed by both acts and omissions.

The *"public official"* and *"person acting in an official capacity"* requirement

A defining element of torture under section 134 is the requirement that it is inflicted by, or at the behest of a *"public official"* or a *"person acting in an official capacity"*. This requirement does not feature in the elements of torture as a war crime or a CAH.[120] The *"public official or person acting in an official capacity"* requirement under section 134 is identical to that found in the definition of torture in Article 1(1) UNCAT.[121] Neither the Statute, nor UNCAT define these terms. However, their meaning has been examined by the House of Lords in *Pinochet No. 3*, and more recently by the Supreme Court in *R v RTA* [2019] UKSC 51 (hereinafter, "*RTA*"), which concerned the prosecution of Agnes Taylor at the Central Criminal Court in relation to charges under section 134 CJA. The following principles emerge from the case law:

[120] The elements of torture as a war crime and a CAH are set out in the corresponding chapters.

[121] *R v RTA* [2019] UKSC 51 para. 23 in which Lord Lloyd-Jones noted that the words *"person acting in an official capacity"* must bear the same meaning in section 134 as in article 1, UNCAT"; and *Pinochet (No. 3)*, per Lord Browne-Wilkinson at p. 200 A-B.

- *"Public official"* or a *"person acting in an official capacity"*, excludes the liability of persons acting in a private capacity, which would involve an offence under regular domestic criminal law, rather than the international crime of torture. [122]

- *"Public official"* or a *"person acting in an official capacity"*, *"covers any such person whether acting in peace time or in a situation of armed conflict".*[123]

- *A "Public official"* includes persons acting for, or on behalf of, the state or government of a state.[124]

- *A "person acting in an official capacity"* is not limited to those acting for, or on behalf of, the government of a State and can include conduct on behalf of *"a de facto authority, which seeks to overthrow the government of the State".*[125]

- *A "person acting in an official capacity"* includes a person who acts *"for or on behalf of an organisation or body which exercises, in the territory controlled by that organisation or body and in which the relevant conduct occurs, functions normally exercised by governments over their civilian populations".* [126]

- The *"exercise of governmental functions is a core requirement"*, meaning that the functions being exercised by the organisation

122 *R v RTA* [2019] UKSC 51 paras. 31 and 36.

123 *R v RTA* [2019] UKSC 51 para. 76.

124 *Pinochet* (No. 3) Lord Browne-Wilkinson, p.200A-E and 201B who stated that this included the head of state. Although, Lord Goff took the view that a head of state would be more appropriately categorised as an *"other person acting in a public capacity"* at p.213A-B.

125 *R v RTA* [2019] UKSC 51 para. 76.

126 *R v RTA* [2019] UKSC 51 para. 76.

or body *"must be governmental in character"* and that merely *"purporting to exercise such functions would not be sufficient."*[127]

- There is an important distinction between the exercise of governmental functions and *"purely military activity not involving any governmental function"*.[128] On the one hand it may be that a rebel group has not *"acquired a sufficient degree of control, permanence, authority or organisation to fulfil criteria sufficient to be recognised"* as a *de facto* authority. On the other hand, an *"insurrectional force engaged in fighting the forces of the central government of a State may nevertheless exercise sufficient governmental authority over territory and persons under their control for acts done on their behalf to be official acts for this purpose"*.[129]

In *RTA*, the Appellant argued that the term *"person acting in an official capacity"* applied only to *"those acting for or on behalf of the government of a State"* and could not apply to a *"member of an armed opposition group fighting against or seeking to overthrow the government of a State"*.[130] This argument was rejected in a majority judgment by the Supreme Court. Lord Lloyd-Jones noted that the dichotomy in Article 1 of UNCAT and therefore also under section 134 CJA was, *"between official conduct and purely private conduct, not between State and non-State activity"*.[131] Lord Lloyd-Jones observed that:

> *"[w]hile in most normal circumstances, such as those prevailing in the United Kingdom [...] official conduct will usually be performed on behalf of a State, it is necessary to consider the applicability of the Convention in less stable situations, including those where more than*

---

[127] *R v RTA* [2019] UKSC 51 para. 77.

[128] *R v RTA* [2019] UKSC 51 para. 78.

[129] *R v RTA* [2019] UKSC 51 para. 78. But note that in para. 79, Lord Lloyd-Jones queries whether an entity is required to achieve a degree of *"permanence"* and that, *"the fact that the long-term entity may be an unlikely prospect should not prevent it from being considered a de facto government"*.

[130] *R v RTA* [2019] UKSC 51 para. 20.

[131] *R v RTA* [2019] UKSC 51 para. 25.

> *one body may be performing administrative or governmental functions within the territory of the State [...] the words "person acting in an official capacity" are apt to include someone who holds an official position or acts in an official capacity in an entity exercising governmental control over a civilian population in a territory over which it holds de facto control".*[132]

Assessing whether someone is a *"person acting in an official capacity"* is a distinctly fact-specific exercise. The approach taken to the exercise by Treacy J in the case of *R v Faryadi Zardad* (another prosecution of torture under section 134 CJA at the Central Criminal Court) was cited with approval in the Supreme Court judgment in *RTA*. Lord Lloyd-Jones stated that:

> *"I consider that Treacy J in Zardad correctly identified the required approach when he observed that it is necessary to look at the reality of any particular situation and to consider whether, at the relevant time, the entity in question had a sufficient degree of organisation and actual control over an area and whether it exercised the type of functions which a government or governmental organisation would exercise. This will require an examination of evidence as to the position on the ground. In doing so it will be necessary to make allowance for the particular conditions which may make administration difficult and for different views of appropriate structures of government. The question will be whether the entity has established a sufficient degree of control, authority and organisation to become an authority exercising official or quasi-official powers, as opposed to a rebel faction or a mere military force".*[133]

132 *R v RTA* [2019] UKSC 51 para. 25.

133 *R v RTA* [2019] UKSC 51 para. 79.

R v Faryadi Zardad

The case of *Zardad* provides a good example of an evidential examination of whether a person is acting in an official capacity and it was referred to in detail in the Supreme Court judgment in *RTA*.[134] Zardad was convicted of conspiracy to torture and conspiracy to take hostages in Afghanistan.[135] The case concerned events between 1992 and 1996, when Zardad was a chief commander of Hezb-I-Islami and the military controller of the area of Sarobi. In a preparatory hearing before Treacy J, Zardad argued that he was not a public official because there was a recognised government in Afghanistan at that time and Hezb-I-Islami was not part of that government and was actively opposed to it.[136] Treacy J rejected Zardad's argument and ruled that there was evidence upon which a jury could find that Zardad was a *de facto* public official in an area which was totally controlled by his organisation and which was exercising governmental or quasi-governmental functions in that area.[137] The following features of the evidence were held by Treacy J to support his conclusion that Zardad was a *de facto* public official:

- Zardad's admission that he was a general within Hekmatyar's army (Hekmatayar being the leader of the Hezb-I-Islami faction;
- That the Hezb-I-Islami faction controlled the Sarobi area;

134 Notably, the defence argument before the Supreme Court in Taylor, that Zardad was wrongly decided was flatly rejected (*R v RTA* [2019] UKSC 51 para. 64).

135 Zardad was sentenced to 20 years imprisonment, upheld on appeal (*R. v Faryadi Sarwar Zardad* [2007] EWCA Crim 279).

136 *R v RTA* [2019] UKSC 51 para. 62, referring to Treacy J in *R v Zardad*, Case No T2203 7676, 7 April 2004 ("Treacy J's ruling").

137 *R v RTA* [2019] UKSC 51 paras. 63 and 65, referring to Treacy J's ruling at para. 35. Also see Treacy J's ruling para. 33 quoted at *R v RTA* [2019] UKSC 51 para. 63.

- That the Hezb-I-Islami faction had a clear command structure;
- That prisons in the controlled area were run by the Hezb-I-Islami faction;
- Zardad was personally involved in arresting and imprisoning lawbreakers and in mediating and resolving disputes between individuals;
- Representatives of international organisations and aid agencies would make representations to Zardad, as opposed to any central government authority, if equipment was seized or delayed at any of the checkpoints for which Zardad's force was responsible;
- Those who complained of ill-treatment, torture and hostage taking regarded Zardad and Hekmatyar as the only official authority in the area, which was dominated and controlled by them.

R v Agnes Taylor / RTA

Agnes Taylor faced several charges of torture under section 134 at the Central Criminal Court. The alleged crimes occurred in 1990, during the initial stages of the first civil war in Liberia, when an armed rebel group, the National Patriotic Front of Liberia ("NPFL") led by Charles Taylor (Agnes' then husband) sought to take control of the country and to depose the then President, Samuel Doe. The prosecution argued that the NPFL was a *de facto* military government or government authority and that Agnes Taylor was acting in an official capacity on behalf of the NPFL.[138] The prosecution relied upon on an expert witness, who had provided a report about the historical development of the conflict. He initially stated that the location where the alleged crimes occurred, namely Nimba county was under NPFL control by the end of May 1990.[139] However, during the course of the appellate litigation, the expert revised his evidence, clarifying that when he used of the term *"control"* in his initial report he intended to refer to military rather than administrative control over Nimba county.[140] After the Supreme Court judgement in *RTA*, the case returned to the Central Criminal Court, where Sweeney J was asked to consider an application to dismiss the case based on the revised expert evidence. Sweeney J dismissed the case because, in his view, the evidence presented indicated that the NPFL exercised only military, rather than governmental functions, at the time and place of the alleged crimes.[141]

---

[138] *R v RTA* [2019] UKSC 51 para. 4.

[139] *R v RTA* [2019] UKSC 51 para. 6.

[140] *R v RTA* [2019] UKSC 51 paras. 7 and 80.

[141] There are a number of media reports about this hearing. See for example: https://www.bbc.co.uk/news/uk-50685426. As noted by the Supreme Court in *R v RTA* [2019] UKSC 51 para. 20 because the allegations related to 1990, they could only be charged under section 134 CJA 1988 and not under the ICCA whose jurisdiction begins on 1 January 1991.

"Acting in the performance or purported performance of his official duties"

The offence under section 134 requires that the conduct is committed when the public official or person acting in an official capacity is *"acting in the performance or purported performance of his official duties"*. In other words, there is a requirement that the acts of torture should be committed for a purpose connected to the person's public or official function. Purely private acts of torture with no official character or connection are excluded.[142] This means that private conduct, such as the conduct of an off-duty police officer, would not constitute an offence under section 134.

"Severe pain and suffering"

Section 134 requires the conduct inflicted to reach the level of *"severe pain and suffering"*. Notably, this requirement is shared with the crime of torture as a war crime and torture as a CAH.[143] What constitutes *"severe pain and suffering"* is not defined in section 134, save that it expressly states that it can include both physical and mental suffering. Likewise, Article 1 UNCAT does not provide any further elaboration. In a Crown Court trial, the judge will want to direct the jury on the meaning of *"severe pain and suffering"* so that the jury can decide whether the conduct alleged reaches this threshold. In that regard, assistance may be found in international jurisprudence from the international criminal courts and the ECtHR. In particular, there are a number of cases from the ICTY which consider the elements of the offence of torture, including the requirement of *"severe pain and suffering"*. The Appeals Chamber at the ICTY has stated that whether or not an act inflicts severe pain or suffering is a fact-specific inquiry and that inflicting physical pain may amount to torture even where it does not cause pain of the type accompanying serious injury. Further, that there is no exhaustive classification of acts

142 *R v RTA* [2019] UKSC 51 para. 36.

143 Unlike other elements of torture as a war crime and as a CAH which are different. See the chapters on war crimes and CAH.

which may constitute torture and that whether allegations of torture reach the *"severe pain and suffering"* threshold should be considered on a case-by-case basis.[144] It is well established in international jurisprudence that rape amounts to torture, as it necessarily involves the infliction of severe pain or suffering on the complainant. This was specifically considered at the ICTY in the case of *Prosecutor v. Kunarać and Others* (IT-96-23 and I-96-23/1 AC) Appeal Judgment, 12 June 2002.[145]

Direct and secondary liability

Section 134 refers to liability for commission of the offence of torture. It expressly provides for two ways of committing the offence:

(1) Where (i) a public official, or (ii) person acting in an official capacity intentionally inflicts severe pain or suffering on another, in the performance of, or purported performance of his official duties; or,

(2) Where a person intentionally inflicts severe pain or suffering on another person, at the instigation, or with the consent or acquiescence of (i) a public official, or (ii) a person acting in an official capacity, who is acting in the performance of, or purported performance of their official duties when they instigate the commission of the offence, or consent or acquiesce to the offence.

144 *Naletilić and Martinović* (IT-98-34-A), Appeal Judgment, 3 May 2006 para. 299, endorsed by the Appeals Chamber in *Brđanin* (IT-99-36-A), Appeal Judgment, 3 April 2007, para. 251.

145 *Prosecutor v. Kunarać and Others* (IT-96-23 and I-96-23/1 AC) AC, 12 June 2002, para. 150-151, also noting at para. 150 that sexual violence likewise necessarily gives rise to severe pain and suffering *"and in this way justifies its characterisation as… torture"*. See also *Brđanin* (IT-99-36-T), Trial Judgment, 1 September 2004, para. 485.

Secondary or accessorial liability is not expressly referred to in section 134 CJA. However, secondary liability flows for the offence under section 134 in the same way as any other inchoate offence under domestic criminal law. This is consistent with the terms of UNCAT which envision not only the liability of principals but also that of accessories through complicity, as well as attempts to commit torture.[146] Secondary liability under section 134 was considered by the Divisional Court in *R (Equality and Human Rights Commission) v Prime Minister* [2011] EWHC 2401 (Admin).[147] Sir Anthony May, delivering the judgment, noted that the *"secondary party has to encourage or assist the principal offender, and has at least to foresee that the commission of the crime by the principal was a real or substantial risk"* but that, *"[i]t is not necessary for the secondary party to know, believe or intend that the principal will commit the indictable offence".*[148] The only conviction so far under section 134 in the case of *Zardad* involved a charge of conspiracy to torture.[149] The Crown's case was that Zardad had responsibility for checkpoints at which people had been tortured, and that actions of soldiers committing acts of torture at the checkpoints had taken place with Zardad's knowledge and approval and in some cases his presence, or with his direct involvement.[150] The extradition proceedings in relation to Senator Pinochet concerned charges from the Spanish Court including conspiracy to torture.[151]

---

[146] Article 4 UNCAT requires state parties to the Convention to ensure that all acts of torture, including attempts and complicity are criminalised.

[147] *R (Equality and Human Rights Commission) v Prime Minister* [2011] EWHC 2401 (Admin), see Sir Anthony May, President of the Queen's Bench Division, delivering the judgment of the Divisional Court, at para. 37, referring to secondary liability under domestic law by virtue of section 8 of the Accessories and Abettors Act 1861, which provides that whoever aids, abets, counsels or procures the commission of an indictable offence shall be criminally liable as a principal offender; see further paras. 61-63 and 66-70.

[148] *R (Equality and Human Rights Commission) v Prime Minister* [2011] EWHC 2401 (Admin) at para. 37.

[149] *R v Zardad* [2007] EWCA Crim 279 para. 1.

[150] *R v Zardad* [2007] EWCA Crim 279 paras. 3 – 11, esp. 11.

[151] *Pinochet (No. 3)*, per Lord Browne-Wilkinson p.190 D: *"Although it is not alleged that Senator Pinochet himself committed any of those acts, it is alleged that they were*

Defence of "lawful authority, justification or excuse"

Section 134 creates a specific defence of *"lawful authority, justification or excuse"* and the specific terms of the defence are defined in the legislation. Section 134(5)(a) concerns conduct in the UK. Section 134(5)(b) concerns conduct outside of the UK. Notably, section 134(5)(b)(iii) provides a potential defence in relation to conduct outside the UK in circumstances where there was *"lawful authority, justification or excuse under the law of the place where it was inflicted"*. This provision appears to permit a defendant charged with torture in the Crown Court to argue that they have a defence in circumstances where torture is permitted by the law of a foreign state. It is difficult to square this provision with the purpose of UNCAT and the defence does not find its genesis in UNCAT, which only excludes *"pain of suffering arising only from, inherent in or incidental to lawful sanctions"*.[152] Moreover, UNCAT specifically provides that *"no exceptional circumstances whatsoever, whether a state of war or a threat of war, internal political instability or any other public emergency may be invoked as a justification of torture"* (Article 2(2)) and that *"an order from a superior officer or a public authority may not be invoked as a justification of torture"* (Article 2(3)). Issues surrounding the defence under section 134 have yet to be litigated in the courts of the UK, but it is controversial,[153] and there have been calls for this particular sub-section (section 134(5)(b)(iii)) to be repealed.[154] There are also, of

---

done in pursuance of a conspiracy to which he was a party, at his instigation and with his knowledge".

152 UNCAT, Article 1(1).

153 See Dr. Kate Grady, *"International crimes in the courts of England and Wales"*, Criminal L.R. 693 2014, at p.11-12 and also Sir Nigel Rodley and Matt Pollard, *"Criminalisation of Torture: State Obligations under the United Nations Convention against Torture and Other Cruel, Inhuman or Degrading Treatment or Punishment"* [2006] E.H.R.L.R 2, 115-141 at pp.121-122, which also notes that there is also *"controversy"* in relation to the *"lawful sanctions"* provision under Article 1, UNCAT.

154 In terms of a call to repeal this sub-section, see for example, a July 2008 publication, *"Ending Impunity in the United Kingdom for genocide, crimes against humanity, war crimes and torture and other crimes under international law - the urgent need to strengthen universal jurisdiction legislation and to enforce it vigorously"*

course, potential defences available under the common law and these too are yet to be considered in relation to a charge under section 134 in domestic proceedings.

---

by Carla Ferstmen and Daniel Machover, at page 12 and which at page 13 calls for the amendment of section 134 to include the incorporation of the provision in Article 2(3) of UNCAT that *"an order from a superior officer or a public authority may not be invoked as a justification of torture"*.

CHAPTER THREE

WAR CRIMES UNDER THE ICCA

What is a war crime under the ICCA?

It is often said that it is the link to an armed conflict which transforms what might otherwise be an offence under ordinary domestic criminal law into a war crime. For example, if murder is committed in peacetime it can be tried contrary to The Homicide Act 1957. Whereas, if murder is committed in the context of and in association with an armed conflict, it can be tried as a war crime under the ICCA.

Article 50 ICCA explains that a war crime means a war crime as defined in Article 8.2 of the Rome Statute of the ICC, which is set out in Schedule 8 to the ICCA. [155] Schedule 8 lists the many different war crimes offences, which are set out in the second half of this chapter.

It is important to note that neither Article 8 of the Rome Statute, nor Schedule 8 to the ICCA reflect a complete statement of all of the war crimes recognised under international law. The Rome Statute codified, to a significant extent, the applicable customary international law in relation to war crimes. However, the Rome Statute was the product of negotiation and agreement could not be reached in relation to a number of offences, which resulted in their omission from the Statute. For example, *"collective punishments"*[156] and *"acts of terrorism"*[157] which have

[155] Schedule 8 ICCA does not incorporate Article 8.1 of the Rome Statute, which indicates that the ICC has jurisdiction in relation to war crimes committed as part of a plan of policy, or as part of a large-scale commission of offences.

[156] Collective punishments are a violation of common article 3.

[157] Acts of terrorism is a violation of common article 3.

been tried by other international criminal tribunals.[158] Also, omitted from the Statute were offences relating to nuclear weapons.[159] On the other hand, the Rome Statute advanced earlier articulations of war crimes. It recognised crimes, such as the war crime of *"recruiting child soldiers"*[160] and" *"attacks on peacekeepers"*.[161] The ICC Statute also codified war crimes committed in non-international armed conflict ("NIAC") for the first time.[162]

Historical origins of the war crimes provisions in the ICCA

IHL is a conglomeration of both treaty and customary international law. In terms of treaty law, it primarily comprises of 'Geneva law', which is concerned with the Geneva Conventions and 'Hague law', which is concerned with the Hague Conventions.[163]

---

158 For example, the crime of *"collective punishments"* was successfully prosecuted at the SCSL (see *Prosecutor v Fofana and Kondewa* Trial Judgment, 2 August 2007, para.178, *Prosecutor v Fofana and Kondewa* (SCSL-04-14-A) Appeal Judgment, 28 May 2008, para.222 and the crimes of *"acts of terrorism"* has been successfully prosecuted at the ICTY (see *Prosecutor v Galic* (IT-98-29-T) Trial Judgment, 5 December 2003, paras. 63 - 138, *Prosecutor v. Galic* (IT-98-29-A) Appeal Judgment, 30 November 2006, paras. 70 – 104.

159 See, *The International Criminal Court: A Commentary on the Rome Statute*, William A. Schabas, pp. 195 and 198.

160 ICC Statute, Article 8(2)(b)(xxvi) and Article 8(2)(e)(vii).

161 ICC Statute, Article 8(2)(b)(iii) and Article 8(2)(e)(iii).

162 See, *The International Criminal Court: A Commentary on the Rome Statute*, William A. Schabas, p. 195.

163 As noted in *International Law*, Malcolm N. Shaw, ninth ed., Cambridge University Press, at pp.1030-1031 a number of the international conventions from which IHL is derived also represent in whole or in part rules of customary international law. See also p.1033.

The Geneva Conventions of 1949:

The Geneva Conventions of 1949 are the most significant treaty provisions in the corpus of international humanitarian law ("IHL").[164] They consist of four treaties which outline certain protections to be ensured by parties engaged in international armed conflict ("IAC"). Each of the four Geneva Conventions is concerned with different classes of persons who are to be afforded protection. The first Geneva Convention is concerned with the *"wounded and sick in armed forces in the field"*.[165] The second Geneva Convention relates to *"wounded, sick and shipwrecked members of the armed forces at sea"*.[166] The third Geneva Convention concerns *"prisoners of war"*.[167] The Fourth Geneva Convention is concerned with protections to be afforded to *"civilians"*.[168] All four of the Geneva Conventions are primarily concerned with IAC, which is armed conflict between nations, or situations of occupation where there is no armed resistance to that occupation (see discussion on the definition of an IAC below).

Common article 3 to the Geneva Conventions of 1949:

Although the Geneva Conventions of 1949 are principally concerned with IAC, article 3 of each of the conventions outlines some minimum protections in NIAC. This is known as *"common article 3"* because it is common to each of the four Geneva Conventions. Common article 3

164 Cross-reference the discussion about the Geneva Conventions in chapter 1 under the sub-heading, *The Geneva Conventions Act 1957.*

165 Convention for the Amelioration of the Condition of the Wounded and Sick in Armed Forces in the Field, (1950) 75 UNTS 31, arts. 13, 24-26.

166 Convention for the Amelioration of the Condition of the Wounded, Sick and Shipwrecked Members of Armed Forces at Sea, (1950) 75 UNTS 31, arts 13, 24-26.

167 Convention Relative to the Treatment of Prisoners of War, (1950) 75 UNTS 135, arts. 4, 13, 16, 20.

168 Convention Relative to the Protection of Civilian Persons in Time of War, (1950) 75 UNTS 287, arts. 8, 44, 45, 73, 75, 77.

demands that those who have put down their arms, or are out of the conflict due to injury or sickness, are treated humanely, without any adverse discrimination based on race, colour, religion, sex, social status, wealth or any other such criteria, and it specifically prohibits:

> *"violence to life and person, in particular murder of all kinds, mutilation, cruel treatment and torture", "taking of hostages", "outrages upon personal dignity, in particular, humiliating and degrading treatment", "the passing of sentences and the carrying out of executions without previous judgment pronounced by a regularly constituted court, affording all the judicial guarantees which are recognized as indispensable by civilized peoples".*[169]

The grave breach regime:

A grave breach is a particularly serious violation of the Geneva Conventions which imposes on states the obligation to prosecute or extradite persons accused of having committed them, regardless of the nationality of the perpetrator, or the victim, or the place of commission of the crime. The grave breach regime in the four Geneva Conventions is concerned with IAC. Each of the four Conventions contains an article outlining grave breaches: Article 50 of Geneva Convention I, Article 51 of Geneva Convention 2, Article 130 of Geneva Convention III and Article 147 of Geneva Convention IV. (Grave breaches have been considered already in the first chapter, where the text of Article 50 has been set out).

Additional Protocols I and II of 1977:

The Geneva Conventions of 1949 were supplemented by two Additional Protocols in 1977. Additional Protocol I *("Protocol additional to the Geneva Conventions of 12 August 1949 and Relating to the Protection of Victims of International Armed Conflicts")* expanded the protections provided for the civilian population, as well as military and civilian

[169] Wording as per common article 3 to each of the Four Geneva Conventions of 1949.

medical workers in the context of IAC. Additional Protocol II *("Protocol additional to the Geneva Conventions of 12 August 1949 and Relating to the Protection of Victims of Non-International Armed Conflicts")* elaborated protections for victims in NIAC; complementing the minimum guarantees in NIAC contained in common article 3.[170]

Hague Law

During conferences in the Hague in 1899 and 1907 the laws of war were codified with the adoption of a series of conventions, known as the 'Hague Conventions'. The Hague Conventions established rules in relation to the means and methods of warfare. The Hague Conventions concern the rights and duties of belligerents in the conduct of operations and limit the choice of means of doing harm.[171]

Article 8.2 of the ICC Statute and Schedule 8 of the ICCA:

Having considered the principle IHL treaty provisions, we can now return to the ICCA and see how things fit together. As noted above, the definition of war crimes under the ICCA comes from the Rome Statute and is born out of the historical development of ICL from IHL and the negotiations and associated drafting process of the Statute. Schedule 8 ICCA, Article 8, replicating Article 8.2 of the ICC Statute, divides war crimes into four categories:

170 See the American Red Cross, *"Summary of the Geneva Conventions of 1949 and Their Additional Protocols"*, April 2011(https://www.redcross.org/content/dam/redcross/atg/PDF_s/International_Services/International_Humanitarian_Law/IHL_SummaryGenevaConv.pdf), or *International Law,* Malcolm N. Shaw, ninth ed., Cambridge University Press, p.1031 and 1032-1033.

171 *International Law,* Malcolm N. Shaw, ninth ed., Cambridge University Press, pp.1031 and 1033.

(1) [G]rave breaches of the Geneva Conventions of 12 August 1949,[172]

(2) [O]ther serious violations of the laws and customs applicable in international armed conflict,[173]

(3) Serious violations of article 3 common to the four Geneva Conventions of 12 August 1949,[174]

(4) Other serious violations of the laws and customs applicable in armed conflicts not of an international character.[175]

The first two categories apply only in the context of an IAC. The second two categories apply only in the context of an NIAC. The first category of *"grave breaches of the Geneva Conventions of 12 August 1949"* derive directly from the grave breaches regime. As regards the second category of war crimes, *"other serious violations of the laws and customs applicable in international armed conflict"*, this category includes all the other war crimes contained in the four Geneva Conventions and Additional Protocol I, as well as other war crimes provided for by the laws and customs of war, which include the Hauge Conventions and customary international law. As regards the third category of war crimes, *"serious violations of article 3 common to the four Geneva Conventions of 12 August 1949"*, this derives directly from the protections contained in article 3 common to the four Geneva Conventions, which applies to NIAC. Category four, *"other serious violations of the laws and customs applicable in armed conflicts not of an international character"*, captures those war crimes in NIAC that are not contained in article 3 common to the

[172] ICCA, Schedule 8, Article 8(2)(a).

[173] ICCA, Schedule 8, Article 8(2)(b).

[174] ICCA, Schedule 8, Article 8(2)(c).

[175] ICCA, Schedule 8, Article 8(2)(e).

Geneva Conventions. Category four principally derives from the provisions of Additional Protocol II.

Elements of war crimes under the ICCA

"Contextual elements" and elements of offences

In any war crimes case, the prosecution must prove both the *"contextual elements"* of war crimes,[176] and the elements of the underlying offence. Contextual elements are those elements that make the offence in question a war crime, as opposed to an ordinary offence in domestic law unrelated to an armed conflict. The contextual elements of war crimes include:

(1) the existence of an armed conflict;

(2) a link between the offence and the armed conflict;

(3) that the victim is someone who qualifies as a *"protected victim"* of a war crime, or concerns *"protected property"*;

(4) that the perpetrator of the offence is aware of the factual circumstances of the armed conflict; and

(5) that the perpetrator was aware of the protected status of the victim, or property.

In the next part of this chapter, the contextual elements of war crimes will be examined.

Duty to "take into account" the ICC Elements of Crimes document

The ICCA provides that in interpreting and applying the provisions defining war crimes, (as well as CAH and genocide) the court *"shall take*

[176] Note that *"contextual elements"* are also often referred to as *"chapeau"*.

into account" the Elements of Crimes used by the ICC.[177] The ICC Elements of Crimes document is set out as a matter of domestic law in *"The International Criminal Court Act 2001 (Elements of Crimes) Regulations 2001"* (hereinafter, *"ICCA Elements of Crimes Regulations"* or *"Regulations"*).[178] Judges dealing ICCA crimes will have to decide whether, or not, to adopt the elements of crimes as articulated in the Regulations. Where offences already exist in domestic law, for example offences such as murder and rape, the judge will have to consider whether to use the ICC elements, or elements of crimes familiar to domestic criminal law, in addition to the contextual elements of war crimes. Alternatively, it would also be possible to adopt the elements of crimes as articulated by other ad hoc international criminal tribunals, if after consideration, such alternative articulations were preferable. Whilst this is not necessarily the most desirable course, considering the issue of potential fragmentation of international law, there may be circumstances where such an approach is justified. For example, when the ICC Elements of Crimes do not articulate the elements of a certain offence in sufficient detail, or if cogent arguments are advanced for departing from the ICC elements.

Duty to "take into account" ICC jurisprudence and the discretion to take into account other international jurisprudence

The ICCA provides that in interpreting and applying the provisions defining war crimes (as well as CAH and genocide) the court *"shall take into account"* any relevant judgment or decision of the ICC, and that *"account may also be taken"* of any other relevant international jurisprudence.[179] The legislation therefore requires that any relevant judgment or decision of the ICC is considered by the court. As regards

---

177 ICCA, section 50(2) and Schedule 8, Article 9.

178 The *"The International Criminal Court Act 2001 (Elements of Crimes) Regulations 2001"* can be found at https://www.legislation.gov.uk/uksi/2001/2505/made. They entered into force on 1 September 2001.

179 ICCA, section 50(5).

other *"international jurisprudence"*, the court has a discretion about whether or not to take account of that jurisprudence. However, the parties would be well advised to put relevant caselaw before the court. This is because over the last thirty years[180] the ad hoc international criminal tribunals have built a significant body of jurisprudence relating to the elements of offences. In relation to the phrase *"international jurisprudence"* it is of note that this is a broad phrase which is not defined in the Act. Such *"international jurisprudence"* would most obviously be found in the judgments and decisions of the ad hoc international criminal tribunals and the International Court of Justice ("ICJ") but there is nothing in the Act that limits it to the same.

Contextual elements of war crimes

The armed conflict requirement

In order to prove a war crime, the existence of an armed conflict must be established.[181] Neither the ICCA, the ICC Statute nor the ICC Elements of Crimes define *"armed conflict"* and neither do the Geneva Conventions, so it is necessary to look to the case law.[182] The definition of an *"armed conflict"* provided by the Appeals Chamber in the seminal ICTY decision in *Prosecutor v. Tadic ("Tadic")* has been adopted with

180 The ICTY was established in May 1993 and the ICTR November 1994, so at the time of writing it's nearly thirty years.

181 See for example the *Prosecutor v. Thomas Lubanga* (ICC-01/04 – 01/06) Trial Chamber, *"Judgment pursuant to Article 74 of the Statute"*, 14 March 2012 ("*Lubanga*, Trial Judgment") in which the Trial Chamber at para. 504 refer to proving the existence of an armed conflict as a fundamental requirement, without which the prosecution will have failed to prove its charges.

182 *Lubanga*, Trial Judgment, paragraph, 531-532; *Prosecutor v. Germain Katanga* (ICC-01/04-01/07-3436) 7 March 2014 ("*Katanga*, Trial Judgment"), para. 1173.

approval at the ICC.[183] The Appeals Chamber in *Tadic* defined *"armed conflict"* as existing:

- whenever there is a resort to armed force between states, or
- protracted armed violence between governmental authorities and organized armed groups, or
- protracted armed violence between armed groups within a state.

The *Tadic* Appeals Chamber explained that IHL applies from the beginning of armed conflicts, until peace, or a peaceful settlement is reached. IHL applies to the entirety of the territory of the warring states, or that territory under the control of the warring party, whether or not actual fighting takes place there.[184]

International versus non-international armed conflict

The provisions in the ICCA, mirroring the ICC Statute, reflect the historical division in IHL between IAC and NIAC. This distinction will be of significance to prosecutors bringing war crimes charges, as consideration will need to be given about whether to bring charges under the provisions concerning IACs or NIACs. For example, in relation to an allegation of murder, if the murder was committed in the context of an IAC it should be charged under Schedule 8, Article 8(2)(a)(i) as *"wilful killing"* as a grave breach of the Geneva Conventions, whereas if the murder was committed in the context of a NIAC it should be charged under Schedule 8, Article 8(2)(c)(i) as *"murder"* as a serious violation of common article 3. In some scenarios, it will be easy to say whether a conflict is international or non-international. However, in others, it will

[183] *Lubanga,* Trial Judgment, para. 533; *Katanga,* Trial Judgment, para. 1173, *Prosecutor v. Jeanne-Pierre Bemba* (ICC-01/05-01/08), *"Judgment pursuant to Article 74 of the Statute",* 21 March 2016 ("*Bemba,* Trial Judgment"), para. 128.

[184] *Prosecutor v. Tadic* (IT-94-I-AR72), *"Decision on the Defence Motion for Interlocutory Appeal on Jurisdiction",* 2 October 1995, ("*Tadic,* Interlocutory Appeal Decision") para.70.

be more difficult. In such situations, one course may be to plead alternate charges, reflecting both versions of the offence in IAC and NIAC.

International armed conflict

Under the ICCA, war crimes in situations of IAC include: *"grave breaches of the Geneva Conventions of 12 August 1949"*,[185] and *"other serious violations of the laws and customs applicable in international armed conflict"*.[186] Again, it is necessary to look to the case law to find a definition of IAC. ICC case law has confirmed that there are (at least) five categories of situation where IAC can be said to arise:

- Declared war between two states;
- War between two states, where the state of war is not recognized by one of them;
- Partial or total occupation of the territory of a state, whether or not that occupation meets with armed resistance;
- An internal armed conflict, which transforms into an IAC, by virtue of the direct involvement of the armed forces of a foreign state;
- Internal armed conflict, which transforms into an IAC, by virtue of armed groups involved in the armed conflict acting on behalf of a foreign state. [187]

---

185 ICCA, Schedule 8, Article 2(a).

186 ICCA, Schedule 8, Article 2(b).

187 *Lubanga*, Trial Judgment, para. 541; *Katanga*, Trial Judgment, para. 1174; *Bemba*, Trial Judgment para. 130.

Case law from the Trial Chambers of the ICC provides guidance in relation to the assessment of whether a conflict falls into these various categories and thus can be characterized at an IAC.[188]

Non-international armed conflict

Under the ICCA, war crimes in situations of NIAC include *"serious violations of article 3 common to the four Geneva Conventions of 12 August 1949"*,[189] and *"other serious violations of the laws and customs applicable in armed conflicts not of an international character"*.[190] The ICCA provides some assistance in relation to a definition of NIAC. Schedule 8, Article 8(2)(f), which mirrors Article 8(2)(f) of the ICC Statute, refers to *"armed conflicts not of an international character" as:*

> *"armed conflicts that take place in the territory of a State when there is protracted armed conflict between governmental authorities and organized armed groups or between such groups"*.[191]

The ICCA also explicitly provides that situations of NIAC do not include:

> *"internal disturbances and tensions, such as riots, isolated and sporadic acts of violence or other acts of a similar nature"*.[192]

---

188 *Lubanga,* Trial Judgment, para. 541 – 542; *Katanga,* Trial Judgment, paras. 1178-1180. *Prosecutor v. Lubanga* (ICC-01-04/01-06), *"Decision on the Confirmation of Charges"*, 29 January 2007, para. 205 – 212. Note that the Trial Chambers at the ICC have endorsed the *"overall control"* test set out by the ICTY Appeals Chamber in *Tadic,* in relation to the issue of determining whether an armed group is acting on behalf of a state.

189 ICCA, Schedule 8, see Article 2(c) for the full citation.

190 ICCA, Schedule 8, (2)(e).

191 ICCA, Schedule 8, Article 8(2)(d).

192 ICCA, Schedule 8, Article 8(2)(d).

Trial Chambers at the ICC have confirmed that NIAC refers to *"protracted armed conflict"* between: (1) governmental authorities and organised armed groups, and (2) between organised armed groups.[193] In *Katanga*, an ICC Trial Chamber also found that an NIAC would exist where there is a conflict between foreign governmental authorities and organised armed groups and where the foreign state has intervened with the consent of the state on whose territory the armed conflict is taking place.[194] Case law from the Trial Chambers of the ICC provides further guidance in relation to the assessment of whether a conflict is an NIAC.[195]

Determining the nature of the conflict at trial

As noted already above, determining the nature of the armed conflict is important in relation to selecting the appropriate charges under the ICCA. At the trial stage, determining the nature of the armed conflict could be straightforward, but in some circumstances it could be a challenging and potentially cumbersome exercise, requiring evidence, including expert evidence. In such situations there are some potential short cuts that could be taken to obviate the need to spend significant resources on determining the issue.

First, where prosecutions before the Crown Court concern situations of armed conflict which have already been the subject of proceedings before international courts or tribunals, determinations from these courts and tribunals, could direct both prosecutorial strategy and judicial determinations regarding the nature of the conflict. In such a situation, agreement may be reached by the parties by way of admission, or judicial

[193] See for example, *Katanga*, Trial Judgment, para. 1184.

[194] *Katanga*, Trial Judgment, para. 1184.

[195] *Lubanga,* Trial Judgment, paras. 535-538; *Katanga*, Trial Judgment, paras. 1185 - 1187. For example, in relation to the assessment of what constitutes an *"organized armed group"* see *Lubanga,* Trial Judgment, para. 537. In relation to the assessment of whether the *"intensity"* of the conflict is sufficient to reach the standard of a NIAC see *Lubanga,* Trial Judgment, para. 538, *Katanga,* Trial Judgment at para. 1187 and the *Bemba,* Trial Judgment at paras. 137-140.

notice may be taken in relation to the existence and nature of an armed conflict. However, some caution should be taken in adopting such an approach, given that the character of a conflict may change over time. As such, a case-by-case approach is important, which reflects the status of the conflict at the time and place where the crimes charged take place.[196]

Secondly, in situations where the underlying war crimes charged share the same or common elements in both IAC and NIAC, a time saving route could be to invite the court to dispense with the need to make a conclusive determination about the nature of the conflict. This approach was taken in several cases before the ad hoc tribunals, for example, at the ICTY.[197] Notably, in jurisprudence from the ad hoc tribunals, the distinction between IAC and NIAC has been regarded as somewhat academic and not of practical importance.[198] However, this approach has not been endorsed at the ICC,[199] and the distinction between IACs and NIACs is part of the statutory framework at the ICC and is incorporated into our domestic law in the ICCA.

The conduct took place in the context of and was associated with an armed conflict (the "nexus" requirement)

Having established the existence of an armed conflict, it must be proved that the relevant offence took place "*in the context of and was associated with*" either an IAC or NIAC. This is often referred to as a requirement that there be a *"nexus"* between the offence and the armed conflict. The nexus requirement distinguishes war crimes from other violations of

196 In this regard, note for example the discussion in the Trial Chamber Judgment in *Katanga* at paras. 1181-1182, as well as para. 1174.

197 *Prosecutor v Martic* (IT-95-11-T) Trial Judgment, June 10, 2007, paras. 41-43 and *Prosecutor v Oric* (IT-03-68-T) Trial Judgment, June 30 2006, para. 25 where the Trial Chamber noted that it was *"immaterial"* whether the crimes alleged occurred in an IAC or NIAC and see paras. 253-260.

198 See for example, *Tadic, Interlocutory Appeal on Decision*, paras. 96-97 and 128-129.

199 *Katanga*, Trial Judgment, para. 1175.

domestic criminal law.[200] The ICC has adopted the jurisprudence of the ICTY in relation to the nexus requirement, which required that the perpetrators conduct was (a) closely related to the hostilities, and (b) that the armed conflict played a major part (or substantial role) in the perpetrator's decision, or ability to commit the crime.[201]. The ICTY Appeals Chamber has listed the following factors as relevant to assessing the nexus requirement:

- Whether the perpetrator is a combatant,
- Whether the victim is a non-combatant,
- Whether the victim is a member of the opposing party,
- Whether the act may be said to serve the ultimate goal of a military campaign,
- Whether the crime is committed as part of or in the context of the perpetrator's official duties.[202]

It is not necessary for an offence to take place in the midst of actual warfare or fighting. Neither is it necessary that the offence is committed at the same time as actual fighting or warfare.[203] Rather, it is sufficient that the crime took place in the territory of a warring state, or in the

200 *Prosecutor v. Germain Katanga and Mathieu Ngudjolo Chui, "Decision on Confirmation of Charges"*, 30 September 2008, ("*Katanga*, Confirmation of Charges Decision") para. 383.

201 *Katanga*, Trial Judgment, para. 1176, *Bema*, Trial Judgment, para. 142.

202 *Prosecutor v. Kunarac et al.*, (IT-96-23/1-A), Appeal Judgment, 12 June 2002, paras. 58 - 59, endorsed by Pre-Trial Chamber I of the ICC, in *Katanga*, Confirmation of Charges Decision, 30 September 2008, para. 382; and in the *Bemba*, Trial Judgment, para. 143.

203 *Bemba*, Trial Judgment, para. 144. See also *Prosecutor v Tadic* Interlocutory Appeal Decision, para. 70.

territory under the control of a party to the conflict.[204] Although, there is likely to be a relationship between a perpetrator and a party to the conflict, it is not necessarily a requirement that a perpetrator had to be a member of a party to the conflict, rather it is important that there is a nexus between the crime and the armed conflict.[205]

The perpetrator was aware of factual circumstances that established the existence of an armed conflict

Each of the war crimes set out in the ICC (Elements of Crimes) Regulations contains the element that the perpetrator *"was aware of factual circumstances that established the existence of an armed conflict"*. In other words, the prosecution must prove that the perpetrator was aware of the existence of the armed conflict.[206] The Regulations explain that:

> *(1) "There is no requirement for a legal evaluation by the perpetrator as to the existence of an armed conflict or its character as international or non-international;*
>
> *(2) In that context there is no requirement for awareness by the perpetrator of the facts that established the character of the conflict as international or non-international;*
>
> *(3) There is only a requirement for the awareness of the factual circumstances that established the existence of an armed conflict that*

---

[204] *Kunarac* Appeal Judgment, para. 57. See also *Prosecutor v Tadic* Interlocutory Appeal Decision, para. 70.

[205] *Bemba*, Trial Judgment, para. 143.

[206] Note that in the *Bemba*, Trial Judgment, the Trial Chamber at para. 147 confirms that the relevant awareness is that of the perpetrators of the crimes (and that the same applies to the contextual elements for CAH). See also for example, *Katanga* Confirmation of Charges Decision, para. 387.

is implicit in the terms "took place in the context of and was associated with".[207]

Protected status of victim or property

In order to prove the relevant contextual elements of war crimes the prosecution must also establish the protected status of the victims of those crimes – be that person or property. The terminology of *"protected status"* derives from the fact that the international conventions, namely the Geneva Conventions and the Hague Conventions were intended to provide various protections for different categories of persons. The Geneva Conventions were intended to protect the *"victims of war"*. Whereas, the Hague Conventions were concerned with the rights of combatants. In order to understand this more fully it is helpful to consider the relevant background to these Conventions and equipped with that knowledge return to the ICCA.

(i) "Protected Persons" and "Protected Property" - the "Grave Breach" provisions of the Geneva Conventions - Schedule 8, Article 8(2)(a) of the ICCA:

As discussed above, there are four Geneva Conventions each of which relate to a different category of *"victims"*:

- *wounded and sick in armed forces in the field,*[208]

[207] Regulations, War Crimes, Introduction.

[208] Convention for the Amelioration of the Condition of the Wounded and Sick in Armed Forces in the Field, (1950) 75 UNTS 31, arts. 13, 24-26.

- *wounded, sick and shipwrecked members of the armed forces at sea,*[209]
- *prisoners of war,*[210]
- *civilians.*[211]

All of these categories of persons are defined as *"protected persons"*. *"Grave breaches"* of the Geneva Conventions require the prosecution to prove that the victims belonged to one of these categories of *"protected persons"*. Likewise, the relevant provision in the ICCA, Schedule 8, Article 8(2)(a), prohibits *"grave breaches"* when committed against any of the above categories of *"protected persons"* in the four Geneva Conventions. The prosecution will therefore have to prove that the victim of a grave breach offence is a *"protected person"* or *"property"* under one of the four Geneva Conventions. Thus, it is an element of the grave breach offences that: *"Such person or persons were protected under one or more of the Geneva Conventions of 1949"*.[212] In the case of *"property"* it is an element that: *"Such property was protected under the Geneva Conventions of 1949"*.[213]

(ii) *"Persons taking no active part in the hostilities, including member of armed forces who have laid down their arms and those placed hors de combat by sickness, wounds, detention or any other cause"* - violations of

---

209 Convention for the Amelioration of the Condition of the Wounded, Sick and Shipwrecked Members of Armed Forces at Sea, (1950) 75 UNTS 31, arts 13, 24-26.

210 Convention Relative to the Treatment of Prisoners of War, (1950) 75 UNTS 135, arts. 4, 13, 16, 20.

211 Convention Relative to the Protection of Civilian Persons in Time of War, (1950) 75 UNTS 287, arts. 8, 44, 45, 73, 75, 77.

212 See for example the war crime of wilful killing, Regulations, Article 8(2)(a)(i) para. 2.

213 See the war crime of destruction and appropriation of property, Regulations, Article 8(2)(a)(iv) para. 3.

article 3 common to the Geneva Conventions of 12 August 1949 - Schedule 8(2)(c) of the ICCA:

As discussed above, Common article 3 to the Geneva Conventions relates to NIAC. The *"protected status"* of victims under Common Article 3 to the Geneva Conventions, differs from the notion of *"protected persons"* under the four Geneva Conventions. Schedule 8, Article 8(2)(c) of the ICCA, which copies Article 8(2)(c) of the Rome Statute, is based upon Common Article 3 and categorises the *"protected status"* of victims as follows:

> *"Persons taking no active part in the hostilities, including members of armed forces who have laid down their arms and those placed hors de combat by sickness, wounds, detention or any other cause".*

The Regulations provide some elaboration on this definition, explaining that the list includes *"civilians, medical personnel taking no active part in the hostilities"* and that the term *"religious personnel"* includes those non-confessional non-combatant military personnel carrying out a similar function".[214] In the Regulations each violation of Common Article 3 sets out as an element of the offence that: *"Such person or persons were either hors de combat, or were civilians, medical personnel, or religious personnel* [footnote omitted] *taking no active part in the hostilities"*.[215]

(iii) Schedule 8, Article 8(2)(b) of the ICCA and Schedule 8, Article 8(2)(d) of the ICCA:

214 For example, the war crime of murder, Regulations Article 8(2)(c)(1) - 1, para. 2, which provides that: *"Such person or persons were either hors de combat, or were civilians, medical personnel, or religious personnel (1) taking no active part in the hostilities"* (footnote (1) says that : *"The term "religious personnel" includes those non-confessional military personnel carrying out a similar function"*).

215 See for example, the war crime of Murder, Article 8(2)(c)(i)-1, para, 2; and the war crime of Mutilation, Article 8(2)(c)(i)-2, para. 3.

Schedule 8, Article 8(2)(a) ICCA concerning grave breaches, and Schedule 8, Article 8(2)(c) concerning violations of Common article 3, impose the above status criteria regarding the protected status of victims. What then of Schedule 8, Article 8(2)(b) and Schedule 8, Article 8(2)(d) concerning *"Other serious violations of the laws and customs applicable in international armed conflict" and "Other serious violations of the laws and customs applicable in armed conflicts not of an international character"* respectively? These offences cover a large number of wide ranging violations both against persons and property, as diverse as the war crime of using and recruiting child soldiers under the age of 15,[216] to the war crime of attacking objects or persons using the distinctive emblems of the Geneva Conventions.[217] The Regulations set out the relevant requirements in relation to the status of protected persons and property as an element/s of many of the offences under Schedule 8, Article 8(2)(b) and Schedule 8, Article 8(2)(d) . So for example, in relation to the war crime of using and recruiting child soldiers under the age of 15 the prosecution must prove that *"such person or persons were under the age of 15"*.[218] In relation to the war crime of attacking objects or persons using the distinctive emblems of the Geneva Conventions, the prosecution must prove that *"one or more persons, buildings, medical units or transports or other objects"* were attacked.[219] However, in relation to Schedule 8, Article 8(2)(b) and Schedule 8, Article 8(2)(d) war crimes it is important to note that there may be occasions where it is necessary to ascertain from where the offence in question derived (i.e. from which Convention or customary IL rule) in order to ensure that the protected status of the victim or property can be proven.

---

216 Regulations, Article 8(2)(b)(xxvi).

217 Regulations, Article 8 (2) (b)(xxiv).

218 Regulations, Article 8(2)(b)(xxvi), para. 2.

219 Regulations, Article 8(2)(b)(xxiv), para. 1.

The perpetrator was aware of the factual circumstances that established that protected status

Finally, the prosecution must prove that the perpetrator was aware of the factual circumstances that established the protected status of the victim, or property.[220] This does not mean that is has to be established that the perpetrator knew that the victim was protected *per se*. Rather the perpetrator must have been aware of the *"factual circumstances"* that establish that protected status.[221]

Checklist for contextual elements of war crimes

- Can the existence of an armed conflict be established?
- Did the offence take place in the context of or was associated with the armed conflict?
- Was the perpetrator aware of the existence of an armed conflict?
- Is the victim a qualifying victim or the property qualifying property?
- Was the perpetrator aware of the victims protected status, or the protected status of the property?

---

[220] See for example the war crime of wilful killing, Regulations, Article 8(2)(a), Article 8(2)(a)(i) para 3. *"the perpetrator was aware of the factual circumstances that established that protected status"* and note footnotes (2) and (3).

[221] *Katanga*, Decision on Confirmation of Charges, para. 297, explaining that it is not necessary for the perpetrator to have considered and concluded that the victim was a protected person under any of the Geneva Conventions.

Elements of the underlying war crimes offences

The ICC (Elements of Crimes) Regulations set out the elements of the various underlying offences that can be charged as war crimes. There are more than 70 different war crimes offences in the Regulations. A prosecutor considering charges for war crimes will need to consider which of the different war crimes to include in the indictment. A Crown Court judge trying a defendant for war crimes will need to direct the jury about the elements of the war crime charged. Given that the Crown Court judge has a duty to "*take into account*" the ICC Elements of Crimes document, the Regulations is an indispensable document. For reasons of length, this chapter will not set out all of the elements of all of the war crimes in the Regulations. Rather, all of the elements will be listed for the first few war crimes to familiarise the reader with the way in which the elements of the war crimes offences are structured. Thereafter, only the elements of the *actus reus* and *mens rea* (where there are *mens rea* requirements in addition to intent and knowledge) will generally be listed. In some instances, the elements of some of the war crimes are not set out but a reference to the Regulations is included.[222]

In this Chapter the various war crimes are listed under the following eight categories which link similar types of crime:

- **Offences against the Person**
- **Sexual Offences**
- **Offences against personal freedoms**
- **Theft and offences against property, objects and places**
- **False imprisonment, deportation, transfer and displacement**

---

222 The reader may find it helpful to cross-refer to the text of the ICCA (Elements of Crimes) Regulations to see not only the elements of the *actus reus* and *mens rea* but also the contextual elements.

- **Offences against protected parties: (1) civilians, (2) peacekeepers, (3) POWs and combatants**

- **Denial of due process / fair trial rights**

- **Violations of the rules and means of combat**

In grouping the various war crimes in this way, the Chapter does not follow the flow of Article 8 in Schedule 8 in the ICCA, nor the ICC (Elements of Crimes) Regulations, in which the different war crimes are grouped on the basis of the sources of law from which they derive. It is hoped that grouping the different war crimes in terms of similar types of offence will make it easier for the reader to consider the relevant war crimes.

The structure of the elements of the underlying offences

To understand the offences in the ICCA (Elements of Crimes) Regulations it is worth pausing to consider how the elements of the offences are structured. The elements of each offence include: the contextual elements of the offence (addressed in the first part of this chapter) and the *actus reus* of the offence. The *mens rea* of the offence is not set out as a separate element of the offence. Under the ICC regime, *mens rea* is governed by Article 30 of the ICC Statute, which has been incorporated into domestic law by section 66 ICCA (see below). However, where a crime is one of specific intent, or strict liability, this is set out in the elements of the offence in the Regulations. By way of example, the elements of torture as a war crime in the context of IAC are set out in the Regulations as follows [footnote omitted]:

1. *The perpetrator inflicted severe physical or mental pain or suffering upon one or more persons.*

2. *The perpetrator inflicted the pain or suffering for such purposes as: obtaining information or a confession, punishment,*

intimidation or coercion or for any reason based on discrimination of any kind.

3. *Such person or persons were protected under one or more of the Geneva Conventions of 1949.*

4. *The perpetrator was aware of the factual circumstances that established that protected status.*

5. *The conduct took place in the context of and was associated with an international armed conflict.*

6. *The perpetrator was aware of factual circumstances that established the existence of an armed conflict.* [223]

Element 1 in bold represents the *actus reus* of the offence of torture as a war crime. Element 2 in bold represents the specific intent element of the *mens rea* of the crime. The remaining elements of the offence represent the contextual elements: element 3 represents the protected person requirement; element 5 represents the armed conflict and nexus to the armed conflict requirements; elements 4 and 6 represent the *mens rea* requirements as regards the contextual elements of the offence. It is worth noting that the level of detail in which the *actus reus* of each underlying offence is set out varies considerably in relation to the different war crimes in the Regulations.

Mens rea under the ICCA

Section 66 ICCA incorporates Article 30 of the Rome Statute, which sets out the *mens rea* that applies to international crimes under the ICC regime. The default position under section 66(2) (like Article 30(2) of the Rome Statute) is that a person is regarded as committing a crime, where the *actus reus* of the offence is committed *"with intent and knowledge"*, except where the offence in question specifically provides

[223] Regulations, Article 8(2)(a)(ii).

that a different *mens rea* applies to that offence.[224] Section 66(3) ICCA sets out that:

> *"For this purpose –*
>
> (a) *A person has intent –*
>
> (i) *In relation to conduct, where he means to engage in the conduct, and*
>
> (ii) *In relation to a consequence, where he means to cause the consequence or is aware that it will occur in the ordinary course of events; and*
>
> (b) *"knowledge" means awareness that a circumstance exists or a consequence will occur in the ordinary course of events."*

Section 66(4) ICCA underscores that, *"in interpreting and applying the provisions of this section (which corresponds to article 30) the court shall take into account any relevant judgment or decision of the ICC"* and that *"account may also be taken of any other relevant jurisprudence"*. The Regulations state that the *"existence of intent and knowledge can be inferred from relevant facts and circumstances"*.[225]

The *mens rea* as articulated in section 66 ICCA (taken from Article 30 of the Rome Statute) does not include recklessness. The inclusion of recklessness was proposed in early drafts of the Rome Statute but ultimately was not included after the process of lengthy negotiations to agree on the text of the Statute.[226] However, section 66(4) ICCA seems to leave open the possibility that a domestic court considering the *mens rea* of an offence could apply recklessness. Jurisprudence at the ad hoc tribunals has included the standard of recklessness in relation to the *mens*

224 See the *'General Introduction'* section to the Regulations, para. 2.

225 Regulations, *'General Introduction'*, para. 3, which mirrors the ICC Elements of Crimes document (2011), General Introduction, para. 2.

226 William A. Schabas, *"Oxford Commentaries on International Law, The International Criminal Court, A Commentary on the Rome Statute"*, OUP, 2010 ed., p. 473.

rea of numerous war crimes.[227] As for the ICC, there are conflicting decisions from Pre-Trial Chambers at the ICC in respect of whether Article 30 of the Rome Statute can be interpreted to include recklessness.[228] However, in *Katanga*, an ICC Trial Chamber preferred the reasoning of the Pre-Trial Chamber in *Bemba*, which held that Article 30 of the Statute included *"oblique intent"* but not recklessness.[229]

Offences against the person

The following war crimes fall under the category of offences against the person:[230]

- **Murder (NIAC) and wilful killing (IAC)**
- **Killing or wounding a person *hors de combat* (IAC)**
- **Treacherously killing or wounding (IAC and NIAC)**
- **Torture (IAC and NIAC)**

227 For example, the war crime of murder (noted below).

228 Pre-Trial Chamber II in *Prosecutor v. Jean-Pierre Bemba Gombo* (ICC-01/05-01/08), *"Decision Pursuant to Article 61(7)(a) and (b) of the Rome Statute on the Charges of the Prosecutor Against Jean-Pierre Bemba Gombo"*, ("*Bemba*, Confirmation of Charges Decision") 15 June 2009, para. 360-368, came to the clear conclusion that recklessness was not captured by Article 30 of the Statute based on a textual interpretation of Article 30 and a review of the *travaux preparatoires* of the Statute. By contrast, Pre-Trial Chamber I in *Prosecutor v. Lubanga* (ICC-01/04-01/06), *"Decision on the Confirmation of Charges"*, 29 January 2007 paras. 352-355 referring to the jurisprudence of the ICTY and ICTR considered that Article 30 included *"dolus eventualis"*, which ostensibly is recklessness, as it covers a situation where a defendant is aware of the risk that a crime may result from their conduct and consents to taking that risk.

229 *Katanga* Trial Judgment, para. 776 and discussion at paras. 773-339.

230 For ease of reference, I have included in brackets which are offences in an IAC and a NIAC and which in both IAC and NIAC.

- **Mutilation (IAC and NIAC)**
- **Inhuman treatment and cruel treatment (IAC)**
- **Wilfully causing great suffering (IAC)**
- **Outrages upon personal dignity (IAC and NIAC)**
- **Biological experiments (IAC)**
- **Medical or scientific experiments (IAC and NIAC)**

As can be seen from the list above, rather than a single war crime of murder, there are in fact four different war crimes which concern murder. The four different offences relate to whether the crime was committed in an IAC or an NIAC, as well as the different categories of protected person.

Murder and Wilful Killing

As a war crime in the context of an IAC, murder is prohibited as *"wilful killing"*, a grave breach of the Geneva Conventions.[231] As a war crime in the context of NIAC, murder is prohibited as *"murder"*, a serious violation of article 3 common to the four Geneva Conventions.[232]

The Regulations state that the elements of the war crime of *"wilful killing"*, a grave breach of the Geneva Conventions, are as follows:

1. *The perpetrator killed one or more persons.*[233]

---

231 ICCA, Schedule 8, Article 8(2)(a)(i).

232 ICCA, Schedule 8, Article 8(2)(c)(i).

233 A footnote to this element provides that: *"the term "killed" is interchangeable with the term "caused death"*. This footnote applies to all elements which use either of these concepts.

2. *Such person or persons were protected under one or more of the Geneva Conventions of 1949.*

3. *The perpetrator was aware of the factual circumstances that established that protected status.*[234]

4. *The conduct took place in the context of and was associated with an international armed conflict.*[235]

5. *The perpetrator was aware of factual circumstances that established the existence of an armed conflict.*

The Regulations provide that the elements of the war crime of *"murder"*, a serious violation of article 3 common to the four Geneva Conventions are:

1. *The perpetrator killed one or more persons.*

2. *Such person or persons were either hors de combat, or were civilians, medical personnel, or religious personnel*[236] *taking no active part in the hostilities.*

3. *The perpetrator was aware of the factual circumstances that established this status.*

---

234 A footnote to this element provides that: *"This mental element recognizes the interplay between articles 30 and 32. This footnote also applies to the corresponding element in each crime under article 8(2)(a), and to the element in other crimes in article 8(2) concerning the awareness of factual circumstances that establish the status of persons or property protected under the relevant international law of armed conflict. With respect to nationality it is that the perpetrator needs only to know that the victim belonged to an adverse party to the conflict"*.

235 A footnote to this element provides that: *"The term "international armed conflict" includes military occupation"*.

236 A footnote to this element provides that: *"The term "religious personnel" includes those non-confessional non-combatant military personnel carrying out a similar function"*.

4. *The conduct took place in the context of and was associated with an armed conflict not of an international character.*

5. *The perpetrator was aware of factual circumstances that established the existence of an armed conflict.*

The Regulations simply provide that the *actus reus* of the offence of wilful killing / murder requires that *"the perpetrator killed one or more persons"*. A judge in the Crown Court will, of course, want to decide whether to use this definition, or the *actus reus*, familiar to domestic criminal practitioners. Unsurprisingly, murder as a war crime, has been charged on countless occasions at the international criminal tribunals. So, there is a wealth of jurisprudence in relation to the elements of murder as a war crime.

As regards the *actus reus* of the crime the following propositions emerge from the international jurisprudence:

- the crime can be committed by either an act or omission; [237]
- there must be a cause and effect relationship between the perpetrator's conduct and the death of the victim; [238]
- proof of death does not necessarily require proof that the dead body of the person has been recovered, provided that the victim's death is the only reasonable conclusion that can be drawn.[239]

As regards *mens rea*, the relevant requirement under the ICC regime is intent and knowledge, as articulated in Article 30 of the Statute

---

237 See for example: *Katanga*, Trial Judgment, 7 March 2014, para. 767.

238 *Katanga*, Trial Judgment, para. 767 referring to ICC and ICTY caselaw in footnote 1813; *Katanga*, Confirmation of Charges Decision, para. 296, where the Pre-Trial Chamber adopted the ICTY conclusion that the conduct of the perpetrator must have been a *"substantial cause"* of the death of the victim (referring to case law from the ICTY at footnote 400).

239 See for example: *Katanga*, Trial Judgment, para. 768.

(incorporated by section 66 ICCA).[240] Trial and pre-trial Chambers at the ICC have interpreted Article 30 as encompassing circumstances where the perpetrator either intends to kill, or is aware that the death of the person will occur in the ordinary course of events.[241] As with the *actus reus*, the Crown Court judge will likewise have to decide whether to use the *mens rea* familiar to the domestic offence of murder, or the *mens rea* in section 66 ICCA.[242] Notably, at the *ad hoc* international criminal tribunals the *mens rea* requirement has been satisfied in circumstances including where a perpetrator either intends to kill, or intends to cause serious bodily harm, in the reasonable knowledge that death would likely result and/or with reckless disregard for human life.[243]

As regards proceedings at the ICC, there have been convictions for murder as a war crime in the cases of: Germain Katanga (as an accessory),[244] Bosco Ntaganda for murder and attempted murder, in part as a direct perpetrator and in part as an indirect perpetrator,[245] and

---

240 See for example, *Katanga* Trial Judgment, para. 773 and *Katanga,* Confirmation of Charges Decision, para. 295.

241 See for example: *Katanga* Trial Judgment, para. 793 and note the discussion in the context of murder as a CAH at paras. 773 – 779; *Bemba*, Confirmation of Charges Decision, paras. 352-369.

242 As noted above, section 66(4) ICCA seems to leave open the possibility that a domestic court considering the *mens rea* of an offence could apply recklessness.

243 For example: *Prosecutor v. Emmanuel Ndindabahizi* (ICTTR-2001-71-I), Trial Judgement, 15 July 2004, para. 487, referring to recklessmss and see the refences at footnote 618 to other ICTR cases and sources of law. Alternatively, see: *Kordić and Čerkez* Appeal Judgement, para. 36, referring to the intent to cause death or serious bodily injury and an understanding that death was likely to result.

244 *Katanga*, Trial Judgment.

245 *Prosecutor v. Bosco Ntaganda* (ICC-01/04-02/06) 8 July 2019, Trial Chamber VI, *"Judgment"* and the *Appeal Chamber's Judgment of 30 March 2021 "Judgment on the appeals of Mr Bosco Ntaganda and the Prosecutor against the decision of the Trial Chamber VI of 8 July 2019 entitled 'Judgment'"* (*"Ntaganda,* Trial Judgment*" and "Ntaganda* Appeal Judgment*"*).

Dominic Ongwen.[246] Acquittals in relation to murder as a war crime were recorded in the cases of Mathieu Ngudjolo Chui [247] and Jean-Pierre Bebma Gombo (in which the Appeals Chamber overturned the decision of the Trial Chamber, finding by a majority, that the Trial Chamber had erred in its application of command responsibility).[248] There are three ongoing trials at the ICC which include charges of murder as a war crime: Abd-Al-Rahman,[249] Abdallah Banda,[250] and the cases of Alfred Yekatom and Patrice-Edouard Ngaïssona (which are joined).[251]

---

246 Trial Chamber IX convicted Ongwen of 61 counts of the 70 counts indictment (*Prosecutor v. Dominic Ongwen* (ICC-02/04-01/15), *'Trial Judgment'*, 4 February 2021 (*"Ongwen Trial Judgment'*) (confirmed on appeal).

247 *Prosecutor v. Mathieu Ngudjolo Chui* (ICC-01/04-02/12) 18 December 2012, Trial Chamber II *"Judgment pursuant to article 74 of the Statute"*, upheld by an Appeals Chamber on 7 April 2015 in *"Judgement on the Prosecutor's appeal against the decision of the Trial Chamber II entitled, "Judgment pursuant to article 74 of the Statute" "* (*"Chui,* Trial Judgment*" and "Chui* Appeal Judgment*"*).

248 *Prosecutor v. Jean-Pierre Bemba Gombo* (ICC-01/05-01/08 A) 8 June 2018, *"Judgment on the appeal of Mr Jean-Pierre Bemba Gombo against Trial Chamber III's "Judgment pursuant to Article 74 of the Statute" ("Bemba,* Appeal Judgment*")*

249 *Prosecutor v Ali Muhammed Ali Abd-Al-Rahman ('Ali Kushayb')* (ICC-02/05-01/20) 9 July 2021, *Public with confidential Annex 1, Decision on the confirmation of charges against Ali Muhammed Ali Abd-Al-Rahman ('Ali Kushayb')* (hereinafter, *"Abd-Al-Rahman confirmation of charges decision"*) at paras. 33-35.

250 *Prosecutor v Abdallah Banda* (ICC-02/05-03/09), charges including under article 8(2)(c)(i) of the Rome Statute were confirmed by Pre-Trial Chamber I on 7 March 2021 but the accused is currently at large.

251 *Prosecutor v Alfred Yekatom and Patrice-Edouard Ngaissona* (ICC-01/14-01/18) Pre-Trial Chamber II, 11 December 2011, *"Redacted Version Published 20 December 2019, Decision on the Confirmation of Charges against Alfred Yekatom and Patrice-Edouard Ngaissona*" (*"Confirmation of Charges Decision, Yekatom and Ngaissona*").

Killing or Wounding a Person Hors De Combat

The murder of persons *hors de combat*[252] in the context of NIAC can be charged under the auspices of the offence of "*murder*" (above).[253] However, in the context of an IAC the murder of persons *hors de combat* cannot be charged as "*wilful killing*".[254] Rather, there is a separate provision in the context of an IAC under which the murder of persons *hors de combat* must be charged, namely Article 8(2)(b)(vi) which provides for the "*war crime of killing or wounding a person hors de combat*". The first element of the offence, the *actus reus*, is the same as "*murder*" and "*wilful killing*", namely, that "*the perpetrator killed or injured one or more persons*". The second element of the offence expressly states that "*such person or persons were hors de combat*".[255] Care must therefore be taken to charge the murder of a person *hors de combat* under the correct provision: in the context of a NIAC under the ICC Act, Schedule 8, Article 8(2)(c)(i), and in the context of IAC under the ICC Act, Schedule 8, Article 8(2)(b)(vi).

Treacherously Killing or Wounding

A further offence of murder which does not concern the murder of civilians, but rather the murder of combatants, is the offence of "*Treacherously Killing or Wounding*". This offence is a war crime in the context of both IAC (Schedule 8, Article 8(2)(b)(xi)) and NIAC (Schedule 8, Article 8(2)(e)(ix)) and the elements of the underlying offence are the same in both types of conflict.[256]

---

252 Persons who are '*hors de combat*' means persons who are '*out of combat*', for example because they are injured or incapacitated or have laid down their arms.

253 ICCA, Article 8(2)(C)(i).

254 ICCA, Article 8(2)(a)(i).

255 Regulations, Article 8(2)(b)(vi).

256 Regulations, Article 8(2)(b)(xi) and Article 8(2)(e)(ix) respectively.

Torture as a war crime

Torture is a war crime in the context of IAC and NIAC. It is a grave breach of the Geneva Conventions punishable under Schedule 8, Article 8(2)(a)(ii) ICCA. It is also a serious violation of common article 3 to the Geneva Conventions punishable under Schedule 8, Article 8(2)(c)(i) ICCA. The elements of the underlying offence of torture are the same in relation to both IAC[257] and NIAC.[258]

The *actus reus* of the offence is:

> *"The perpetrator inflicted severe physical or mental pain or suffering upon one or more persons".*

The *mens rea* of the offence is:

> *"The perpetrator inflicted the pain or suffering for such purposes as: obtaining information or a confession, punishment, intimidation or coercion or for any reason based on discrimination of any kind".*

Additionally, the Regulations expressly note that, *"with respect to mental elements associated with elements involving value judgment, such as those using the terms "inhumane" or "severe", it is not necessary that the perpetrator personally completed a particular value judgment, unless otherwise indicated below".*[259]

Torture as a war crime is a crime of specific intent. It requires that the perpetrator inflicted *"severe physical or mental pain or suffering"* upon one

[257] Regulations, Article 8(2)(a)(ii)-1 war crime of torture. Note that in a footnote (35) attached to the elements of this offence it is stated that: *"As element 3 requires that all victims must be "protected persons" under one or more of the Geneva Conventions of 1949, these elements do not include the custody and control requirement found in the elements of article 7(1)(e)"* (Article 7(1) is the CAH of imprisonment or other severe deprivation of physical liberty).

[258] Article 8(2)(c)(i)-4, war crime of torture.

[259] Regulations, *'General Introduction'*, para. 4.

or more persons, for a specific purpose, such as *"obtaining information or a confession, punishment, intimidation or coercion or for any reason based upon discrimination"*. Significantly, the elements of torture as a war crime differ from the elements of torture as a CAH and as a crime under section 134 CJA 1988 because the latter categories do not require torture to have been inflected for a specific purpose i.e., they are not crimes of *"specific intent"*.

Just one accused at the ICC has been convicted of torture as a war crime (Dominic Ongwen).[260] However, it has also been charged as a war crime in three ongoing cases at the ICC: Al Hassan,[261] Mahamat Said Abdel Kain[262] and Yekatom and Ngaïssona.[263] Torture as a war crime has also featured in cases before the ad hoc tribunals,[264] so that case law will also be instructive in cases involving torture under the ICCA.

Mutilation

Mutilation is a war crime in both IAC and NAC. The elements of the underlying offence are identical in relation to both types of conflict. In IAC, *"Subjecting persons who are in the power of an adverse party to physical mutilation or to medical or scientific experiments of any kind which are neither justified by the medical, dental or hospital treatment of the person concerned nor carried out in his or her interest, and which cause death to or seriously endanger the health of such person or persons"* is prohibited in Schedule 8, Article 8(2)(b)(x) ICCA, as *"Other serious violations of the*

---

260 *Ongwen*, Trial Judgment.

261 *Prosecutor v. Al Hassan* (ICC-01/12 – 01/18) (the decisions on the confirmation of charges are available in French only).

262 *Prosecutor v. Mahamat Said Abdel Kani* (ICC-01/14-01/21), Pre-Trial Chamber II, *"Decision on the confirmation of charges against Mahamat Said Abdel Kani"*, 9 December 2021 (, *"Said,* Confirmation of Charges Decision").

263 See Confirmation of Charges Decision, *Yekatom and Ngaissona*.

264 See for example: *Kunarać et al.* (IT-96-23/1-A), Judgment, 12 June 2002, paras.142-156 discussing the elements of torture and referring also to the ICTR case law as well as that of the ICTY.

laws and customs applicable in international armed conflict, within the established framework of international law".

The Regulations state that the elements of the offence in IAC are:

1. *The perpetrator subjected one or more persons to mutilation, in particular by permanently disfiguring the person or persons, or by permanently disabling or removing an organ or appendage.*

2. *The conduct caused death or seriously endangered the physical or mental health of such person or persons.*

3. *The conduct was neither justified by the medical, dental or hospital treatment of the person or persons concerned nor carried out in such person's or persons 'interest.*[265]

4. *Such person or persons were in the power of an adverse party.*

5. *The conduct took place in the context of and was associated with an international armed conflict.*

6. *The perpetrator was aware of factual circumstances that established the existence of an armed conflict.*[266]

The equivalent offence in the context of NIAC is prohibited in Schedule 8, Article 8(2)(e)(xi) ICCA and the Regulations.[267] The elements of the war crime of mutilation are set out in detail in the Regulations. In essence the war crime prohibits acts of mutilation, which either cause death, or seriously endanger the health of the victim (who must be in the power of an adverse party) and which are not justified by the medical, dental or hospital treatment of the person concerned or carried out in his/her

[265] Also note footnote 46 appended to this element in the Regulations which explains that consent is not a defence to this crime, and that the same element for article 8 (2) (b) (x)-2.

[266] Regulations, Article 8(2)(b)(x)-I.

[267] Regulations, Article 8(2)(e)(xi)-1 war crime of mutilation.

interest. The phrase *"in particular"* signals that *"permanently disfiguring the victim, permanently disabling or removing an organ or appendage of the victim"* are illustrative examples of mutilation. No charges in relation to the war crime of mutilation have yet been confirmed in proceedings before the ICC.[268] However, the war crime of mutilation featured in cases before the SCSL. Indeed, one of the hallmarks of the conflict in Sierra Leone was the amputation of civilian limbs by the rebel forces - the Revolutionary United Front (RUF) and the Armed Forces Revolutionary Council (AFRC). The analysis and application of the law in relation to the war crime of mutilation in the judgments from the Special Court for Sierra Leone are therefore helpful in relation to this crime.[269]

Inhuman Treatment and Cruel Treatment

"Inhuman treatment" is a war crime in IAC. It is a grave breach of the Geneva Conventions punishable under Schedule 8, Article 8(2)(a)(iii) ICCA. The equivalent offence in NIAC is *"Cruel treatment"*, which is a serious violation of article 3 common to the four Geneva Conventions punishable under Schedule 8, Article 8(2)(c)(i) ICCA. Aside from the contextual elements of the offences, the elements of the offences of *"Inhuman treatment"* and *"Cruel treatment"* are identical.[270] The *actus reus* of the offence is that:

> *"The perpetrator inflicted severe physical or mental pain or suffering upon one or more persons".*

---

[268] A confirmation of charges hearing in the *Mokom* case is scheduled for January 2023 in relation to which a Pre-Trial Chamber is due to consider whether or not to confirm charges including mutilation as a war crime (as per the case information sheet).

[269] See for example, *Prosecutor v. Sesay, Kallon and Gbao* (SCSL-04-15-), Trial Judgment, 2 March 2009 ("the RUF Trial judgment"), discussing the war crime of mutilation and the elements of the offence at paras. 178-182.

[270] Regulations, Article 8(2)(a)(ii)-2 War Crime of inhuman treatment, and Article 8(2)(c)(i)-3 War crime of cruel treatment.

The war crimes of *"Inhuman treatment"* and *"Cruel treatment"* have been charged on numerous occasions at the ad hoc international criminal tribunals and other war crimes tribunals. There is therefore an abundance of case law regarding both the law and its practical application in relation to these crimes.[271] *"Inhuman treatment"* and *" Cruel treatment"* act as a residual category for a broad range of serious acts and offences which are not otherwise specifically enumerated in the Statutes of the various courts and tribunals.[272] At the ICC, *"Cruel Treatment"* has been charged in the following cases: Al Hassan,[273] Ongwen,[274] Said[275] and Yekatom and *Ngaïssona*.[276]

Wilfully Causing Great Suffering

The crime of *"Wilfully causing great suffering or serious injury to body or health"* is prohibited under Schedule 8, Article 8(2)(a)(iii) ICCA, as a grave breach of the Geneva Conventions. *"Wilfully causing great suffering"* is a crime in IAC and there is no equivalent in NIAC.

The *actus reus* of the offence is that:

> *"The perpetrator caused great physical or mental pain or suffering to, or serious injury to body or health of, one or more persons".*[277]

---

271 See for example, *Prosecutor v. Kordić & Čerkez* (IT-95-14/2-A) Appeal Judgment, 17 December 2004, para. 39 for a definition of *"inhuman treatment"* and *Prosecutor v Kordic et al.,* (IT-95-14/2-T), Trial Judgment, 26 February 2001, para. 265, for a definition of *"cruel treatment"*.

See for example, *Prosecutor. v. Delalić et al.,* Trial Judgement, 16 November 1998, para. 552.

273 *Prosecutor v. Al Hassan* (ICC-01/12 – 01/18).

274 *Ongwen* Trial Judgment (Ongwen was acquitted of charges of cruel treatment).

275 *Said,* Confirmation of Charges Decision.

276 Confirmation of Charges Decision in *Yekatom and Ngaïssona.*

277 Regulations, Article 8(2)(a)(iii) para. 1.

"Wilfully Causing Great Suffering" is similar, but distinct from the war crimes of torture and "Inhuman treatment", which are also grave breaches of the Geneva Conventions. Unlike torture there is no specific intent requirement. Unlike *"Inhuman treatment"* there is a requirement that *"great physical or mental pain or suffering"* be proven. *"Wilfully Causing Great Suffering"* is yet to be charged at the ICC. However, it has been prosecuted in a handful of cases before the ICTY, and guidance should therefore be sought from the jurisprudence of that Tribunal.[278]

Outrages upon Personal Dignity

"Outrages Upon Personal Dignity" is a war crime in IAC and NIAC. The elements of the underlying offence are the same in both types of conflict. In IAC *"Outrages upon Personal Dignity"* are prohibited by Schedule 8, Article 8(2)(b)(xxi), as an *"Other serious violation of the laws and customs applicable in the context of international armed conflict"*. Schedule 8, Article 8(2)(c)(ii) prohibits *"Outrages upon Personal Dignity"* as a *"violation of article 3 common to the four Geneva Conventions"* in NIAC.

The *actus reus* of the offence is that:

1. *The perpetrator humiliated, degraded or otherwise violated the dignity of one or more persons (1).*[279]

2. *The severity of the humiliation, degradation or other violation was of such degree as to be generally recognized as an outrage upon personal dignity.*

---

278 See for example: *Prosecutor v. Blaškić* (IT-95-14-T) Trial Judgment, 3 March 2000, para.156; *Prosecutor v Delalić* (IT-96-21-T) Trial Judgment, 16 November 1998, para.442; and *Prosecutor v Kordić. et al.,* (IT-95-14/2-T), Trial Judgment, 26 February 2001, para. 245.

279 Regulations, Article 8(2)(b)(xxi) footnote 1 and see also Article 8(2)(c)(ii) and footnote 1, which is the same.

Footnote (1) states that:

> *"For this crime, "persons" can include dead persons. It is understood that the victim need not personally be aware of the existence of the humiliation or degradation or other violation. This element takes into account relevant aspects of the cultural background of the victim."*

Notably, Article 8(2)(b)(xxi) in the Regulations like the corresponding provision in the ICC (Elements of Crimes) Document omits the contextual element describing the victim of the crime. This omission was considered by an ICC Pre-Trial Chamber in *Katanga*, which clarified that the contextual elements are that the perpetrator must have caused the humiliation, degradation, or violation of the personal dignity to individuals: (i) who are aligned to or whose allegiance is to a party to the conflict who is adverse or hostile to the perpetrator, and (ii) who are in the hands of the party to the conflict to which the perpetrator belongs.[280]

The offence can be committed through either an act or an omission.[281] The types of acts or omissions which can constitute *"Outrages upon Personal Dignity"* are *"left undefined"*.[282] So long as the acts of humiliation, degradation or violation to the person's dignity are *"real and serious"*, there is no requirement that such suffering be lasting.[283] Although the types of conduct that can amount to *"Outrages upon Personal Dignity"* are undefined, there are numerous examples provided in the case law. The ICC Pre-Trial Chamber in *Katanga* noted that the following acts have been recognised as *"Outrages upon Personal Dignity"* in the ICTY and ICTR jurisprudence:

- compelling victims to dance naked on a table,

[280] *Katanga,* Confirmation of Charges Decision, para. 368.

[281] *Katanga,* Confirmation of Charges Decision, paras. 368 - 369.

[282] *Katanga,* Confirmation of Charges Decision, para. 369.

[283] *Katanga,* Confirmation of Charges Decision, para. 369.

- using detainees as human shields or trench diggers,
- forcing detainees to relieve bodily functions in their clothing,
- imposing conditions of constant fear or being subject to physical violence,
- mental or sexual violence on detainees,
- forced incest,
- burying corpses in latrine pits, and
- leaving infants without care after killing their guardians.[284]

The war crime of *"Outrages upon Personal Dignity"* has featured in many cases before the ad hoc international criminal tribunals. At the ICC Dominic Ongwen has been convicted of *"Outrages against personal dignity"* by a Trial Chamber.[285] The crime has also been charged in *Abd-Al-Rahman*,[286] and *Al Hassan* at the ICC.[287] In addition, it has been prosecuted in a sizeable number of domestic war crimes prosecutions in European countries, in particular in circumstances involving the posting of photographs of crimes on Facebook. For example, the Federal Supreme Court in Frankfurt upheld a conviction of a German national who joined the *"armed Jihad"* in Syria. He posed for photographs with the heads of enemy combatants impaled on metal rods and then uploaded

---

[284] *Katanga,* Confirmation of Charges Decision, para. 371. Notably, *"forced incest"* and *"sexual violence"* would now be charged under the provisions in relation to *"any other form of sexual violence"* (see the discussion further below in relation to sexual violence crimes).

[285] *Ongwen,* Trial Judgment (confirmed on appeal).

[286] *Abd-Al-Rahman confirmation of charges decision, paras. 40-45.*

[287] *Prosecutor v. Al Hassan* (ICC-01/12 – 01/18).

them to Facebook after he returned to Germany.[288] Another example comes from a First Instance Court in Finland, which convicted a corporal from the Iraqi army of *"Outrages upon Personal Dignity"*. The corporal had uploaded a video to Facebook, which showed him cutting the head off a dead ISIL fighter, dangling it in his hands and displaying a *"victory sign"*.[289]

Biological Experiments

Schedule 8, Article 8(2)(a)(ii) ICCA prohibits *"Torture or inhuman treatment, including biological experiments"*. The war crime of conducting *"biological experiments"* upon protected persons is prohibited as a grave breach of the Geneva Conventions. There is no equivalent provision in NIAC. The elements of this war crime are set out in the Regulations at Article 8(2)(a)(ii) *"War crime of biological experiments"*. There haven't been any cases to date at the ICC featuring this war crime.

Medical or Scientific Experiments

The war crime of subjecting persons to *"medical or scientific experiments"* is prohibited in both IAC and NIAC. The elements of the underlying offence are the same in both types of conflict. In IAC the crime is prohibited under Schedule 8, Article 8(2)(b)(x) ICCA as an *"Other serious violations of the laws and customs applicable in international armed conflict"*. In NIAC the crime is prohibited by Article 8(2)(e)(xi) as an *"Other serious violation of the laws and customs applicable in non-international armed conflict"*. The elements of the offences are set out in the Regulations under Article 8(2)(b)(x)-2 and Article 8(2)(e)(xi)-2. The war crime of medical or scientific experiments is associated with the war

---

288 Federal Supreme Court, Frankfurt 27 July 2017, case number StR57/17. Found at: https://www.eurojust.europa.eu/document/case-number-str-57-17-federal-court-justice-germany-july-2017

289 First Instance Court, Finland, 10 January 2019, case number R 18/6593. Found at: https://www.eurojust.europa.eu/document/case-number-r18-6593-helsinki-district-court-finland-january-2019

crime of physical mutilation.[290] This war crime has not been charged in any cases before the ICC.

Sexual Offences

The following acts of sexual violence linked to an armed conflict are prohibited as war crimes in both IAC[291] and NIAC[292] by the ICCA:

- **Rape**
- **Sexual slavery**
- **Enforced prostitution**
- **Forced pregnancy**
- **Enforced sterilization**
- **Any other form of sexual violence ("also constituting a grave breach of the Geneva Conventions" (IAC), or "also constituting a serious violation of article 3 common to the four Geneva Conventions" (NIAC).**

As a matter of background, it is useful to be aware that at the ad hoc international criminal tribunals, rape as a war crime was initially charged

290 The crimes are prohibited under the same provisions in the ICCA and ICC Statute respectively. See: Schedule 8, Articles 8(2)(b)(x) and 8(2)(e)(xi) which concern both mutilation and medical or scientific experiments in IAC and NIAC respectively.

291 In IAC these crimes are prohibited as as a serious violation of the laws and customs applicable in international armed conflict (ICCA, Schedule 8, Article 8(2)(b)(xxii)).

292 In NIAC these crimes are prohibited as as a serious violation of the laws and customs applicable in armed conflicts not of an international character (ICCA, Schedule 8, Article 8(2)(e)(vi)).

as *"Outrages upon personal dignity"*. This was because rape had not been previously been recognised as a distinct war crime and so was not set out as a distinct war crime in the statutes of the tribunals. Jurisprudence from the ICTY and ICTR swiftly made clear that rape was a war crime under customary international law. Consequently, when the Rome Statute was drafted, rape, as well as the other forms of sexual violence listed in the provision above, were codified as distinct war crimes. In view of the above, offences of sexual violence should be charged under the provisions specifically relating to sexual violence offences, and not as *"Outrages upon personal dignity"*. Notably, in an early case at the ICC, Pre-Trial Chamber II in *Bemba* refused to confirm charges in circumstances where the prosecution charged *"Outrages upon personal dignity"* in respect of conduct which was fully encompassed in counts of rape also charged in the case. The Pre-Trial Chamber correctly took the view that rape was the most appropriate legal characterisation of the conduct presented.[293] There is a wealth of jurisprudence at the ad hoc international criminal tribunals in relation to sexual violence crimes, in particular rape and sexual slavery. Much of that jurisprudence considers the underlying sexual violence crimes in the context of CAH. Notably, the elements of the underlying offences of rape, sexual slavery, enforced prostitution, forced pregnancy, enforced sterilization and sexual violence are the same for war crimes and CAH.

Rape

Rape is a war crime in both IAC and NIAC. The elements of the underlying offence are the same in both types of conflict. In IAC, rape is prohibited by Schedule 8, Article 8(2)(b)(xxii) ICCA. In NIAC, rape is prohibited by Schedule 8, Article 8(2)(e)(vi) ICCA. The Regulations set out the elements of the *actus reus* as follows:

---

293 *Bemba*, Confirmation of Charges Decision, paras. 301-313, esp. at 308, 310 and 312.

> 1. *The perpetrator invaded*[294] *the body of a person by conduct resulting in penetration, however slight, of any part of the body of the victim or of the perpetrator with a sexual organ, or of the anal or genital opening of the victim with any object or any other part of the body.*
>
> 2. *The invasion was committed by force, or by threat of force or coercion, such as that caused by fear of violence, duress, detention, psychological oppression or abuse of power, against such person or another person, or by taking advantage of a coercive environment, or the invasion was committed against a person incapable of giving genuine consent.*[295]

Rape has been charged in numerous cases at the ad hoc international criminal tribunals and other war crimes tribunals.[296] At the ICC, a Trial Chamber convicted Bosco Ntaganda as an *'indirect perpetrator'* in relation to the war crime of rape arising from charges in relation to the situation in the D.R.C.[297] Another Trial Chamber convicted Dominic Ongwen of several counts of rape as a war crime (and as a CAH) in the context of a

---

294 Regulations, Article 8(2)(b)(xxii)-1. A footnote to this element provides that: *"The concept of "invasion" is intended to be broad enough to be gender-neutral*". Article 8(2)(b)(xxii)-1 is the relevant provision in IAC. In NIAC the relevant provision is Article 8(2)(e)(vi)-1.

295 *Ibid.* A footnote to this element provides that: *"It is understood that a person may be incapable of giving genuine consent if affected by natural, induced or age-related incapacity. This footnote also applies to the corresponding elements of article 8(2)(b)(xxii)3, 5 and 6)".*

296 The first case at the ad hoc tribunals to define rape was *Prosecutor v Jean-Paul Akayesu* (ICTR-96-4-T), Trial Judgment, 2 September 1998. At paras. 325-326 the ICTR Trial Chamber in *Akayesu* defined rape in broad terms. This case was followed shortly thereafter by *Prosecutor v. Furundžija* (IT-95-17/1-T) Trial Judgment, 10 December 1998, at the ICTY, which at para. 185 adopted a narrower definition of rape; which was confirmed by the ICTY Appeals Chamber in *Prosecutor v Kunarać et al. (IT-96-23*/1-A) Appeal Judgment, 12 June 2002 at para. 128. The ICTY definition is similar to that adopted in the ICC Elements of Crimes Document and replicated in the Regulations.

297 *Ntaganda,* Trial Judgment and Appeal Judgment.

lengthy indictment arising from the situation in Northern Uganda.[298] Rape has also been charged as a war crime in the cases of Abd-Al-Rahman[299] and Al Hassan.[300] As with murder, rape is another example of an offence where a Crown Court judge may consider whether or not to use elements of the familiar domestic offence, rather than those set out in the Regulations.

Sexual Slavery

Sexual slavery is a war crime in IAC and NIAC and the elements of the underlying offence are the same in both types of conflict. In IAC sexual slavery is prohibited under Schedule 8, Article 8(2)(b)(xxii). In NIAC, sexual slavery is prohibited under Schedule 8, Article 8(2)(vi) ICCA. The Regulations sets out the following as elements of the *actus reus*:

1. *The perpetrator exercised any or all of the powers attaching to the right of ownership over one or more persons, such as by purchasing, selling, lending or bartering such a person or persons, or by imposing on them a similar deprivation of liberty.* [301]

2. *The perpetrator caused such person or persons to engage in one or more acts of a sexual nature.*

---

298 *Ongwen,* Trial Judgment (confirmed on appeal).

299 *Abd-Al-Rahman,* Confirmation of Charges Decision, paras. 46-47.

300 *Prosecutor v. Al Hassan* (ICC-01/12 – 01/18).

301 Regulations, Article 8(2)(b)(xxii)-2. Footnote 54 appended to this element provides that: *"It is understood that such deprivation of liberty may, in some circumstances, include exacting forced labour or otherwise reducing a person to servile status as defined in the Supplementary Convention on the Abolition of Slavery, the Slave Trade, and Institutions and Practices Similar to Slavery of 1956. It is also understood that the conduct described in this element includes trafficking in persons, in particular women and children".* The relevant provision in NIAC is Article 8(2)(vi)-2 and there is an equivalent footnote.

The crime of sexual slavery has featured in a significant number of cases at the ICTY and the SCSL.[302] At the ICC, a Trial Chamber convicted Bosco Ntaganda as an *'indirect perpetrator'* in relation to the war crime of sexual slavery and as a CAH.[303] Dominic Ongwen was also convicted of charges including sexual slavery as a war crime and a CAH.[304] Sexual slavery is also amongst the charges in the case of *Al Hassan.*[305]

Enforced Prostitution

Enforced prostitution is a war crime in IAC and NIAC. The elements of the underlying offence are the same in both types of conflict. In IAC enforced prostitution is prohibited under Schedule 8, Article 8(2)(b)(xxii) ICCA. In NIAC, enforced prostitution is prohibited under Schedule 8, Article 8(2)(vi) ICCA. The Regulations set out the elements of the *actus reus* as follows:

> 1. *The perpetrator caused one or more persons to engage in one or more acts of a sexual nature by force, or by threat of force or coercion, such as that caused by fear of violence, duress, detention, psychological oppression or abuse of power, against such person or persons or another person, or by taking advantage of a coercive environment or such person's or persons' incapacity to give genuine consent.*

302 Note that the statute of the SCSL expressly listed *"sexual slavery"* as a CAH but not a war crime. At the SCSL there were convictions for sexual slavery including in *Prosecutor v Charles Taylor* (SCSL-03-01-T) Trial Chamber, Judgment, 18 May 2022 and Sentencing Judgment, 30 May 2012. Note that at the ICTY sexual slavery was charged as *"enslavement"* because *"sexual slavery"* was not expressly listed as a CAH in the ICTY statute. See for example: *Prosecutor v. Kvočka et al.* (IT-98-30/1-T) Trial Judgment, 2 November 2001, para. 541, see also *Prosecutor v. Kunarać* (discussed below in relation to *"enslavement"*).

303 *Bosco Ntaganda,* Trial Judgment.

304 *Ongwen,* Trial Judgment.

305 *Prosecutor v. Al Hassan* (ICC-01/12 – 01/18).

2. *The perpetrator or another person obtained or expected to obtain pecuniary or other advantage in exchange for or in connection with the acts of a sexual nature.*[306]

This war crime has not been charged in any of the cases at the ICC.

Forced Pregnancy

Forced Pregnancy is a war crime in IAC and NIAC. The elements of the underlying offence are the same in both types of conflict. In IAC forced pregnancy is prohibited under Schedule 8, Article 8(2)(b)(xxii) ICCA. In NIAC, forced pregnancy is prohibited under Schedule 8, Article 8(2)(vi) ICCA. The *actus reus* of the offence is that:

1. *The perpetrator confined one or more women forcibly made pregnant, with the intent of affecting the ethnic composition of any population or carrying out other grave violations of international law.*[307]

So far there has only been one conviction at the ICC in relation to the war crime of forced pregnancy in the case of *Dominic Ongwen.*[308]

Enforced Sterilization

Enforced Sterilization is a war crime in IAC and NIAC. The elements of the underlying offence are the same in both types of conflict. In IAC enforced sterilization is prohibited under Schedule 8, Article 8(2)(b)(xxii). In NIAC enforced sterilization is prohibited under Schedule 8, Article 8(2)(vi) of the ICC Act. The *actus reus* of the offence in the Regulations is:

306 Regulations, Article 8(2)(b)(xxii)-3 (IAC) and Article 8(2)(e)(vi)-4 (NIAC).

307 Regulations, Article 8(2)(b)(xxii)-4 (IAC) and Article 8(2)(e)(vi)-4 (NIAC).

308 *Ongwen,* Trial Judgment.

1. *The perpetrator deprived one or more persons of biological reproductive capacity.*[309]

2. *The conduct was neither justified by the medical or hospital treatment of the person or persons concerned nor carried out with their genuine consent.* [310]

This war crime has not been charged in any of the cases at the ICC.

Sexual Violence

The crimes of sexual violence set out in the paragraphs above are specifically enunciated in the war crimes provisions in the ICCA and ICC Statute. However, the ICCA and ICC Statute also contains a *"catch-all"* provision in respect of other acts of sexual violence which are not specifically referred to, but which can be prosecuted as war crimes. Thus, Schedule 8, Article 8(2)(b)(xxii) and Schedule 8, Article 8(2)(vi) ICCA prohibit *"any other form of sexual violence"*. In order to qualify as *"any other form of sexual violence"* the offence must be of *"a gravity comparable to that of a grave breach of the Geneva Conventions or of common article 3"*. This is a useful provision as it enables other sexual violence crimes which are not otherwise enunciated to be prosecuted as crimes of sexual violence, rather than as, for example *"outrages upon personal dignity"* or *"cruel [or] inhuman treatment"*. One example of a crime that might be prosecuted under this provision is the crime of forced marriage. This has been recognised as a distinct war crime in the jurisprudence of the

309 Regulations, Article 8(2)(b)(xxii)-5. Footnote 55 to this element which explains that: *"The deprivation is not intended to include birth-control measures which have a non-permanent effect in practice"*. Article 8(2)(e)(vi)-5, in NIAC has the same footnote.

310 Footnote 56 to this element in the Regulations provides that: *"It is understood that "genuine consent" does not include consent obtained through deception"*.

SCSL.[311] Although forced marriage is not prohibited in its own right under the ICCA, in appropriate factual circumstances it could be charged as *"any other form of sexual violence"*.[312]

The Regulations sets out the elements of the *actus reus* of the offence in IAC as follows:

1. *The perpetrator committed an act of a sexual nature against one or more persons or caused such person or persons to engage in an act of a sexual nature by force, or by threat of force or coercion, such as that caused by fear of violence, duress, detention, psychological oppression or abuse of power, against such person or persons or another person, or by taking advantage of a coercive environment or such person's or persons' incapacity to give genuine consent.*

2. *The conduct was of a gravity comparable to that of a grave breach of the Geneva Conventions.*[313]

The requirement is the same in NIAC, save that the second element requires that the *"conduct was of a gravity comparable to that of a serious violation of article 3 common to the four Geneva Conventions"* rather than a *"grave breach of the Geneva Conventions"*.[314] At the time of writing there haven't been any charges under this provision at the ICC.

---

311 *Prosecutor v. Brima et al.,* (SCSL-2004-16-A) Appeal Judgment, 22 February 2008, paras. 175 - 203, esp. at 195 and 198.

312 Alternatively, it could be charged as sexual slavery. The jurisprudence from the SCSL makes interesting reading in relation to this issue. Alternatively, at the ICC Dominic Ongwen was convicted by the Trial Chamber of forced marriage charged as a CAH, as an *"inhumane act of a similar character under Article 7(1)(a)-(j)"*.

313 Regulations, Article 8(2)(b)(xxii)-6 (IAC).

314 Regulations, Article 8(2)(e)(vi)-6 (NIAC).

Offences against Personal Freedoms

The category of offences against personal freedoms has been chosen to group together four war crimes which have as a common theme an affront to the personal freedom of the victim. These are the war crimes of:

- **Compelling service in hostile forces (IAC)**
- **Compelling participation in military operations (IAC)**
- **Hostage taking (IAC and NIAC)**
- **Using, Conscripting or Enlisting Child Soldiers (IAC and NIAC)**

Compelling a Prisoner of War to Serve in Forces of a Hostile Power

The war crime of *"Compelling a prisoner of war or other protected person to serve in the forces of a hostile Power"* is prohibited as a grave breach of the Geneva Conventions,[315] and is set out in Schedule 8, Article 8(2)(a)(v) ICCA. There is no equivalent provision in NIAC. There is no jurisprudence from the ICC or the ad hoc tribunals in relation to this war crime. Prisoners of war are defined by article 4 of the third Geneva Convention[316] and articles 43 to 45 of Additional Protocol I[317] (the provisions are lengthy, so are not set out here but it is, of course, an important definition in the context of IHL). The *actus reus* of the offence as set out in the Regulations, requires that, *"the perpetrator coerced one or more persons, by act or threat, to take part in military operations against that*

315 This war crime is drawn from articles 130 and 147 of the third Geneva Convention Relative to the Treatment of Prisoners of War, (1950) 75 UNTS 279.

316 The Third Geneva Convention Relative to the Treatment of Prisoners of War (1950) 75 UNTS 135.

317 Protocol Additional to the 1949 Geneva Conventions and Relating to the Protection of Victims of International Armed Conflicts (1979) 1125 UNTS 3.

person's own country or forces or otherwise serve in the forces of a hostile power".[318]

Compelling Participation in Military Operations

"*Compelling Participation in Military Operations*"[319] is prohibited as a serious violation of the laws and customs applicable in IAC[320] under Schedule 8, Article 8(2)(b)(xv) ICCA. This is a similar offence to the war crime of "*Compelling Service in Hostile Forces*". Like that offence, there is no equivalent in IAC. Similarly, neither is there any jurisprudence from the ICC or the ad hoc criminal tribunals dealing with this offence. The *actus reus* requires that, "*the perpetrator coerced one or more persons by act or threat to take part in military operations against that person's own country or forces*" and that "*such person or persons were nationals of a hostile party*".[321]

Hostage Taking

"*Taking of hostages*" is prohibited by the ICCA in situations of IAC as a grave breach of the Geneva Conventions,[322] and in NIAC as a serious violation of article 3 common to the Geneva Conventions of 1949.[323] The elements of the *actus reus* of the crime, as set out in the Regulations, are the same in both IAC and NIAC and are as follows:

1. *The perpetrator seized, detained or otherwise held hostage one or more persons.*

318 Regulations, Article 8(2)(a)(v).

319 See ICCA, Schedule 8(2)(b)(xv) for the full title of this war crime.

320 This war crime is drawn from article 23(h) of the 1907 Hague Convention.

321 Regulations, Article 8(2)(b)(xv).

322 ICCA, Schedule 8(2)(a)(viii).

323 ICCA, Schedule 8(2)(c)(iii).

2. *The perpetrator threatened to kill, injure or continue to detain such person or persons.*

3. *The perpetrator intended to compel a State, an international organization, a natural or legal person or a group of persons to act or refrain from acting as an explicit or implicit condition for the safety or the release of such person or persons.*[324]

The war crime of *"taking of hostages"* has not yet been charged at the ICC. However, there are numerous examples of the prosecution of this crime over the last century. The widespread use of the practice of hostage taking in Nazi Germany led to a number of post-war prosecutions of the crime,[325] and more recently there have been prosecutions at the ICTY (*Prosecutor v Blaskic,* [326] *Prosecutor v Kordic and Cerkez*[327] and *Prosecutor v Karadzic*[328]) and at the SCSL. At the SCSL, the crime was considered

324 Regulations, Article 8(2)(a)(viii) (IAC) and Article 8(2)(c)(iii) (NIAC).

325 See Cassese, *The Oxford Companion to International Criminal Justice*, Oxford University Press, 2009, 1st ed., pp. 795 - 797.

326 *Prosecutor v. Blaškić* (IT-95-14-T), Trial Judgment, 3 March 2000, para. 158, in relation to the crime of taking civilian hostages and noting that detention may be lawful in some circumstances. Note that the crimes is not limited to civilian hostages as confirmed by the Appeals Chamber decision in *Karadžić* (below). See also para. 187 of *Blaskic*.

327 *Prosecutor v. Kordić and Čerkez* (IT-95-14/2-T) Trial Judgment ("*Kordić*, Trial Judgment") 26 February 2001, para. 314.

328 See for example, *Prosecutor v Radovan Karadžić*, IT-95-5/18-AR72.5, *"Decision on Appeal of Trial Chamber's Decision on Preliminary Motion to Dismiss Count 11 of the Indictment"* 9 July 2009, where the Appeals Chamber confirmed that the war crime of taking hostages was not limited to civilian hostages. The prosecution had identified the victims of hostage-taking in the indictment as *"UN personnel"* and *"UN military observers and peacekeepers"*, as *"persons taking no active part in the hostilities"*. The Appeals Chamber dismissed a challenge made by the defence that such persons were not captured by the war crime of *"taking hostages"*. Note also the discussion in *Kordic,* Trial Judgment, paras. 311-314.

by the Appeals Chamber in *Prosecutor v Sesay et al.*[329] Notably, in relation to the third element the Appeals Chamber held that the communication of a threat to a third party was not an element of the offence, but rather the communication of a threat to a third party could provide a means by which to evidence the third element of the offence.[330]

Using, Conscripting or Enlisting Child Soldiers

"*Conscripting or enlisting children under the age of fifteen years into the national armed forces or using them to participate actively in hostilities*" is prohibited in IAC, as a serious violation of the laws and customs of war,[331] and in NIAC as a serious violation of the laws and customs of law applicable in armed conflict not of an international character.[332]

The *actus reus* of the offence in IAC is set out in the Regulations as follows:

1. *The perpetrator conscripted or enlisted one or more persons into the national armed forces or used one or more persons to participate actively in hostilities.*

2. *Such person or persons were under the age of 15 years.*

3. *The perpetrator knew or should have known that such person or persons were under the age of 15 years.*[333]

The elements of the offence in an NIAC are the same, save the first element of the *actus reus* is that:

---

329 *Prosecutor v Sesay, Kallon and Gbao* (SCSL-04-15 A) Appeal Judgment, ("RUF Appeal Judgment") 26 October 2009, paras. 550-609.

330 RUF Appeal Judgment, paras. 580.

331 ICCA, Schedule 8(2)(b)(xxvi).

332 ICCA, Schedule 8(2)(e)(vii).

333 Regulations, Article 8(2)(b)(xxvi) (IAC) and Article 8(2)(e)(vii).

> 1. *The perpetrator conscripted or enlisted one or more persons into an armed force or group or used one or more persons to participate actively in hostilities (emphasis added).*

The war crime (or war crimes) of using, conscripting or enlisting child soldiers was first prosecuted at the SCSL,[334] and has been prosecuted in several cases before the ICC.[335] The first case at the ICC in which an accused was convicted of the crimes was that of Thomas Lubanga Dylio and the Appeal Chamber judgment in this case is essential reading in relation to this war crime.[336] Since then, there have been further convictions in the cases of Bosco Ntaganda[337] and Dominic Ongwen.[338] The offence has also been charged in the case of Yekatom and *Ngaïssona.*[339]

The first element of the offence makes it clear that the offence can be committed in three different ways and some Trial Chambers at the ICC have referred to this as encompassing three different war crimes:[340]

- *"conscripting"* children into armed forces;
- *"enlisting"* children into armed forces; and,

---

334 The crime was charged in every case at the SCSL. See also *Prosecutor v. Norman* (Fofana Intervening) SCSL-2003-14-AR72(E) *"Decision on Preliminary Motion based on Lack of Jurisdiction (Child Recruitment)"* 31 May 2004.

335 Mathieu Ngudjolo Chui was acquitted of charges under Article 8(2)(b)(xxvi) arising from the situation in the D.R.C. by the Trial Chamber on 18 December 2012.

336 Lubanga was found guilty on 14 March 2012 and sentenced to 14 years imprisonment, which was upheld on appeal.

337 *Prosecutor v. Bosco Ntaganda*, Trial Judgment and Appeal Judgment.

338 *Ongwen,* Trial Judgment.

339 See Confirmation of Charges Decision, *Yekatom and Ngaïssona.*

340 Note *Lubanga,* Appeal Judgment at paras. 37 and 38, referring to the approach of the Trial Chamber.

- *"using"* children to participate actively in hostilities.

"Conscripting" and "enlisting" are two forms of "recruitment".[341] "Conscripting" is "forcible recruitment",[342] whereas "enlisting" "pertains more to voluntary recruitment".[343] A child's consent cannot constitute a valid defence to the crime.[344] As regards the use of children to participate actively in hostilities, this refers not only to direct participation in hostilities,[345] but also covers active participation in combat related activities such as scouting, spying, sabotage and the use of children as decoys, couriers or at military checkpoints.[346]

---

341 *Lubanga*, Confirmation of Charges Decision, para. 246 and *Lubanga*, Trial Judgment, para. 609.

342 *Lubanga*, Appeal Judgment, para. 278 and see paras. 278-282 discussing the elements of compulsion necessary and how it can be established, note also the references to the SCSL jurisprudence in relation to this war crime.

343 *Lubanga*, Confirmation of Charges Decision, para. 246. Pre-Trial Chamber I pointed out that this distinction was also made by Judge Robertson in his Separate Opinion appended to the judgment rendered by the Appeals Chamber of the SCSL on 31 May in the case of *Prosecutor v. Sam Hinga Norman*. See also *Lubanga*, Trial Judgment, para. 609.

344 *Lubanga*, Confirmation of Charges Decision, para. 247. See also the discussion in the Appeal Judgment in Lubanga in relation to consent at paras. 301-302.

345 *Lubanga*, Appeals Judgment, para. 328.

346 *Lubanga*, Confirmation of Charges Decision, para. 261, referring at footnote 339 to the Draft Statute for the International Court, Report of the Preparatory Committee on the establishment of an International Criminal Court, addendum 1, UN Doc. A/CONF.183/2/Add.1, p.21. See also *Lubanga*, Appeal Judgment, at para. 304.

Theft and Offences against Property, Objects and Places

The following war crimes are grouped together under the category of theft and offences against property, objects and places:

- **Pillage (IAC and NIAC)**
- **Destruction and appropriation of property (IAC)**
- **Attacking protected objects (IAC and NIAC)**
- **Attacking civilian objects (IAC)**
- **Destroying or seizing the enemy's property (IAC and NIAC)**
- **Attacking undefended places (IAC)**

Pillage

Pillage is prohibited by Schedule 8, Article 8(2)(b)(xvi) ICCA, as a crime in IAC as *"Pillaging a town or place, even when taken by assault"*,[347] a serious violation of the laws and customs applicable in IAC. It is prohibited in exactly the same terms in NIAC, as a serious violation of article 3 common to the four Geneva Conventions, contrary to Schedule 8, Article 8(2)(c)(v) ICCA.[348]

The *actus reus* of pillage, as set out in the Regulations is the same in IAC as NIAC and is as follows:

1. *The perpetrator appropriated certain property.*

---

[347] ICCA Schedule 8, Article 8(2)(b)(xvi).

[348] ICCA, Schedule 8, Article 8(2)(c)(v), which prohibits *"Pillaging a town or place, even when taken by assault"*.

2. *The perpetrator intended to deprive the owner of the property and to appropriate it for private or personal use.*[349]

3. *The appropriation was without the consent of the owner.*[350]

The ICL definition of pillage is broad and embraces a potentially wide range of theft-based offences, from a single appropriation by a soldier for private gain to situations such as the large-scale illegal appropriation of natural resources by a warring party.[351] At the ICC, the Trial Chamber in *Katanga* confirmed that the war crime *"comprises all forms of appropriation"*.[352] As such, the war crime of pillage provides a potentially flexible tool with which to prosecute a wide range of offending. Pillage has been prosecuted in a number of cases before the ICC, as well as in other international criminal tribunals. At the ICC there have been convictions for pillage as a war crime in *Katanga*[353] and *Ongwen*.[354]

---

349 Regulations, Article 8(2)(b)(xvi) (IAC), footnote 48 appended to this element in the Regulations provides that: *"As indicated by the use of the term "private or personal use", appropriations justified by military necessity cannot constitute the crime of pillaging"*. The same footnote appears in relation to the elements of the offence in a NIAC at Article 8(2)(e)(v) (NIAC) of the Regulations.

350 Regulations, Article 8(2)(b)(xvi) (IAC) and Article 8(2)(e)(v) (NIAC).

351 See Antonio Cassese, *"The Oxford Companion to International Criminal Justice"*, Oxford University Press, 2009 ed., pp.454-455, as well as some of the examples given in relation to the prosecution of pillage at the ICTY and at other tribunals.

352 *Katanga*, Trial Judgment, para. 905, referring to public and private appropriation and organised and systematic appropriation as well as acts committed by combatants in their own interest.

353 *Katanga*, Trial Judgment.

354 *Ongwen*, Trial Judgment.

Pillage has also been charged in the following cases: *Abd-Al-Rahman*,[355] *Banda*,[356] and *Ngudjolo Chui*.[357]

Destruction and Appropriation of Property

As a war crime in the context of an IAC, the ICCA, Schedule 8, Article 8(2)(a)(iv) prohibits the "*extensive destruction and appropriation of property, not justified by military necessity and carried out unlawfully and wantonly*", as a grave breach of the Geneva Conventions. The Regulations set out the following as elements of the offence:

1. *The perpetrator destroyed or appropriated certain property.*
2. *The destruction or appropriation was not justified by military necessity.*
3. *The destruction or appropriation was extensive and carried out wantonly.*
4. *Such property was protected under one or more of the Geneva Conventions of 1949.*
5. *The perpetrator was aware of the factual circumstances that established that protected status.*[358]

---

355 *Abd-Al-Rahman*, Confirmation of Charges Decision, *paras. 36-37*.

356 *Prosecutor v. Abdallah Banda (ICC-02/05- 03/09)* (although charges were confirmed in this case on 7 March 2021, the accused is at large (as per the case information sheet)).

357 *Chui*, Trial Judgment (Chui was acquitted of charges the charge of pillage (alongside other war crimes and CAH) by a Trial Chamber on 18 December 2012.

358 Regulations, Article 8(2)(a)(iv). The last two contextual elements are omitted.

There have not been any cases at the ICC specifically in relation to this offence,[359] although there have been several ICC cases in relation to the destruction of property charged under other articles of the Rome Statute. The crime of *"destruction and appropriation of property"* can be distinguished from other war crimes grouped together in this section by virtue of the fact that the chief mischief it is intended to remedy is the *"extensive"* and *"wanton"* unlawful destruction or appropriation of property.[360] Although, a single act is capable of satisfying that requirement in exceptional cases, by and large the appropriation or destruction must be large scale to satisfy the requirements of this offence.[361]

Destroying or Seizing the Enemy's Property

"Destroying or seizing the enemy's property unless such destruction or seizure be imperatively demanded by the necessities of war" is prohibited as a serious violation of the laws and customs of IAC under ICCA, Schedule 8, Article 8(2)(b)(xiii). A similar offence of *"Destroying or seizing the property of an adversary unless such destruction or seizure be imperatively demanded by the necessities of the conflict"* is prohibited as a serious violation of the laws and customs applicable in NIAC, under the ICCA Schedule 8, Article 8(2)(e)(xii).

The Regulations set out the following elements of the *actus reus* of the offence in IAC:

---

359 There were a number of cases at the ICTY in relation to this offence. See for example *Prosecutor v. Kordić et al.*, (IT-95-14/2-T), Trial Judgment, 26 February 2001, paras. 335 – 341.

360 *Katanga,* Confirmation of Charges Decision, para. 314, referring to *Prosecutor v. Radoslav Brđanin* (IT-99-36-T) Trial Judgment, 1 September 2004, paras. 584-585.

361 *Katanga,* Confirmation of Charges Decision, para. 314, referring to *Prosecutor v. Blaškić* (IT-95-14-T) Trial Judgment, 1 September 2004, paras. 584-585.

1. *The perpetrator destroyed or seized certain property.*

2. *Such property was property of a hostile party.*

3. *Such property was protected from that destruction or seizure under the international law of armed conflict.*

4. *The perpetrator was aware of the factual circumstances that established the status of the property.*

5. *The destruction or seizure was not justified by military necessity.*[362]

The elements of the *actus reus* of the offence are the same in NIAC, save that the second element requires that *"such property was property of an adversary"*, rather than *"property of a hostile party"*.[363] According to the ICC Trial Chamber in *Katanga*, the requirement that the property must have belonged to an adversary means that the property, whether it is moveable or immoveable, public or private, must belong to persons or to entities aligned with or with an allegiance to a party to the conflict, which is adverse or hostile to the perpetrator.[364] The elements of the offence are wide enough to cover not only the destruction or attacks against property belonging to an *"enemy"* or *"hostile party"* but also civilian property protected from destructions under the international law of armed conflict. [365]

[362] Regulations, Article 8(2)(b)(xiii). The final two contextual elements are omitted above.

[363] Regulations, Article 8(2)(e)(xii).

[364] *Katanga*, Trial Judgment, para 892.

[365] *Katanga,* Confirmation of Charges Decision, paras. 309-317, especially at 310-313. See also *Katanga*, Trial Judgment, paras. 892-895.

There have been a number of convictions for this war crime at the ICC,[366] one acquittal[367] and it also features in *Abd-Al-Rahman* which is in trial. [368]

Attacking Protected Objects

The war crime of *"attacking protected objects"* is prohibited in both IAC and NIAC. It prohibits attacking buildings dedicated to religion, education, art, science or charitable purposes, historic monuments and public health. Schedule 8, Article 8(2)(b)(ix) ICCA, prohibits: *"Intentionally directing attacks against buildings dedicated to religion, education, art, science or charitable purposes, historic monuments, hospitals and places where the sick and wounded are collected, provided they are not military objectives"*, as a serious violation of the laws and customs applicable in IAC. In NIAC the offence is set out in the ICCA in similar terms in Schedule 8, Article 8(2)(e)(iv) and is prohibited as a serious violation of the laws and customs applicable in NIAC. The elements of the underlying offences are the same.

The Regulations, sets out the *actus reus* of the offence as follows:

1. *The perpetrator directed an attack.*
2. *The object of the attack was one or more buildings dedicated to religion, education, art, science or charitable purposes, historic monuments, hospitals or places where the sick and wounded are collected, which were not military objectives.*[369]

---

366 *Katanga*, Trial Judgment; *Ntaganda*, Trial Judgment; *Ongwen*, Trial Judgment.

367 *Chui*, Trial Judgment.

368 *Abd-Al-Rahman, Confirmation of Charges Decision, paras. 38-39.*

369 Regulations, Article 8(2)(b)(ix). Note that Footnote 46 appended to the short title in the Regulations provides that: "*The presence in the locality of persons specially protected under the Geneva Conventions of 1949 or of police forces retained for the sole purpose of maintaining law and order does not by itself render the locality a military*

The *mens rea* of the offence is that:

> 3. *The perpetrator intended such building or buildings dedicated to religion, education, art, science or charitable purposes, historic monuments, hospitals or places where the sick and wounded are collected, which were not military objectives, to be the object of the attack.*

This war crime has featured in cases before the ICC arising from the situation in Timbuktu, Mali. Ahmad Al Faqi Al Mahdi pleaded guilty, as a co-perpetrator, to the war crime of intentionally directing attacks against historic monuments and buildings dedicated to religion, including nine mausoleums and one mosque in Timbuktu in June – July 2021.[370] Bosco Ntaganda was also convicted of this offence arising from the situation in the D.R.C.[371] This crime is also charged in the joined cases of *Yekatom and Ngaïssona*, which are ongoing.[372] Case law from the ICTY is helpful in relation to the historical origins and legal requirements of this war crime.[373]

Attacking Civilian Objects

Schedule 8, Article 8(2)(b)(ii) ICCA, prohibits *"Intentionally directing attacks against civilian objects, that is objects which are not military*

---

objective." The NIAC provision is found in Article 8(2)(e)(iv), which has an equivalent footnote 61.

370 *Prosecutor v. Al Mahdi* (ICC-01/12 – 01/13), as per the case information sheet, the confirmation of charges decision took place on 2 May 2016 and Trial Chamber III unanimously found him guilty on 27 September 2016. This crime is also charged in *Al Hassan* (ICC-01/12 – 01/18), which is in trial.

371 *Ntaganda*, Trial Judgment.

372 *Prosecutor v. Al Hassan* (ICC-01/12 – 01/18) (the decisions on the confirmation of charges are available in French only); and Confirmation of Charges Decision, *Yekatom and Ngaïssona*.

373 See for example: *Prosecutor v Kordić et al.* (IT-95-14/2-A), Appeal Judgment, 17 December 2004, paras. 85 - 92, and the Trial Judgment, *Prosecutor v Kordić et al.* (IT-95-14/2-T), 26 February 2001, at paras. 354 - 362.

objectives", as a serious violation of the laws and customs applicable in IAC. The crime is only punishable in IAC.

The Regulations set out the following elements of the offence

1. *The perpetrator directed an attack.*
2. *The object of the attack was civilian objects, that is, objects which are not military objectives.*
3. *The perpetrator intended such civilian objects to be the object of the attack.*[374]

The war crime of *"attacking civilian objects"* derives from article 52 of Additional Protocol I which mandates that civilian objects shall not be the object of attack or reprisals,[375] and that attacks shall be limited strictly to military objectives.[376] The Appeals Chamber of the ICTY in the case of *Kordic et al.*, observed that the prohibition against attacking civilians stems from a fundamental principle of IHL, called, *"the principle of distinction"*. The *"principle of distinction"* obliges warring parties to distinguish, at all times, between the civilian population and combatants, and between civilian objects and military objectives, and to direct military operations only against military objectives.[377] None of the cases at the ICC have featured this war crime.

Attacking Undefended Places

The war crime of *"attacking undefended places"* is prohibited by Article 8(2)(b)(v) of Schedule 8 ICCA, which refers in full to an offence of

---

374 Regulations, Article 8(2)(b)(II), the two final elements (contextual elements) are omitted from the quotation.

375 Civilian objects are defined as all objects which are not military objectives – see paras. 1 and 2 of article 52 of Additional Protocol I.

376 Military objectives are then defined in article 52 of Additional Protocol I, para. 2.

377 *Prosecutor v Kordić et al* (IT-95-14/2-A), Appeal Judgment, 17 December 2004, para. 54.

"Attacking or bombarding, by whatever means, towns, villages, dwellings or buildings which are undefended and which are not military objectives". It is an offence in IAC. The Regulations set out the following elements of the offence:[378]

1. *The perpetrator attacked one or more towns, villages, dwellings or buildings.*

2. *Such towns, villages, dwellings or buildings were open for unresisted occupation.*

3. *Such towns, villages, dwellings or buildings did not constitute military objectives.*[379]

The war crime of attacking undefended places has not yet been charged at the ICC.

False Imprisonment, Deportation, Transfer and Displacement

The ICCA includes four war crimes which concern the movement and or restrictions upon the movement of individuals against their choosing in situations of war:

- **Unlawful deportation and transfer (IAC)**

- **Unlawful confinement (IAC)**

- **Transfer by an occupying power of its own civilian population, or the deportation or transfer of the population of the occupied territory (IAC)**

[378] Regulations, Article 8(2)(b)(v). Footnote 1 appended to this title in the Regulations, provides that: *"The presence in the locality of persons specially protected under the Geneva Conventions of 1949 or of police forces retained for the sole purpose of maintaining law and order does not by itself render the locality a military objective."*

[379] Two final elements (the contextual elements) are omitted.

- **Displacing civilians (NIAC)**

In IAC *"unlawful deportation or transfer or unlawful confinement",*[380]is prohibited as a grave breach of the Geneva Conventions. This crime incorporates both the unlawful deportation of an individual, and the unlawful transfer of an individual to another location not necessarily beyond the border of the State. It also concerns situations where civilians are being unlawfully confined i.e. the confinement of civilians in circumstances that do not amount to lawful internment during situations of military occupation. Also prohibited in IAC is the *"transfer of populations to an occupied territory".*[381]This war crime is prohibited as a serious violation of the laws and customs applicable in IAC. It prohibits the direct or indirect transfer of a civilian population into or outside of an occupied territory. The war crimes provisions in relation to NIAC are not as extensive as those referred to above which apply only to IAC. In NIAC there is a single war crime, which prohibits *"ordering the displacement of the civilian population for reasons related to the conflict, unless security of the civilians involved or imperative military reasons so demand"*, as *"a serious violation of the laws and customs applicable in armed conflicts not of an international character".*[382] Only of the war crime of *"displacing civilians"* has been charged before the ICC. [383]

Unlawful Deportation and Transfer and Unlawful Confinement

In the Regulations, the offence of *"unlawful deportation or transfer or unlawful confinement"* under ICCA, Schdule 8(2)(a)(vii) is divided into two separate offences; with the elements of *"unlawful deportation and transfer"* being set out as one offence, and the elements of *"unlawful confinement"* as another offence. The *actus reus* of *"unlawful deportation*

380 ICCA, Schedule 8(2)(a)(vii).

381 ICCA, Schedule 8(2)(b)(viii).

382 ICCA, Schedule 8(2)(e)(viii).

383 See Confirmation of Charges Decision, *Yekatom and Ngaïssona.*

and transfer" is that, *"the perpetrator deported or transferred one or more persons to another State or to another location".*[384] The *actus reus* of *"unlawful confinement"* is that, *"the perpetrator confined or continued to confine one or more persons to a certain location".*[385] Although, the confinement of civilians in situations of IAC is a war crime, it is important to be aware of the fact that under IHL, specifically Articles 42 - 43 of the Geneva Conventions, the practice of internment of civilians during military occupation is a potentially legitimate one, but only as an exceptional measure, when the conditions in those two Articles are met. This was confirmed by the by the Appeals Chamber of the ICTY in the case of *Delalić et al.*[386]

Transfer by an Occupying Power of its own civilian population, or the Deportation or Transfer of the Population of an Occupied Territory[387]

This war crime is prohibited as a serious violation of the laws and customs applicable in IAC. It derives from article 49(6) of the fourth Geneva Convention and is deemed a grave breach, in accordance with article 85(4)(a) of Additional Protocol I. The elements of the offence are set out in the Regulations at Article 8(2)(b)(viii).

Displacing Civilians

In NIAC the ICCA prohibits *"Ordering the displacement of the civilian population for reasons related to the conflict, unless the security of the civilians*

---

384 Regulations, Article 8(2)(a)(vii)-I.

385 Regulations, Article 8(2)(a)(vii)-2.

386 *Delalić et al.*, (IT-96-21-A), Appeal Judgment, 20 February 2001, paras. 320 - 322 and see also the Appeal Chambers application of the law in relation to the civilians who were held at Čelebići camp at paras. 323 - 330. For further analysis of this war crime, see the Trial Chamber Judgment in *Delalić* (*Delalić et al.* (IT-96-21-A), Judgment, 16 November 1998, paras. 564 – 583).

387 ICCA, Article 8(2)(b)(viii) (note the long title for this offence is set out in that provision).

involved or imperative military reasons so demand".[388] This war crime derives from article 8(2)(e)(iv) of article 17 of Additional Protocol II. The Regulations sets out the *actus reus* of the offence as follows:

1. *The perpetrator ordered a displacement of a civilian population.*

2. *Such order was not justified by the security of the civilians involved or by military necessity.*

3. *The perpetrator was in a position to effect such displacement by giving such order.*[389]

Offences against Protected Parties - Civilians

The following war crimes fall into the category of offences against civilians and concern attacks, or acts of violence, directed against civilians who are not taking a direct part in hostilities, or a civilian population:

- **Attacking civilians (IAC and NIAC)**

- **Using human shields (IAC)**

- **Starvation as a method of warfare (IAC)**

- **Excessive incidental Death, Injury, or Damage (IAC)**

Attacking Civilians

The war crime of *"Attacking Civilians"* derives from the absolute prohibition against attacking civilians under IHL.[390]" Attacking

388 ICCA, Schedule 8(2)(e)(viii).

389 Regulations, Article 8(2)(e)(viii), the two contextual elements are omitted above.

390 Under this absolute prohibition civilians only lose their protection if and when they take a direct part in hostilities (see Additional Protocol I, Article 51(3) and Additional Protocol II, Article 13(3) and customary international law).

Civilians" is a war crime in both IAC and NIAC. In IAC the, the ICCA prohibits *"Intentionally directing attacks against the civilian population as such or against individual civilians not taking part in hostilities"*, as a serious violation of the laws and customs applicable in IAC under Schedule 8, Article 8(2)(b)(i).[391] In NIAC Schedule 8, Article 8(2)(e)(i) prohibits the same crime as a serious violation of the laws and customs applicable in armed conflicts not of an international character.[392] The elements of the underlying offence are the same in IAC and NIAC.

The Regulations set out the following elements of the *actus reus* of the offence:

1. *The perpetrator directed an attack.*

2. *The object of the attack was a civilian population as such or individual civilians not taking direct part in hostilities.*[393]

The Regulations set out the following *mens rea*:

3. *The perpetrator intended the civilian population as such or individual civilians not taking direct part in hostilities to be the object of the attack.*

"Attacking civilians" has features in several cases before the ICC, including *Bosco Ntaganda* (convicted),[394] *Katanga* (convicted),[395] *Ngudjolo Chui* (acquitted),[396] *Dominic Ongwen* (convicted by the Trial

---

[391] The prohibition in the context of IAC derives from Article 85(3)(a) of Additional Protocol and is a grave breach of that Protocol.

[392] The prohibition in the context of NIAC derives from Article 13(2) of Additional Protocol II.

[393] Regulations, Article 8(2)(b)(i) (IAC) and Article 8(2)(e)(i) (NIAC).

[394] Bosco Ntaganda was convicted of war crimes including intentionally directing attacks against a civilian population as well as CAH.

[395] *Katanga,* Trial Judgment.

[396] Chui was acquitted of charges the charges under Article 8(2)(b)(i) (alongside other war crimes and CAH) by a Trial Chamber on 18 December 2012.

Chamber),[397] *Abd-Al-Rahman*[398] and *Yekaton and Ngaissona.*[399] *"Attacking civilians"* was also charged in a number of cases at the ICTY.[400] Consequently, there is plenty of case law to consult in relation to this war crime.

Using Human Shields

The *"War Crime of Using Protected Persons as Shields"* is prohibited as a war crime in IAC, as an *"other serious violation of the laws and customs applicable in international armed conflict"* under Article 8(2)(b)(xxiii) of the ICCA which refers to *"Utilizing the presence of a civilian or other protected person to render certain points, areas or military forces immune from military operations"*. There is no equivalent provision in NIAC. The prohibition on the use of human shields derives from the Geneva Conventions and from Additional Protocol I.

The Regulations sets out the following as elements of the offence:

1. *The perpetrator moved or otherwise took advantage of the location of one or more civilians or other persons protected under the international law of armed conflict.*

2. *The perpetrator intended to shield a military objective from attack or shield, favour or impede military operations.*[401]

There are yet to be any cases at the ICC in relation to *"using human shields"*. Furthermore, despite the long history of the practice of using

---

397 *Ongwen,* Trial Judgment.

398 *Abd-Al-Rahman,* Confirmation of Charges Decision, paras. *31-32.*

399 *Yekatom and Ngaissona,* Confirmation of Charges Decision (currently in trial).

400 See for example, the Appeals Chamber Judgment and Trial Chamber Judgment in *Prosecutor v Galić* (IT-98-29) 30 November 2006 and 5 December 2003 respectively; and *Prosecutor v. Blaškić* (IT-95-14-T) Trial Judgment, 3 March 2000, para. 180.

401 Regulations, Article 8(2)(b)(xxiii). The two contextual elements are omitted.

civilians and other protected persons as human shields, the case law on this war crime is sparse. There have been a number of prosecutions at the ICTY which have dealt with various factual scenarios involving human shielding. However, in these cases, the use of human shields was not been charged under the rubric of the "*War Crime of Using Protected Persons as Shields*" but rather as crimes including *"Inhuman Treatment",*[402] *"Cruel Treatment",*[403] *" Hostage Taking"*[404] *and "Outrages against Personal Dignity"*[405]*;* the reason for charging the crime under these alternate headings being the absence of the more specific crime of *"Using Human Shields"* in the ICTY Statute. The fact that the war crime of *"Using Human Shields"* has been charged under the auspices of other more general war crimes, is of potential relevance to proceedings in the Crown Court. Should the prosecution wish to charge *"Using Human Shields"* in the context of IAC, then Article 8(2)(b)(xxiii) will obviously be the appropriate provision under which to do so. However, in a NIAC the prosecution would have to find an alternate provision under which to do so, and here the jurisprudence from the ICTY may assist because it provides precedent under the auspices of other war crimes.

The *actus reus* of the war crime in the Regulations covers at least two factual scenarios. First, the scenario where a perpetrator shields a legitimate military target from attack by placing civilians in the location of that military target, and secondly, the situation where military operations are moved into an area where civilians are present. In practice, there is also another scenario where the use of human shields may arise, and that is when civilians are literally used as a shield to protect combatants by forcing civilians to march in front and thus shield combatants who are under attack. Although this scenario is perhaps not

---

402 *Prosecutor v. Kordić* (IT-95-14/2) Trial Judgment, 3 March 2000, para. 264.

403 *Prosecutor v. Blaškić* (IT-95-14-T) Trial Judgment, 3 March 2000, para. 716.

404 *Prosecutor v. Blaškić* (IT-95-14-T) Trial Judgment, 3 March 2000, para. 750.

405 *Prosecutor v. Aleksovski* (IT-95-14/1-T) Trial Judgment, 25 June 1999, para. 225.

obviously covered by the ICC elements of the crimes, there would be a strong argument that it should be so covered. The *mens rea* for this offence requires the specific intent to *"shield a military objective from attack or shield, favour or impede military operations"*. Notably the victims of this crime can include not only civilian victims, but also other protected persons such as peace keeping and humanitarian personnel.

Starvation as a Method of Warfare

The war crime of *"Starvation as a Method of Warfare"* is prohibited as a crime in IAC by Schedule 8, Article 8(2)(b)(xxv) of the ICCA, which refers to *"Intentionally using starvation of civilians as a method of warfare by depriving them of objects indispensable to their survival, including wilfully impending relief supplies as provided for under the Geneva Conventions"*. There is no equivalent provision in NIAC. This crime has not been charged at the ICC. The elements of the offence as set out in the Regulations.[406]

Excessive Incidental Death, Injury or Damage

The war crime of *"Excessive Incidental Death, Injury or Damage"* is prohibited in IAC by Schedule 8, Article 8(2)(b)(iv) as another serious violation of the laws and customs applicable in the context of IHL. Article 8(2)(b)(iv) refers to *"Intentionally launching an attack in the knowledge that such attack will cause incidental loss of life or injury to civilians or damage to civilian objects or widespread, long term and severe damage to the natural environment which would be clearly excessive in relation to the concrete and direct overall military advantage anticipated"*. It derives from Additional Protocol I of the Geneva Conventions.[407] None

Regulations, Article 8(2)(b)(xxv).

407 Protocol Additional to the 1949 Geneva Conventions and Relating to the Protection of Victims of International Armed Conflicts, (1979) 1125 UNTS 3, art. 85(3), article 57(2)(a)(iii).

of the accused at the ICC have been charged with this offence. The elements of the offence are set out in the Regulations. [408]

Offences against Protected Parties – Peacekeepers and Humanitarian Workers

The ICCA contains two offences in relation to protected parties, namely peacekeepers and humanitarian workers operating under the auspices of the United Nations:

- **Attacking Personnel or Objects Involved in a Humanitarian Assistance or Peacekeeping Mission (IAC and NIAC)**
- **Attacking Objects or Persons using the Distinctive Emblem of the Geneva Conventions (IAC and NIAC)**

Attacking Personnel or Objects Involved in a Humanitarian Assistance or Peacekeeping Mission

The ICCA, Schedule 8, Article 8(2)(b)(iii) prohibits: *"Intentionally directing attacks against personnel, installations, material, units or vehicles involved in a humanitarian assistance or peacekeeping mission in accordance with the Charter of the United Nations, as long as they are entitled to the protection given to civilians or civilian objects under the international law of armed conflict"*, as a serious violation of the laws and customs applicable in IAC.[409] The equivalent offence in NIAC is prohibited by Schedule 8, Article 8(2)(e)(iii) as a serious violation of the laws and customs applicable in armed conflicts not of an international character.[410]

The Regulations set out the elements of the offence, which are the same in IAC and NIAC, as follows:

---

408 Regulations, Article 8(2)(b)(iv).

409 ICCA, Schedule 8(2)(b)(iii).

410 ICCA, Schedule 8(2)(e)(iii).

1. *The perpetrator directed an attack.*

2. *The object of the attack was personnel, installations, material, units or vehicles involved in a humanitarian assistance or peacekeeping mission in accordance with the Charter of the United Nations.*

3. *The perpetrator intended such personnel, installations, material, units or vehicles so involved to be the object of the attack.*

4. *Such personnel, installations, material, units or vehicles were entitled to that protection given to civilians or civilian objects under the international law of armed conflict.*[411]

This offence was charged at the ICC in the case against Abdallah Banda (who despite initially voluntarily surrendering to the jurisdiction of the court is now at large).[412] Although, the ICC has not yet registered any convictions for this war crime, the offence has been successfully prosecuted elsewhere. At the SCSL, in the case against members of the Revolutionary United Front, the three defendants in that case were convicted of the offence in the first prosecution of this crime before an international criminal tribunal.[413]

---

411 Regulations, Article 8(2)(b)(iii) (IAC) and Article 8(2)(e)(iii) (NIAC). The three contextual elements are omitted.

412 *Prosecutor v Abdallah Banda* (ICC-02/05-03/09) on 7 March 2021 Pre-Trial Chamber I confirmed the charges.

413 *Prosecutor v Sesay, Kallon and Gbao* (SCSL-04-15-T) Trial Judgment, ("AFRC, Trial Judgment)" 2 March 2009. Notably, the approach of the SCSL in this judgment is endorsed at para. 84 of the *Abu Gharda* Confirmation of Charges Decision. For a helpful analysis of this war crime see also the following article: "*Prosecuting the Crime of Attack on Peacekeepers: A Prosecutor's Challenge*", Mohamed A. Bangura, Leiden Journal of International Law 23 (2010) pp. 165-181.

Attacking Objects or Persons Using the Distinctive Emblems of the Geneva Conventions

"Attacking Objects or Persons Using the Distinctive Emblems of the Geneva Conventions" is prohibited in both IAC and NIAC by Schedule 8, Article 8(2)(b)(xxiv) and Article 8(2)(e)(ii) respectively. This war crime prohibits intentionally directing attacks against personnel, buildings, material, medical units and transport or *"any other objects"* using the distinctive emblems of the Geneva Conventions *"or any other method of identification indicating protection under the Geneva Conventions"*. This war crime has not yet been charged at the ICC. The *actus reus* and *mens rea* are the same in both IAC and NIAC and are set out in Regulations, Article 8(2)(b)(xxiv) (IAC) and Article 8(2)(e)(ii) (NIAC).

Offences against Protected Parties – Prisoners of War and Combatants

As a war crime in IAC, the ICCA prohibits:

- **"Compelling a prisoner of war or other protected person to serve in the forces of a hostile Power"** (a grave breach of the Geneva Conventions),[414]
- **"Wilfully depriving a prisoner of war or other protected person of the rights of fair and regular trial"** (a grave breach of the Geneva Conventions),[415]
- **"Killing or wounding a combatant who, having laid down his arms or having no longer means of defence, has surrendered at**

[414] ICCA, Schedule 8, Article 8(2)(a)(v).

[415] ICCA, Schedule 8(2)(a)(vi).

discretion" (as a serious violation of the laws and customs applicable in IAC),[416]

- "**Killing or wounding treacherously individuals belonging to the hostile nation or army**" (as a serious violation of the laws and customs applicable in IAC),[417]

- **Killing or wounding treacherously a combatant adversary**" (as a serious violation of the laws and customs applicable in armed conflicts not of an international character).[418]

The various "Killing or wounding" offences have been set out at the beginning of this chapter in the context of *"Offences against the Person"*. *"Compelling a prisoner of war or other protected person to serve in the forces of a hostile Power"* has been considered above in the sub-section *"Offences Against Personal Freedoms"*. *"Wilfully depriving a prisoner of war or other protected person of the rights of fair and regular trial"* is referred to below under *"Denial of Due Process / Fair Trial Rights"*.

Fair Trial Rights / Denial of Due Process

The ICCA includes provisions which concern the protection of due process and fair trial rights of protected persons in IAC and NIAC. In IAC the war crime of *"Denying a Fair Trial" ("Wilfully depriving a prisoner of war or other protected person of the rights of fair and regular trial")* is prohibited under Schedule 8, Article 8(2)(a)(vi) as a grave breach of the Geneva Conventions. In addition, in IAC there is also the war crime of *"Denying the Nationals of the Hostile Power of Rights or Actions"*

416 ICCA, Schedule 8(2)(b)(vi).

417 ICCA, Schedule 8(2)(b)(xi).

418 ICCA, Schedule 8(2)(e)(ix).

("Declaring abolished, suspended or inadmissible in a court of law the rights and actions of the nationals of the hostile party"), which is prohibited by Schedule 8, Article 8(2)(xiv) of the ICCA. This war crime derives from the Hague Convention of 1907.[419] In NIAC, Schedule 8, Article 8(c)(i)(v) provides for the war crime of *"The Passing of sentences and the carrying out of executions without previous judgment pronounced by a regularly constituted court, affording all judicial guarantees which are generally recognised as indispensable" ("Sentencing or Execution without Due Process")*. This war crime derives from common article 3 to the Geneva Conventions. At the ICC, charges were brought in *Al-Hassan* for *"passing of sentences without previous judgment pronounced by a regularly constituted court, affording all judicial guarantees which are generally recognised as indispensable"*.[420] The elements of these various crimes can be found in the Regulations.

Violations of the Rules and Means of Combat

This section groups together a number of crimes under the category, *"Violations of the Rules and Means of Combat"*. These crimes have as a central and connecting theme prohibitions concerning the rules and means of combat. The crimes in this section can be divided into three sub-categories. First, prohibitions in relation to the use of certain types of weapons in situations of IAC. Secondly, offences relating to the improper use of flags, insignia, uniforms or emblems. Thirdly, the offence of *"denying quarter"* in situations of both IAC and NIAC. None of these crimes have been charged in any of the cases before the ICC.

419 The Hague Convention (IV) Respecting the Laws and Customs of War by Land, [1910] UKTS 9, annex, art. 23(h)

420 *Prosecutor v. Al Hassan* (ICC-01/12 – 01/18). This case in in trial.

Using illegal weapons in an IAC

"Employing poison or poisoned weapons",[421] *" Employing asphyxiating, poisonous or other gases, and all analogous liquids, materials or devices"*[422] *and "Employing bullets which expand or flatten easily in human body, such as bullets with a hard envelope which does not entirely cover the core or is pierced with incisions",*[423] are prohibited as serious violations of the laws and customs applicable in IAC. Notably, the same offences are not criminalised in the ICCA as offences in the context of NIAC. This is because agreement was only reached about the criminality of these offences in NIAC at the Review Conference of the Rome Statute of the ICC in Kampala, in 2010. These crimes were not contained in earlier incarnations of the Rome Statute, upon which the ICCA is based. These offences are not therefore criminalised in our domestic criminal legislation, although they are now found in the Rome Statute and the ICC Elements of Crimes document.[424] The elements of the offences in the context of IAC are set out in the Regulations.[425]

Improper use of a flag, truce, insignia, uniform or emblem

The ICCA prohibits the following as serious violations of the laws and customs applicable in IAC: *"Making improper use of a flag of truce, or of the flag of the military insignia and uniform of the enemy of the United Nations, as well as the distinctive emblems of the Geneva Conventions, resulting in death or serious personal injury".*[426] This war crime is only

---

[421] ICCA, Schedule 8(2)(b)(xvii).

[422] ICCA, Schedule 8(2)(b)(xviii).

[423] ICCA, Schedule 8(2)(b)(xix).

[424] See the ICC (Elements of Crimes) document, 2011 ed. and Article 8(2)(e)(xii), Article 8(2)(e)(xiv) and Article 8(2)(e)(xv), which observes that these Articles were amended as a result of the conference in Kampala in 2010.

[425] Employing Poison or Poisoned Weapons: Regulations, Employing Prohibited Gases, Liquids, Materials or Devices: Article 8(2)(b)(xvii), Regulations, Article 8(2)(b)(xviii), Employing Prohibited Bullets: Regulations, Article 8(2)(b)(xix).

[426] ICCA, Schedule 8(2)(b)(vii).

punishable when committed in the context of IAC. The Regulations divide this offence into the following four separate offences:

- **Improper use of a flag or truce**[427]
- **Improper use of a flag, insignia or uniform of the hostile party**[428]
- **Improper use of a flag, insignia or uniform of the United Nations**[429]
- **Improper use of the distinctive emblems of the Geneva Conventions**[430]

The elements of the four offences are set out in the Regulations. They concern the situation where, as a result of the perpetrator falsely using a flag, truce, insignia, uniform or emblem, death or serious injury occurs.

Denying Quarter

"Declaring that no quarter will be given" ("Denying Quarter") is a war crime in the context of IAC and NIAC. This war crime is committed when a person in a position of effective command and control declares and/or orders that there shall be no survivors, in circumstances where that declaration and/or order is made in order to threaten an adversary or to conduct hostilities on the basis that that there shall be no survivors. The prohibition derives from article 23(d) of the Hague Convention of 1907.[431] *"Denying Quarter"* is prohibited in IAC by Schedule 8, Article 8(2)(b)(xii) as an other serious violation of the laws and customs

427 Regulations, Article 8(2)(b)(vii)-1.

428 Regulations, Article 8(2)(b)(vii)-2.

429 Regulations, Article 8(2)(b)(vii)-3.

430 Regulations, Article 8(2)(b)(vii)-4.

431 The Hague Convention (IV) Respecting the Laws and Customs of War by Land [1910] UKTS 9, annex, art.23(b).

applicable in IAC. In NIAC, the crime is prohibited under Schedule 8, Article 8(2)(e)(x) as an *"other serious violation of the laws and customs applicable in armed conflicts not of an international character"*. The elements of the crime, which are the same in IAC and NIAC are set out in the Regulations.[432]

[432] Regulations, Article 8(2)(b)(xii) (IAC) and Article 8(2)(e)(x)(NIAC).

CHAPTER FOUR

CRIMES AGAINST HUMANITY UNDER THE ICCA

The definition of a crime against humanity under the ICCA

The ICCA makes crimes against humanity ("CAH") an offence under domestic law.[433] CAH are defined in Schedule 8, Article 7 of the ICCA as follows:

> *"Crimes against humanity" means any of the following acts when committed as part of a widespread or systematic attack directed against any civilian population, with knowledge of the attack:*
>
> *(a) Murder;*
>
> *(b) Extermination;*
>
> *(c) Enslavement;*
>
> *(d) Deportation or forcible transfer of population;*
>
> *(e) Imprisonment or other severe deprivation of physical liberty in violation of the fundamental rules of international law;*
>
> *(f) Torture;*
>
> *(g) Rape, sexual slavery, enforced prostitution, forced pregnancy, enforced sterilization, or any other form of sexual violence of comparable gravity;*
>
> *(h) Persecution;*

433 ICCA, Article 51.

(i) Enforced disappearance of persons;

(j) Apartheid;

(k) Other inhumane acts of a similar character intentionally causing great suffering, or serious injury to body or to mental and physical health.

(Footnotes omitted but addressed below).

In essence, a CAH means any one of the above acts *"committed as part of a widespread or systematic attack directed against any civilian population, with knowledge of the attack"*. Unlike war crimes, a CAH can be committed either during an armed conflict, or in peacetime. The concept of a widespread, or systematic attack, directed against a civilian population is at the heart of the concept of a CAH. Thus, CAH address offences (a) – (k) committed on a massive scale, or repeatedly over time.

ICCA, Schedule 8, Article 7 comprises of three sections:

- Article 7(1) sets out the meaning of CAH,
- Article 7(2) is a definitional section, which sets out definitions of both the contextual elements of CAH and the underlying crimes,
- Article 7(3) defines the term *"gender"* for the purposes of Article 7 and in the Statute generally.[434]

Schedule 8, Article 7 which defines CAH for the purposes of the ICCA derives from Article 7 of the Rome Statute. The definition of CAH in domestic law is the same as the definition in the Rome Statute.

---

[434] Schedule 8, Article 7(3) provides that: *"For the purpose of this Statute, it is understood that the term "gender" refers to the two sexes, male and female, within the context of society. The term "gender" does not indicate any meaning different from the above"*.

Historical origins of crimes against humanity

War crimes derive from IHL. Genocide derives from the Genocide Convention. By contrast the historical origins of CAH have been described by eminent scholars such as Antonio Cassese as less certain.[435] CAH, first arose as a political rather than a legal concept at the beginning of the last century. Its first incarnation as a legal concept came in the wake of World War II in the Charter of the International Military Tribunal (IMT) at Nuremberg, which translated the political idea into a legal concept to which individual criminal responsibility attached.[436] The next significant articulation of CAH came in the 1990s with the Statute of the ICTY.[437] The first judgment at the ICTY in the seminal case of *Prosecutor v. Duško Tadić* examined CAH. The Trial Chamber in *Tadić* stated that the IMT Charter had in effect created a new crime of CAH,[438] and that by the time of the atrocities in the former Yugoslavia in the early 1990s, individual criminal responsibility for CAH had been firmly established in customary international law.[439] The Trial Chamber held, and the ICTY Appeals Chamber confirmed, that there was no requirement under customary international law that CAH occur in the context of an armed conflict.[440] CAH were later included in the Statutes of the other ad hoc tribunals: the ICTR, the SCSL and the Extraordinary Chambers of Cambodia, and finally the ICC. The Statutes of those ad

[435] *International Criminal Law, Cases & Commentary*, Antonio Cassese and others, Oxford University Press, 2011 ed., p. 155.

[436] Cassese, *ibid.*

[437] Article 5 ICTY Statute.

[438] *Prosecutor v. Tadić*, (IT-94-1-T) Trial Chamber Judgment, 7 May 1997, para. 618.

[439] *Ibid.*, para. 623.

[440] *Prosecutor v. Tadić*, (IT-94-1-T) *"Decision on the Defence Motion on Jurisdiction"*, 10 August 1995, paras. 77-83, and *Prosecutor v. Tadić*, (IT-94-1-AR72), *"Decision on the Defence Motion for Interlocutory Appeal on Jurisdiction"*, 2 October 1995, para. 141 noting that it was a settled ruled of customary IL that CAH do not require a connection to an IAC. Notably, this ruling was despite the fact that the ICTY Statute required a connection between a CAH and an armed conflict.

hoc tribunals and Article 7 of the Rome Statute make plain that a CAH can be committed either in connection with an armed conflict, or during peacetime.

Elements of crimes against humanity under the ICCA

The ICCA (Elements of Crimes) Regulations sets out the elements of the sixteen CAH offences.[441] The elements of each offence in the Regulations include: the contextual elements of the offence and the *actus reus* of the underlying offence. The *mens rea* of the underlying offence is not repeated as a distinct element of each offence, rather this is governed by section 66 ICCA (which reflects Article 30 of the Rome Statute).[442] Although, where a crime is one of specific intent or strict liability, this is specifically set out in the elements of crimes. For example, sexual slavery as a CAH is set out in the Regulations, Article 7(1)(g)-2, as follows:

> 1. *The perpetrator exercised any or all of the powers attaching to the right of ownership over one or more persons, such as by purchasing, selling, lending or bartering such a person or persons, or by imposing on them a similar deprivation of liberty [footnote omitted].*
>
> 2. *The perpetrator caused such person or persons to engage in one or more acts of a sexual nature.*
>
> 3. *The conduct was committed as part of a widespread or systematic attack directed against a civilian population.*

---

[441] As noted in the prior chapters the ICCA (Elements of Crimes) Regulations set out the ICC Elements of Crimes Document in domestic law, which section 50(2) ICCA requires the Crown Court to *"take into account"*, as well as the case law of the ICC (ICCA, section 50(5)).

[442] Article 30 of the Rome Statute provides that as a general rule the mental element of each offence is *"intent"* and *"knowledge"*. Cross-reference the prior chapter where Article 30 and section 66 ICCA is addressed.

4. *The perpetrator knew that the conduct was part of or intended the conduct to be part of a widespread or systematic attack directed against a civilian population.*

The first two elements represent the element of the underlying offence of sexual slavery. The remaining two elements reflect the contextual elements of CAH. The prosecution must prove both the *"contextual elements"* of CAH, and the elements of the underlying offence. *"Contextual elements"* are those elements that make the offence in question a CAH, as opposed to a war crime, or genocide, or any ordinary offence under domestic law. The contextual elements of CAH relate to the requirement that acts are committed by a perpetrator *"as part of a widespread or systematic attack directed against any civilian population, with knowledge of the attack"*.

Contextual elements of crimes against humanity

In any case, be it international or domestic, it is crucial that the contextual elements of CAH are proven. The contextual elements of CAH are yet to be examined in a domestic criminal case. However, they have been examined in this jurisdiction in immigration proceedings, in relation to Article 1F of the Refuge Convention 1951. Article 1F provides that the provisions of the Refugee Convention do not apply to a person in relation to whom there are serious reasons for considering that they have committed CAH.[443] *KM (exclusion; Article 1F(a); Article 1F(b)) Democratic Republic of Congo* [2022] UKUT 00125 (IAC) (hereinafter, *"KM"*) is a decision from the Upper Tribunal (Immigration and Asylum Chamber). The Secretary of State had decided that KM should be excluded from refugee status under Article 1F of the Refugee Convention. The Upper Tribunal concluded that the Secretary of State had failed to prove the contextual elements of CAH to the necessary standard, rendering the Secretary of State's decision on this aspect of the

[443] This exclusionary clause also applies to war crimes and crimes against peace (see Article 1F Convention on the Protocol Relating to the Status of Refugees, 1951).

case unlawful.[444] The Upper Tribunal cited the following cautionary example from the ICC:

> *"The importance of satisfying the contextual elements of the chapeau of Article 7 is illustrated by the trial of the former President of Côte d'Ivoire, Laurent Gbagbo. He was brought to trial in the ICC but was found to have no case to answer. He was acquitted of charges of crimes against humanity allegedly committed during post-election violence in 2010 and 2011 on the ground that the prosecution had failed to produce sufficient evidence to satisfy the contextual elements of the chapeau of Article 7. The acquittal was upheld by the appeal chamber in early 2021".*[445]

Both the case of *KM* (in the Immigration and Asylum Tribunal) and *Gbagbo* (at the ICC) therefore highlight the importance of establishing the contextual elements of CAH. The contextual elements applicable to CAH are examined below and a checklist of contextual elements for CAH is included at the end. The contextual elements of CAH have been considered in several cases at the ICC including in the Trial Chamber judgments in *Katanga,*[446] *Bemba,*[447] *Ntaganda*[448] and *Ongwen,*[449] as well as numerous cases from the ad hoc international criminal tribunals. The relevant principles that emerge are summarised below.

---

[444] *KM,* paras. 147 and 163.

[445] *KM,* paras. 132. Note that what are referred to in this book as *"contextual elements"* are also referred to as *"chapeau",* as in this para 132, *KM*. See: Prosecutor v. *Laurent Gbagbo and Charles Ble Goude* (ICC-02/11-01/15), *"Reasons for oral decision of 15 January 2019…",* 16 July 2019, para. 28

[446] *Katanga,* Trial Judgment, paras. 1094 - 1125. Note that the Trial Chamber in *Katanga* suggest a three-stage process in the analysis of the contextual elements of CAH (paragraphs 1096- 1099).

[447] *Bemba,* Trial Judgment, paras 148 – 169.

[448] *Ntaganda,* Trial Judgment, paras. 660-697.

[449] *Ongwen,* Trial Judgment, paras.2673-2682.

There must be an attack

CAH require that there is *"an attack"*. An attack refers to a course of conduct which involves the mistreatment of civilians. ICCA, Schedule 8, Article 7(2)(a) defines an *"Attack against a civilian population"* as:

> *"a course of conduct involving the multiple commission of acts referred to in paragraph 1 against any civilian population, pursuant to or in furtherance of a State or organsational policy to commit such attack."*[450]

The concepts of *"attack"* and *"armed conflict"* are distinct and separate notions.[451] An *"attack"* does not need to be military in nature and it can encompass any form of violence against the civilian population.[452] The *"attack"* can precede, outlast, or continue during an armed conflict, thus it may, but need not be part of an armed conflict.[453] An *"attack"* refers to *"a course of conduct"* and is not intended to capture a single isolated act.[454] It is the *"multiple commission"* of the crimes in paragraph 1 that constitutes the *"attack"*.[455]

---

450 See the *"Introduction"* to CAH in the Regulations.

451 The *"Introduction"* to CAH in the Regulations confirms that *"the acts need not constitute a military attack"*.

452 *Katanga,* Trial Judgment, para. 1101. See also *Bemba,* Trial Judgment, para. 149.

453 *Prosecutor v. Tadić* (IT-94-1-A), Appeal Judgement, ("*Tadic,* Appeal Judgment") 15 July 1999, para. 251; *Prosecutor v. Tadic* (IT-94-1-AR72), *"Decision on the Defence Motion for Interlocutory Appeal on Jurisdiction"*, 2 October 1995, para. 141; *Prosecutor v. Kunarać* (IT-96-23/1-A) Appeal Judgement, 12 June 2002, (*"Kunarać, Appeal Judgment")* para. 86.

454 *Katanga,* Trial Judgment, para. 1101, *Bemba,* Trial Judgment, para. 149.

455 *Katanga,* Trial Judgment, para. 1101; *Prosecutor v. Bemba* (ICC-01/05-01/08), *"Decision Pursuant to Article 61(7)(a) and (b) of the Rome Statute on the Charges of the Prosecutor Against Jean-Pierre Bemba Gombo"*, ("*Bemba,* Confirmation of

The attack must be widespread or systematic

The *"attack"* must be *"widespread"* or *"systematic"*. The terms *"widespread"* and *"systematic"* are not specifically defined in either the Rome Statute or the ICCA but have been examined in the case law. The two conditions are disjunctive. An *"attack"* need only be either *"widespread"* or *"systematic"* but need not be both.[456] Further, it is the *"attack"* that must be either *"widespread"* or *"systematic"* and not the specific crime with which the accused is charged. Thus, a single act of murder may constitute a CAH provided it is committed within the context of a widespread or systematic attack directed against the civilian population.[457] *"Widespread"* refers to the large-scale nature of the attack, as well as the large number of targeted persons. *"Systematic"* refers to the organized nature of the acts, as well as the improbability of the random occurrence of the acts of violence. [458]

The attack must be directed against any civilian population

The contextual elements of CAH require the attack to be *"directed against any civilian population"*. *"Directed against"* means that the civilian population must be the primary target of the attack and not an incidental victim.[459] Factors that the ICC and the ad hoc tribunals have held to be

---

Charges Decision")15 June 2009, para. 75, and also *Bemba*, Trial Judgment, paras. 149 - 152.

456 Thus, the Pre-Trial Chamber of the ICC in *Bemba* found that the attack was *"widespread"* so did not need to go onto consider whether it was also *"systematic"* - *Bemba*, Confirmation of Charges Decision, para. 82. This approach was later confirmed by the Trial Chamber.

457 *Bemba,* Confirmation of Charges Decision, para. 151.

458 *Katanga* Trial Judgment, para. 1123.

459 *Katanga* Trial Judgment, para. 1104, *Bemba*, Trial Judgment, para. 154.

relevant to determining whether the attack was so directed include the following non-exhaustive list:

- the means and methods used during the attack,
- the status and number of victims,
- the discriminatory nature of the attack,
- the nature of the crimes committed during the attack,
- the resistance to the assailants at the time and the extent to which the attacking force may be said to have complied or attempted to comply with the precautionary requirements of the laws of war.[460]

The victims may belong to *"any civilian population"*, regardless of nationality, ethnicity or other distinguishing features.[461] The entire *"civilian population"* of a geographical entity need not be targeted by the attack.[462] However, the object of the attack must be a civilian *"population"* rather than a limited and randomly selected number of individuals.[463] The targeted population must be predominantly civilian in nature, although non-civilians may be present.[464] The *"civilian population"* includes persons who are not members of the armed forces,

460 *Katanga* Trial Judgment, para. 1104, quoting from the ICTY Appeals Chamber in *Kunarać,* Appeal Judgement at para. 91.

461 *Katanga,* Trial Judgment, para. 1103, confirming the approach taken by the Pre-Trial Chamber, *Bemba,* Trial Judgment, para. 155.

462 *Katanga,* Trial Judgment, para. 1105, *Bemba,* Trial Judgment, para. 154.

463 *Katanga,* Trial Judgment, para. 1105, *Bemba,* Trial Judgment, para. 154.

464 *Katanga,* Trial Judgment, para. 1105, *Bemba,* Trial Judgment, para. 153. See also for example: *Tadić,* Appeal Judgement, 15 July 1999, para. 644.

or otherwise recognized as combatants.[465] Persons *hors de combat* do not *prima facie* fall within this definition.[466] However, where a person *hors de combat* is the victim of an act which objectively forms part of a broader attack directed against a civilian population, this act can amount to a CAH provided that the remaining general requirements of CAH are satisfied in respect of the particular incident.[467]

The attack must be pursuant to a state or organisational policy under the ICC and ICCA regimes

Under the ICC regime the contextual elements of CAH require that the attack must be *"pursuant to a state or organisational policy"*. The ICC regime diverges from the ad hoc tribunals in relation to this requirement. The ICTY and other modern day ad hoc tribunals have stated that the existence of a policy or a plan is not a requirement of CAH;[468] although, it is noted that a policy or plan to carry out such acts/ crimes, may be evidentially relevant to establish the widespread or systematic nature of

---

465 *Katanga*, Trial Judgment, para. 1102 endorsing the definition of *"civilian population"* found in article 50(2) of Additional Protocol I of the Geneva Conventions of 12 August 1949, as did the Trial Chamber in *Bemba*, at para. 152 of the *Bemba*, Trial Judgment. At the ICTY see for example: *Prosecutor v. Martić* (IT-95-11-A) Appeal Judgement ("*Martić*, Appeal Judgement") 8 October 2008, para. 297.

466 *Martić*, Appeal Judgement, paras. 291-302 and 307.

467 See for example, *Martić*, Appeal Judgement, 8 October 2008, paras. 303 -314. In *Martić* the Appeals Chamber entered convictions for crimes committed against persons *hors de combat*, considering that they were victims of a widespread and systematic attack against the civilian population, and that all elements of the offences were met (see *Martić* Appeal Judgement, paras. 318-319, 346,355). Note the *Bemba*, Trial Judgment, para. 156, which states that there is no requirement that individual victims of CAH be *"civilians"*.

468 See for example, *Prosecutor v. Tihomir Blaškić* (IT-95-14-A), Appeal Judgment, ("*Blaškić*, Appeal Judgment) 29 July 2004, paras. 100, 120; *Prosecutor v. Kunarać*, Appeal Judgment, para. 79.

the attack.[469] By lifting Article 7 from the ICC Statute into domestic law, via Schedule 8, the ICCA has incorporated the ICC requirement that the attack must be *"pursuant to a state or organizational policy"* into our domestic law. Schedule 8, Article 7(2), mirroring Article 7(2) of the ICC Statute provides that an *"[a]ttack directed against any civilian population"* means:

> *"a course of conduct involving the multiple commission of acts referred to in paragraph 1 against any civilian population,* ***pursuant to or in furtherance of a State or organizational policy*** *to commit such attack"* (emphasis added).

The Regulations (mirroring the ICC Elements of Crimes Document) provide that:

> *"It is understood that "policy to commit such attack" requires that the State or organization actively promote or encourage such an attack against a civilian population [1]."*[470]

A footnote appended to that provision further provides that:

> *"A policy which has a civilian population as the object of the attack would be implemented by State or organizational action. Such a policy may, in exceptional circumstances, be implemented by a deliberate failure to take action, which is consciously aimed at encouraging such attack. The existence of such a policy cannot be inferred solely from the absence of governmental or organizational action".*

In *Katanga*, the Trial Chamber explained that it needs to be shown: (1) that a policy existed, and (2) that the policy was connected to a state or

---

469 *Blaškić,* Appeal Judgement, paras. 100 and 120; *Kunarać,* Appeal Judgment, para. 98.

470 Regulations, Article 7, CAH, *"Introduction"*, para. 3.

an organisation.[471] *"Policy"* is not defined in either the Rome Statute, or the Elements of Crimes document. The Trial Chamber in *Katanga* stated that:

- a *"policy"* refers to a state or organization's intention to carry out an attack against a civilian population, either through action, or deliberate inaction;[472]
- there is no requirement that a formal policy or design exist;[473]
- a *"systematic"* attack against a civilian population will in principle presuppose the existence of a "policy";[474]
- to establish a *"policy"* all that needs to be established is that the state or organisation meant to commit an attack against a civilian population.[475]

In *Bemba*, the Trial Chamber explained that a *"policy"* can be inferred from a variety of factors, which are listed in the judgment.[476] It must be established that the *"course of conduct"* was carried out in furtherance of, or pursuant to the *"policy"*;[477] thus, the course of conduct must reflect a link to the state or organisational policy.[478] This could be satisfied by the perpetrator deliberately acting in furtherance of the policy, or by the

---

[471] *Katanga* Trial Judgment, para. 1098. See in general the Trial Chamber's analysis of this contextual element in paras. 1106 -1122.

[472] *Katanga* Trial Judgment, para. 1108.

[473] *Katanga* Trial Judgment, para. 1108, and note also in particular paras. 1109 – 1110 about proof of existence of a *"policy"*. Also, *Bemba*, Trial Judgment at para. 160.

[474] *Katanga* Trial Judgment, para. 1111 and see also paras. 1112-1113.

[475] *Katanga* Trial Judgment, para. 1113.

[476] *Bemba*, Trial Judgment, para. 160, which provides a list of relevant factors which could show that a *"policy"* existed.

[477] *Katanga* Trial Judgment, para. 1115 - 1116.

[478] *Bemba*, Trial Judgment, para. 161.

perpetrator engaging in conduct envisaged by the policy, with knowledge.[479] *"Organisation"* is also not defined in the Rome Statute, or Elements of Crimes document. In *Katanga*, the Trial Chamber considered the meaning of *"organisation"*, highlighting that the terms of the Statute and the Elements of Crimes document imply that: (1) an organisation is not the State, and (2) that the organisation must have sufficient means to promote or encourage a campaign involving the multiple commission of acts referred to in article 7(2) of the Statute.[480] The Trial Chamber explained that an *"organisation"* could include a private entity consisting of a group of persons and would not need to have the character of a quasi-State.[481]

There must be a nexus between the acts of the perpetrator / accused and the attack

There must be a nexus between the acts of the accused / perpetrator and the attack against the civilian population.[482] This nexus depends on the factual circumstances of each case. Indicia of a nexus include:

- the similarities between the accused's/ perpetrator's acts and the acts occurring within the attack;
- the nature of the events and circumstances surrounding the accused's/ perpetrator's acts;

479 *Bemba,* Trial Judgment, para. 161.

480 *Katanga* Trial Judgment, para. 1117, and see the further analysis in paras. 1118 - 1122. The Trial Chamber's analysis in *Katanga* was endorsed at para. 158 of the *Bemba,* Trial Judgment.

481 *Katanga* Trial Judgment, paras. 1119 – 1122; but note in particular the comments in 1121 about the jurisprudence of the ad hoc tribunals.

482 *Bemba,* Trial Judgment, paras. 164-165, and *Bemba,* Decision on the Confirmation of Charges, paras. 84-86.

- the temporal and geographic proximity of the accused's/ perpetrator's acts with the attack;

- and the nature and extent of the accused's/ perpetrator's knowledge of the attack when he commits the acts.[483]

A single act perpetrated in the context of a widespread or systematic attack upon a civilian population is sufficient to bestow individual criminal liability - in other words, only the attack and not the individual acts, must be widespread and systematic.[484] Further, the unlawful acts must be related to an attack on a civilian population but need not have been committed in the midst of that attack,[485] thus a crime which is committed before or after the main attack or away from it could still, if sufficiently connected, be part of that attack, provided that it is not an isolated act.[486]

The perpetrator / accused must have knowledge of the attack

Finally, the contextual elements of CAH require that the accused person have knowledge of the attack and that their acts are part of that attack.[487] Thus, an accused who does not have knowledge of the attack cannot be found guilty of CAH. In the Regulations, the final element of each crime provides that:

---

483 *Tadić*, Appeal Judgement, para. 632.

484 *Prosecutor v. Kordić & Čerkez* (IT-95-14/2-A) Appeal Judgement, 17 December 2004, para. 94, referring to the *Kunarać*, Appeal Judgement, para. 96 and *Blaskić* Appeal Judgement, para. 101.

485 *Kunarać,* Appeal Judgement, para.100.

486 *Prosecutor v, Sesay et al.* (SCSL-04-15-A) Trial Judgment, 26 October 2009, para. 89.

487 *Katanga*, Trial Judgment, para. 1125.

> *"The perpetrator knew that the conduct was part of or intended the conduct to be part of a widespread or systematic attack directed against a civilian population".*

The Regulations elaborate upon what is required by this contextual element, stating that:

> *"... the last element should not be interpreted as requiring proof that the perpetrator had knowledge of all characteristics of the attack or the precise details of the plan or policy of the State or organization. In the case of an emerging widespread or systematic attack against a civilian population, the intent clause of the last element indicates that this mental element is satisfied if the perpetrator intended to further such an attack".*[488]

It must be shown that the perpetrator knew that there was an attack on a civilian population, and that his or her acts were part of the attack.[489] Knowledge of the attack and the perpetrator's awareness that his or her conduct formed part of the attack may be inferred from circumstantial evidence.[490] Evidence that the accused has knowledge of the context of the attack can be inferred from factors such as:

- the historical and political circumstances in which the acts of violence occurred,
- the functions of the accused when the crimes were committed,
- the functions of the accused within the political or military hierarchy,

---

488 Regulations, Article 7, CAH, *"Introduction"*, para. 2.

489 *Bemba*, Trial Judgment, para. 167, endorsing the approach of the Pre-Trial Chamber in the Confirmation of Charges Decision (*Bemba,* Confirmation of Charges Decision, para. 88).

490 *Ibid.*

- the direct and indirect relationship between the political and military hierarchy,
- the scope and gravity of acts perpetrated,
- the nature of the crimes committed and the degree to which they are common knowledge.[491]

As indicated in the Regulations, the accused need not know the details of the attack or approve of the context in which his or her acts occurred.[492] The accused must only understand the overall context in which their acts took place.[493] The accused' motivation for participation in the attack are irrelevant; the accused need only know that his or her acts are part of the attack.[494]

Checklist for contextual elements of crimes against humanity

(1) Is there an "attack"?

(2) Is it "widespread" or "systematic"?

(3) Is the attack "directed against any civilian population"?

(4) Is it pursuant to a "State or organizational policy"?

---

491 *Prosecutor v. Blaškić* (IT-95-14-T), Trial Judgment, 3 March 2000, paras. 258-259.

492 *Katanga*, Trial Judgment, paragraph 1125. See also *Kunarac*, Appeal Judgment, para. 102.

493 *Prosecutor v. Kordić and Čerkez* (IT-96-23/1-T), Trial Judgment, 26 February 2001, para. 185.

494 *Katanga*, Trial Judgment, para. 1125. See also: *Tadić*, Appeal Judgment, paras. 270 and 272.

(5) Is the underlying offence part of the attack? / Are the acts of the accused part of the attack?

(6) Did the perpetrator / accused know or have reasons to know that his / her actions formed part of the attack?

The sixteen underlying crimes against humanity offences

The remainder of this chapter will set out the elements of the sixteen different offences that can be charged as CAH.

Murder

The ICCA (Elements of Crimes) Regulations, Article 7(1)(a) set outs the following as the *actus reus* of murder as a CAH:

1. *The perpetrator killed [7]*[495] *one or more persons.*[496]

The elements of the underlying offence of murder as a CAH are exactly the same as the offence of murder (or "wilful killing") as a war crime (so the reader can cross-refer to the previous chapter). The ICC has returned convictions for murder as a CAH in the cases of *Katanga*,[497] *Ntaganda*,[498] and *Ongwen*.[499] The ICC had acquitted accused' in the cases of *Bemba*[500] and *Ngudjolo Chui*.[501] Charges of murder as a CAH also feature in the

---

495 Appended is a footnote "7" in the Regulations, which provides that: *"The term "killed" is interchangeable with the term "caused death". This footnote applies to all elements which use either of these concepts."*

496 The two contextual elements are omitted.

497 *Katanga*, Trial Judgment.

498 *Ntaganda*, Trial Judgment, upheld by Appeal Chamber Judgment (convictions for murder and attempted murder as a CAH).

499 *Ongwen*, Trial Judgment.

500 *Bemba*, Appeal Judgment.

501 *Ngudjolo Chui*, Trial Judgment, upheld by Appeal Judgment.

following ongoing ICC cases: *Abd-Al-Rahman*[502]and *Yekatom* and *Ngaïssona.*[503]

Extermination

The Regulations, Article 7(1)(b) set out the following as the elements of extermination as a CAH:

1. *The perpetrator killed [8]*[504] *one or more persons, including by inflicting conditions of life calculated to bring about the destruction of part of a population. [9]*[505]

2. *The conduct constituted, or took place as part of [3],*[506] *a mass killing of members of a civilian population.*[507]

Schedule 8, Article 7(2)(b) of the ICCA provides that:

> *""Extermination" includes the intentional infliction of conditions of life, inter alia the deprivation of access to food and medicine, calculated to bring about the destruction of part of the population".*[508]

Extermination as a CAH is concerned with mass killing.[509]It is the mass scale of the killing that differentiates this crime with murder as a CAH.[510]

502 *Abd-Al-Rahman*, Confirmation of Charges Decision.

503 *Yekatom and Ngaïssona,* Confirmation of Charges Decision.

504 Appended is a footnote "8"(set out in the main text).

505 Appended is a footnote "9" (set out in the main text).

506 Appended is a footnote "10" (set out in the main text).

507 The two contextual elements are omitted.

508 Emphasis added.

509 *Prosecutor v. Bashir* (ICC-02/05 - 01/09-3) *"Decision on the Prosecution's Application for a Warrant of Arrest against Omar Hassan Ahmed Al Bashir"* para. 96.

510 See for example: *Prosecutor v. Akayesu* (ICTR-96-4-T), Trial Chamber, 2 September 1998, para. 591; *Prosecutor v Ntakirutimana et al.* (ICTR-96-10-A and

The first element of the offence contains two important footnotes. Footnote 8 provides that, *"[t]he conduct could be committed by different methods of killing, either directly or indirectly"*. This footnote clarifies that the killing can either be direct, or indirect. In other words, it incorporates the direct killing of civilians via weapons; and killing of civilians through indirect means, such as those referred to in footnote 9. Footnote [9] provides that, *"[t]he infliction of such conditions could include the deprivation of access to food and medicine"*.

The second element of the offence under the Regulations requires that *"[t]he conduct constituted, or took place as part of [10], a mass killing of members of a civilian population"*. Footnote [10] provides that: *"[t]he term "as part of" would include the initial conduct in a mass killing"*. Thus, extermination requires a significant number of killings. Responsibility for one, or for a limited number of killings, would be insufficient to qualify as extermination.[511]

Extermination as a CAH is similar to the crime of *"Deliberately inflicting on the group conditions of life calculated to bring about its physical destruction in whole or in part"* which is a punishable act as genocide. However, unlike genocide, the accused need not be shown to have intended to destroy a national, ethnic, racial or religious group or part of the group to which the victims belong.[512] There are yet to be any trials in relation to extermination as a CAH at the ICC, although it is contained in the arrest warrant in relation to *Omar Ahmed Al Bashir* (who

---

ICTR-96-17-A) Appeal Judgment, 13 December 2004, para. 542; *Prosecutor v. Krstić* (IT-98-33-T), Trial Judgment, 2 August 2001, para. 501.

511 *Prosecutor v. Kajelijeli* (ICTR-98-44-A), Trial Judgment, 1 December 2003, para. 893.

512 *Prosecutor v. Muesma* (ICTR-96-13-A), Appeal Judgment, 16 November 2001, paras. 366-367.

is at large) and in the arrest warrant in the case of *Mokom* (who is in ICC custody).[513]

Enslavement

The Regulations, Article 7(1)(c) sets out the *actus reus* of enslavement as follows:

> 1. *The perpetrator exercised any or all of the powers attaching to the right of ownership over one or more persons, such as by purchasing, selling, lending or bartering such a person or persons, or by imposing on them a similar deprivation of liberty [11].*[514]

Enslavement is defined in Schedule 8, Article 7(2)(c) of the ICCA as:

> *""Enslavement"" means the exercise of any or all of the powers attaching to the right of ownership over a person and includes the exercise of such power in the course of trafficking persons, in particular women and children".*

At the heart of the crime of enslavement is the idea of the exercise of the powers attaching to the right of ownership over a person.[515] The leading case from the ad hoc tribunals in relation to enslavement as a CAH is *Prosecutor v. Dragoljub Kunarac et al.*, from the ICTY. This case is essential reading in relation to enslavement because the crime is considered at length in both the Trial and Appeal Chamber judgments. The Appeals Chamber in *Kunarac* acknowledged that slavery constitutes a crime under customary international law and that the traditional

---

513 The confirmation of charges hearing in *Mokom* is due to take place in January 2023.

514 Appended is a footnote "1" in the Regulations provides that: *"It is understood that such deprivation of liberty may, in some circumstances, include exacting forced labour or otherwise reducing a person to a servile status as defined in the Supplementary Convention on the Abolition of Slavery, the Slave Trade, and Institutions and Practices Similar to Slavery of 1956. It is also understood that the conduct described in this element includes trafficking in persons, in particular women and children".*

515 *Kunarać*, Appeal Judgment, para. 118.

concept of slavery as defined in the Slavery Convention 1926 had evolved to encompass various contemporary forms of slavery.[516] The Appeals Chamber confirmed that lack of consent is not an element of enslavement.[517] At the ICC, a Trial Chamber has convicted Dominic Ongwen of several counts of enslavement as a CAH in the context of a 70 count indictment. The crime of enslavement includes trafficking of persons and some forms of forced labour. It is important to note that, not all forms of forced labour are illegal under IHL. However, in certain circumstance forced labour is illegal and could thus give rise to a charge of enslavement as a CAH. Forced labour has been prosecuted in several cases before the ad hoc tribunals, including at the ICTY and the SCSL.[518]

Deportation or forcible transfer of population

The Regulations, Article 7(1)(d) set out the following as the elements of deportation or forcible transfer of population as a CAH:

1. *The perpetrator deported or forcibly [12]*[519] *transferred, [13]*[520] *without grounds permitted under international law, one or more*

516 *Kunarać,* Appeal Judgment, para. 117.

517 *Kunarać* Appeal Judgement, para. 120, where the Appeals Chamber elaborated that lack of consent may be relevant in terms of evidence in as far as the prosecution has to prove that the perpetrator exercised the rights of ownership over the victim. However, circumstances which render it impossible to express consent may be sufficient to presume lack of consent, as was the case in *Kunarać.*

518 See for example: *Krnojelać* Trial Judgement, paras. 357 - 359 and *Krnojelać* Appeal Judgment, paras. 189 – 203, *Prosecutor v Sesay et al* (SCSL-04-15-T) Trial Judgment, 2 March 2009, para.195.

519 Appended is a footnote "12"which provides that: *"[t]he term "forcibly" is not restricted to physical force, but may include threat of force or coercion, such as that caused by fear of violence, duress, detention, psychological oppression or abuse of power against such person or persons or another person, or by taking advantage of a coercive environment".*

520 Appended is a footnote "13" which provides that: *"Deported or forcibly transferred" is interchangeable with "forcibly displaced".*

persons to another State or location, by expulsion or other coercive acts.

2. *Such person or persons were lawfully present in the area from which they were so deported or transferred.*

3. *The perpetrator was aware of the factual circumstances that established the lawfulness of such presence.*[521]

ICCA Schedule 8, Article 7(2)(d) explains that *"deportation or forcible transfer means"* the *"forced displacement of the persons concerned by expulsion or other coercive acts from the area in which they are lawfully present, without grounds permitted under international law"*.

The crime of deportation relates to the transfer of persons outside the territory of a state. The crime of *"forcible transfer"* or *"forced displacement"* (apparently interchangeable terms)[522] encompass the transfer of persons within a state territory. Notably, the crime permits the lawful deportation or forcible transfer / forcible deportation under IL. Deportation and forcible transfer / forcible deportation are permitted in certain circumstances under both national and IL. Situations such as the evacuation of civilians owing to security or military necessity provide examples of lawful transfer of persons.[523] This offence has been prosecuted as a CAH in a number of cases before the ICC: *Ntaganda*

521 The two contextual elements are omitted.

522 See footnote "13" in the Regulations.

523 See *Prosecutor v. Blagojević* (IT-02-60-T), Trial Judgment, 17 January 2005, para. 597.

(convicted)[524] *Abd-Al-Rahman* (currently in trial),[525] and *Yekatom* and *Ngaïssona* (currently in trial)[526] as well as the ICTY.[527]

Imprisonment or severe deprivation of liberty[528]

The Regulations, Article 7(1)(e) set out the following as elements of the crime of *"imprisonment or other severe deprivation of physical liberty in violation of fundamental rules of international law":*

1. *The perpetrator imprisoned one or more persons or otherwise severely deprived one or more persons of physical liberty.*

2. *The gravity of the conduct was such that it was in violation of fundamental rules of international law.*

3. *The perpetrator was aware of the factual circumstances that established the gravity of the conduct.*[529]

This offence has been charged in the joined cases of *Yekatom and Ngaïssona*, [530] as well as the case of *Said*,[531] which are in trial.

---

524 *Ntaganda*, Trial Chamber Judgment, confirmed by the Appeals Chamber Judgment.

525 Abd-Al-Rahman, Confirmation of Charges Decision.

526 *Yekatom and Ngaïssona*, Confirmation of Charges Decision.

527 See for example: *Prosecutor v. Krnojelać* (IT-97-25-A), Appeal Judgment, 17 September 2003, para. 218.

528 This act or crime is referred to in full in Schedule 8, Article 7(e) as: *"Imprisonment or other severe deprivation of physical liberty in violation of fundamental rules of international law".*

529 The two contextual elements are omitted.

530 *Yekatom and Ngaïssona,* Confirmation of Charges Decision.

531 *Said*, Confirmation of Charges Decision.

Torture

ICCA Schedule 8, Article 7(2)(e) provides that:

> *""Torture" means the intentional infliction of severe pain or suffering, whether physical or mental, upon a person in the custody or under the control of the accused; except that torture shall not include pain or suffering arising only from, inherent in or incidental to, lawful sanctions".*

The Regulations, Article 7(1)(f) set out the following elements for the crime of torture as a CAH:

1. *The perpetrator inflicted severe physical or mental pain or suffering upon one or more persons.*
2. *Such person or persons were in the custody or under the control of the perpetrator.*
3. *Such pain or suffering did not arise only from, and was not inherent in or incidental to, lawful sanctions.*[532]

Torture as a CAH has no specific purpose element. This is noted in a footnote to the title of the crime in the Regulations, which states *that "[i]t is understood that no specific purpose need be proved for this crime"*. It is to be recalled that torture as a war crime does contain a specific purpose element and thus the underlying offence of torture is different when committed as a war crime as compared to a CAH. At the ICC, Dominic Ongwen was convicted of charges including torture as a CAH,[533] and it has also been charged in the cases of *Al Hassan* and *Said* and the joined cases of *Yekatom and Ngaissona*, all of which are in trial.

[532] The two contextual elements are omitted.

[533] *Ongwen*, Trial Chamber Judgment.

Rape, Sexual Slavery, Enforced prostitution, Forced Pregnancy, Enforced Sterilisation, Sexual Violence

Rape, sexual slavery, enforced prostitution, forced pregnancy, enforced sterilisation and sexual violence can each comprise a CAH. The elements of these offences as CAH, are the same as the elements of these offences as war crimes. The relevant provisions in relation to the elements of the offences as CAH under the ICCA (Elements of Crimes) Regulations are listed below and the reader can cross-refer to the elements of the corresponding provisions in the *War Crimes under the ICCA* chapter.

Rape – Regulations, Article 7(1)(g)-1,

Sexual slavery – Regulations Article 7(1)(g)-2,[534]

Enforced Prostitution – Regulations, Article 7(1)(g)-3,

Forced Pregnancy – Regulations, Article 7(1)(g)-4,

Enforced Sterilization - Regulations, Article 7(1)(g)-5,

Sexual violence – Regulations, Article 7(1)(g)-6.

At the ICC, *Bosco Ntaganda* was convicted of charges including rape and sexual slavery as CAH, [535] as was *Dominic Ongwen*, who was also convicted of crimes of forced pregnancy.[536] *Jean-Pierre Bemba* was acquitted of charges of rape as a CAH,[537] as was *Mathieu Ngudjolo Chui*, who was also acquitted of sexual slavery as a CAH.[538] The ongoing cases

[534] Note that footnote 21 appended to the title of this crime in the Regulations provides that *"Given the complex nature of this crime, it is recognized that its commission could involve more than one perpetrator as a part of a common criminal purpose"*.

[535] *Ntaganda,* Trial Judgment and Appeal Judgment.

[536] *Ongwen,* Trial Judgment. He was also convicted of forced marriage, charged as an *"other inhumane act"* CAH (see below).

[537] *Bemba,* Appeal Chamber Judgment.

[538] *Ngudjolo Chui,* Trial Chamber Judgment (upheld on appeal).

of *Abd-Al-Rahman* and *Ngaïssona* at the ICC involve charges of rape as a CAH. The case of *Al Hassan* involves allegations of rape and sexual slavery, as well as forced marriage charged as an *"other inhumane act"* (see below).[539]

Persecution[540]

ICCA Schedule 8, Article 7(2)(g) provides that:

> *""Persecution" means the intentional and severe deprivation of fundamental rights contrary to international law by reason of the identity of the group or collectivity".*

The Regulations, Article 7(1)(h) provide that the elements of persecution as a CAH are:

1. *The perpetrator severely deprived, contrary to international law[21], one or more persons of fundamental rights.*

2. *The perpetrator targeted such person or persons by reason of the identity of a group or collectivity or targeted the group or collectivity as such.*

3. *Such targeting was based on political, racial, national, ethnic, cultural, religious, gender as defined in article 7, paragraph 3, of the Statute, or other grounds that are universally recognized as impermissible under international law.*

539 *Al Hassan*, Confirmation of Charges Decision.

540 The crime of *"Persecution"* is referred to in full in Schedule 8, Article 7(e) as: *"Persecution against any identifiable group or collectively on political, racial, national, ethnic, cultural, religious, gender as defined in paragraph 3, or other grounds that are universally recognized as impermissible under international law, in connection with any act referred to in this paragraph or any crimes within the jurisdiction of the Court".*

4. *The conduct was committed in connection with any act referred to in article 7, paragraph 1, of the Statute or any crime within the jurisdiction of the Court [22].*[541]

[the two contextual elements are omitted].

At the ICC, *Bosco Ntaganda* was found guilty of persecution as a CAH,[542] as was *Dominic Ongwen*.[543] Charges of persecution as a CAH also feature in a number of cases which are currently in trial: *Abd-Al-Rahman case, Al Hassan, Said, Yekatom and Ngaïssona.*

Enforced disappearance of persons

ICCA Schedule 8, Article 7(2)(i) provides that:

> *""Enforced disappearance of persons" means the arrest, detention or abduction of persons by, or with the authorization, support or acquiescence of, a State or a political organization, followed by a refusal to acknowledge that deprivation of freedom or to give information on the fate or whereabouts of those persons, with the intention of removing them from protection of the law for a prolonged period of time".*

The Regulations, Article 7(1)(i) set out the following elements for the enforced disappearance of persons as a CAH:

1. *The perpetrator:*

---

541 Footnote "22" provides that: *"It is understood that no additional mental element is necessary for this element other than that inherent in element 6".*

542 *Ntaganda*, Trial Chamber Judgment (upheld on appeal).

543 *Ongwen*, Trial Chamber Judgment.

(a) Arrested, detained [25][544] *[26]*[545] *or abducted one or more persons; or*

(b) Refused to acknowledge the arrest, detention or abduction, or to give information on the fate or whereabouts of such person or persons.

2.

(a) Such arrest, detention or abduction was followed or accompanied by a refusal to acknowledge that deprivation of freedom or to give information on the fate or whereabouts of such person or persons; or

(b) Such refusal was preceded or accompanied by that deprivation of freedom.

3. The perpetrator was aware that [27]:[546]

(a) Such arrest, detention or abduction would be followed in the ordinary course of events by a refusal to acknowledge that deprivation of freedom or to give information on the fate or whereabouts of such person or persons [28],[547] *or*

---

544 Footnote "25" provides that: *"[t]he word "detained" would include a perpetrator who maintained an existing detention".*

545 Footnote "26" provides that: *"It is understood that under certain circumstances an arrest or detention may have been lawful".*

546 Footnote "23", which follows the title to this crime provides that: *"This element, inserted because of the complexity of this crime, is without prejudice to the General Introduction to the Elements of Crimes". Footnote "24" follows immediately thereafter, which*

547 Footnote "28" provides that: *"It is understood that, in the case of a perpetrator who maintained an existing detention, this element would be satisfied if the perpetrator was aware that such a refusal had already taken place".*

> (b) *Such refusal was preceded or accompanied by that deprivation of freedom.*
>
> 4. *Such arrest, detention or abduction was carried out by, or with the authorization, support or acquiescence of, a State or a political organization.*
>
> 5. *Such refusal to acknowledge that deprivation of freedom or to give information on the fate or whereabouts of such person or persons was carried out by, or with the authorization or support of, such State or political organization.*
>
> 6. *The perpetrator intended to remove such person or persons from the protection of the law for a prolonged period of time.*
>
> [the two contextual elements are omitted].

Footnote "23" appended to the title of the crime provides that: *"[g]iven the complex nature of this crime, it is recognized that its commission will normally involve more than one perpetrator as a part of a common criminal purpose"*. Footnote "24" appended to the title of the crime provides that: *"[t]his crime falls under the jurisdiction of the Court only if the attack referred to in elements 7 and 8 occurs after the entry into force of the Statute"*.

The CAH has been charged in a single case before the ICC, that of *Mahamat Said Abdel Kani* (known as "*Said*"), which concerns the situation in the Central African Republic.[548]

The crime of apartheid

ICCA Schedule 8, Article 7(2)(h) provides the following:

> *""The crime of apartheid" means inhumane acts of a character similar to those referred to in paragraph 1, committed in the context of an institutionalized regime of systematic oppression and domination by*

548 *Said*, Confirmation of Charges Decision.

> *one racial group over any other racial group or groups and committed with the intention of maintaining that regime".*

The elements of the offence are set out in the Regulations, Article 7(1)(j).

Other inhumane acts

"Other inhumane acts" is referred to in full in Schedule 8, Article 7(e) as: *"Other inhumane acts of a similar character intentionally causing great suffering, or serious injury to body or to mental or physical health".*

The Regulations, Article 7(1)(k) set out the following as the elements of *"Other inhumane acts"* as a CAH:

1. *The perpetrator inflicted great suffering, or serious injury to body or to mental or physical health, by means of an inhumane act.*
2. *Such act was of a character similar to any other act referred to in article 7, paragraph 1, of the Statute [30].*[549]
3. *The perpetrator was aware of the factual circumstances that established the character of the act.*[550]

"Other inhumane acts" as a CAH have been charged in a number of ICC cases, in particular in relation to the practice of forced marriage, in the cases of *Dominic Ongwen* (convicted by a Trial Chamber)[551] and *Al Hassan* (in-trial).[552] Additionally, the case of *Abd-Al-Rahman* also includes charges of *"other inhumane acts"* as a CAH.[553]

---

549 Footnote *"30"* provides that: *"It is understood that "character" refers to the nature and gravity of the act".*

550 The two contextual elements are omitted.

551 *Ongwen,* Trial Chamber Judgment.

552 *Al Hassan,* Confirmation of Charges Decision.

553 *Abd-Al-Rahman,* Confirmation of Charges Decision, paras. 40-45.

CHAPTER FIVE

GENOCIDE UNDER THE ICCA

Historical origins of the crime of genocide

Genocide has been described by eminent scholars of international law and by international courts and tribunals as sitting at the apex in the hierarchy of international crimes.[554] The term genocide was first coined in 1944 by Raphael Lemkin, who was a Polish, Jewish scholar and refugee who had fled the Nazi occupation of his homeland.[555] It was codified into the corpus of international law when, in the wake of World War II, the General Assembly of the UN adopted the Convention for the Prevention and Punishment of the Crime of Genocide on 9 December 1948 *("the Genocide Convention")*.[556] The Genocide Convention has been signed by 152 state parties,[557] and is widely considered to reflect customary international law.[558] It obliges State Parties to prevent and

[554] See for example: William A. Schabas, *The International Criminal Court, A Commentary on the Rome Statute*, Oxford University Press, 2010 at p.119 and Antonio Cassese and others, *International Criminal Law*, Cases and Commentary, Oxford University Press, 2011 at p. 200.

[555] See *ibid.*

[556] Convention for the Prevention and Punishment of the Crime of Genocide, (General Assembly Resolution A/RES/3/260 http://un-documents.net/a3r260.htm). The Genocide Convention was approved and proposed for signature and ratification or accession by General Assembly resolution 260A (III) of 9 December 1948 and entered into force on 12 January 1951.

[557] See: https://www.un.org/en/genocideprevention/genocide-convention.shtml.

[558] See for example, the ICJ Judgment, *Case concerning application of the Convention on the prevention and punishment of the crime of genocide (Bosnia and Herzegovina v. Yugoslavia [Serbia and Montenegro])*, 26 February 2007, para. 161. See also

punish genocide. The Convention defines genocide in Article 2 and makes clear that it can be committed in times of peace or war. The definition of genocide in the Convention was adopted by the ICTY, the ICTR, as well as the ICC in the Rome Statute. The same definition is found in the ICCA. Section 51 ICCA makes genocide an extraterritorial crime under our domestic law and section 52 ICCA criminalises offences ancillary to the commission of genocide. The provisions in relation to jurisdiction under the ICCA have been set out in chapter 1.

Definition of genocide under the ICCA

Schedule 8, Article 6 of the ICCA defines the crime of genocide as follows:

> *For the purposes of this Statute "genocide" means any of the following acts committed with intent to destroy in whole or in part, a national, ethnical, racial or religious group, as such:*
>
> *(a) Killing members of the group;*
>
> *(b) Causing serious bodily or mental harm to members of the group;*
>
> *(c) Deliberately inflicting on the group conditions of life calculated to bring about its physical destruction in whole or in part;*
>
> *(d) Imposing measures intended to prevent births within the group;*
>
> *(e) Forcibly transferring children of the group to another group.*

Genocide does not require the actual extermination of a group in its entirely. Rather, genocide refers to any one of the five acts (above) committed with the specific intent to destroy, in whole or in part, a

---

Prosecutor v Jean-Paul Akayesu (ICTR-96-4-T) Trial Chamber Judgment, 2 September 1999 ("*Akayesu*, Trial Judgment") para. 495.

national, ethnical, racial or religious group, as such. It is the specific intent to destroy a part of humanity which lies at the heart of genocide.

Caselaw

The reader will recall that in interpreting and applying Schedule 8, Article 6 ICCA, which defines genocide, the domestic courts must have regard to the caselaw from the ICC.[559] At the ICC, the Prosecutor has only charged genocide in a single case. That is the case against Omar Hassan Ahmad Al Bashir, the former President of the Republic of Sudan, in relation to alleged crimes against members of the Fur, Masalit and Zaghawa groups in Darfur from March 2003 to July 2008. Initially, a Pre-Trial Chamber declined to issue a warrant in respect of genocide.[560] However, the Appeals Chamber directed the Pre-Trial Chamber to make the decision anew, finding that the Pre-Trial Chamber had erroneously applied the wrong standard of proof.[561] The Pre-Trial Chamber subsequently confirmed charges of genocide in an amended second warrant.[562] Omar Al Bashir is yet to be surrendered to the ICC. Consequently, the ICC jurisprudence in relation to genocide is nascent. However, there is a significant body of jurisprudence from the ICTR in relation to the mass murder of Tutsis in 1994,[563] and the ICTY in

559 ICCA, section 50(5).

560 *The Prosecutor v. Omar Hassan Ahmad Al Bashir*, (ICC-02/05-01/09-3) 4 March 2009, Pre-Trial Chamber, *"Public Redacted Version, Decision on the Prosecution's Application for a Warrant of Arrest against Omar Hassan Ahmad Al Bashir"*.

561 *The Prosecutor v. Omar Hassan Ahmad Al Bashir*, ICC-02/05-01/09-OA, 3 February 2010, Appeals Chamber, *'Judgment on the appeal of the Prosecutor against the "Decision on the Prosecution's Application for a Warrant of Arrest against Omar Hassan Ahmad Al Bashir"*. See the reasoning at paras. 29-39.

562 *The Prosecutor v. Omar Hassan Ahmad Al Bashir* (ICC-02/05-01/09) 12 July 2010, Pre-Trial Chamber, *"Public Document, Second Warrant of Arrest for Omar Hassan Ahmad Al Bashir"*. The charges also include CAH and war crimes.

563 In particular, the first case in which genocide was tried in the modern day ad hoc tribunals, was *Prosecutor v Jean-Paul Akayesu*. The *Akayesu, Trial Judgment* is essential reading in relation to the crime of genocide and the elements of the crime.

relation to the genocide in Srebrenica, Bosnia in 1995, as well as the ICJ.[564] In addition, genocide has been tried domestically in other jurisdictions and such case law and practice could be instructive, should genocide be tried before the Crown Court.[565] Domestically, the Administrative Court decision in the Rwandan extradition proceedings in *Government of Rwanda v. Emmanuel Nteziryayo and four others* [2017] EWHC 1912 (Admin) is of note. In that case, the Divisional Court refused an appeal on behalf of the Rwandan Government to extradite five individuals back to Rwanda to face charges arising from the genocide in 1994. In a nutshell, the basis of the Divisional Court's decision was that there a real risk of a flagrant denial of justice, in violation of their ECHR article 6 right to a fair trial, owing to deemed inadequacies in the criminal justice system in Rwanda. That decision prompted calls for the five individuals to face prosecution for genocide in the Crown Court but to date no such prosecution has taken place.

The elements of the crime of genocide

The elements of the five categories of conduct (or underlying offences) that comprise genocide are set out in the ICC Elements of Crimes document, which has been incorporated into domestic law through the ICCA (Elements of Crimes) Regulations. Should a case alleging genocide proceed to trial in the Crown Court, the judge will have to make a decision about the elements of the offence. The Crown Court has an

[564] Seminal cases from the ICJ in relation to the Genocide Convention and State responsibility are: *Application of the Genocide Convention (Bosnia and Herzegovina v. Serbia and Montenegro) (Merits),* ICJ Reports (2007) (and see as well as the four previous related decisions concerning 'Provisional Measures' and 'Preliminary Objections' and 'Counter-Claims Order')) and *Application of the Genocide Convention (Croatia v. Serbia),* ICJ Reports (2015) 963 (and the prior decision on 'Preliminary Objections').

[565] ICCA, section 50(5) expressly provides that *"account may be taken of any other relevant international jurisprudence"*.

obligation to take the elements of crimes at set out in the Regulations into account.[566]

To establish genocide the following must be proven:

- There must be an underlying offence committed with the requisite *mens rea*;
- The underlying offence must be directed against a protected group – a national, racial, religious or ethnical group;
- The underlying offence must also be committed with the specific intent to destroy all or a substantial part of the group.

The elements of each of the five underlying offences that can be charged as genocide will be set out below, but first the requirement of specific intent, common to the five underlying offences will be considered, as well as the contextual element to the crime of genocide, which is included in the ICC Elements of Crimes Documents and the ICCA (Elements of Crimes) Regulations.

Mens rea and specific intent

It must be established that:

(1) The perpetrator had the requisite mens rea to commit the underlying offence; this has been described as a general subjective element, which consists of intent and knowledge (as per article 30 ICC Statute); and,

[566] ICCA, section 50(2).

(2) The perpetrator committed the underlying offence with the specific intent to destroy the protected group, in whole or in part, as such.[567]

The specific intent requirement is expressed in the ICCA (Elements of Crimes) Regulations as follows:

> *"The perpetrator intended to destroy, in whole or in part, that national, ethnical, racial or religious group, as such".*

The requirement of specific intent, also referred to as *'dolus specialis'*, is at the heart of the crime of genocide. It requires the perpetrator to intend to destroy the protected group as such, in whole or in part.[568] Without that specific intent, no matter how horrific the crime, it will not amount to genocide.[569] The specific intent required for genocide is more extreme than the discriminatory intent required for persecution as a CAH, which is demonstrated by deliberately targeting persons because they are members of a group.[570] The extreme gravity of the crime of genocide is reflected in the requirement to prove specific intent unequivocally.[571]

It can be extremely difficult in practice to prove the requirement of specific intent. The ad hoc tribunals have explained that in the absence of direct evidence, such as a confession, it is necessary to look at the

---

567 *Omar Al Bashir, First Arrest Warrant Decision,* para.139. Note that the introductory section to the crime of genocide in the ICCA (Elements of Crimes) Regulations says that: *"Notwithstanding the normal requirement for a mental element provided for in article 30, and recognizing that knowledge of the circumstances will usually be addressed in proving genocidal intent, the appropriate requirement, if any, for a mental element regarding this circumstance will need to be decided by the Court on a case-by-case basis".*

568 *Akayesu,* Trial Judgment, paras. 498 and 517.

569 *Akayesu,* Trial Judgment, para. 519.

570 *Omar Al Bashir, First Arrest Warrant Decision,* paras. 140 - 143, referring to the ICJ, ICTY and ICTR caselaw.

571 See for example, *Prosecutor v Krstic* (IT-98-33-A) Appeals Chamber Judgment, 19 April 2004 (*Krstic,* Appeal Judgment) para. 37.

surrounding factual circumstances to establish evidence of the specific intent of the perpetrator, including:

- The perpetration of other culpable acts systematically directed against the same group,
- The scale of the atrocities committed,
- The systematic targeting of victims on account of their membership of a particular group,
- The repetition of destructive discriminatory acts.[572]

Proving genocide does not require as a legal ingredient, the existence of a plan or policy but in practice, evidence showing the existence of a plan or policy may facilitate proof of the specific intent requirement.[573]

The ICTY Appeals Chamber in *Prosecutor v. Krstić* ruled that the specific intent requirement of genocide is satisfied where the evidence shows that the perpetrator intended to destroy at least a *"substantial part"* of the protected group.[574] The Appeals Chamber recalled that the aim of the Genocide Convention is to prevent the intentional destruction of entire human groups, and as such the part of the group targeted by the perpetrator must be significant enough to have an impact on the group

---

572 *Prosecutor v Goran Jelisić* (IT-95-10-A) Appeals Chamber Judgment (*"Jelisić*, Appeal Judgment") para. 47. Confirmed in *Prosecutor v. Krstić* (IT-98-33-A) Appeals Chamber Judgement, 19 April 2004, para 34. See also *Akayesu,* Trial Judgment, paras. 523-524.

573 *Jelisić*, Appeal Judgment, para. 48, also noting in footnote 83, that this was also held by the Appeals Chamber for the ICTR in *Obed Ruzindana and Clement Kayishema v Prosecutor* (ICTR-95-1-A) 1 June 2001.

574 *Krstić, Appeal Judgment*, para. 12 and the preceding discussion beginning at para. 8. The Appeals Chamber referred to the rulings of ICTY and ICTR Trial Chambers.

as a whole.[575] The Appeals Chamber held that determining when the targeted part of the group is substantial enough to meet the requirement, may involve a consideration of the following factors:[576]

- The numeric size of the targeted part of the group as the necessary starting point;
- The number of individuals targeted in relation to the overall size of the group;
- The prominence of the targeted group, including if a specific part of the group is emblematic of the overall group, or is essential to its survival;[577]
- The area of the perpetrators' activity and control, as well as the possible extent of their reach – noting, for example, that Nazi Germany may have intended only to eliminate Jews within Europe and that the perpetrators of the genocide in Rwanda did not seriously contemplate the elimination of the Tutsi beyond the borders of Rwanda.[578]

---

575 *Krstić* Appeals Chamber Judgement, 19 April 2004, para. 8.

576 At para. 15, *Krstić, Appeal Judgment*, the Appeals Chamber noted that these considerations were not exhaustive or dispositive but guidelines and that the applicability of the factors would vary depending on the circumstances of the case.

Krstić, Appeal Judgment, para. 12.

Krstić, Appeal Judgment, para. 13.

Prosecutor v Krstić

The *Krstić* case concerned General Radoslav Krstić's responsibility in relation to the mass execution of approximately 7,000 Bosnian Muslim men and boys by Bosnian Serb forces in Srebrenica in July 1995.[579] On appeal, the defence argued that the Trial Chamber had erred by unacceptably narrowing the definition of *"in part"* to encompass the Bosnian Muslims of Srebrenica, or the Bosnian Muslims of Eastern Bosnia. However, the Appeals Chamber rejected this argument and ruled that the Trial Chamber had been correct to deem the Bosnian Muslims of Srebrenica a substantial part of the protected group of Bosnian Muslims. In so ruling, the Appeals Chamber emphasised the prominence of the group. The Appeals Chamber observed that by 1995 most of the Muslim inhabitants in the region had sought refuge in Srebrenica and as such the elimination of the enclave would have accomplished the Bosnian Serb goal of purifying the region of its Muslim population. Furthermore, Srebrenica, which had been declared a UN *"safe area"*. It was important both in the eyes of Bosnian Muslims and the international community and the elimination of the Muslim population of Srebrenica would serve as an example to all Bosnian Muslims. [580] The Appeals Chamber agreed with the Trial Chambers analysis that Krstić had the intent to kill Bosnian Muslim men of military age in Srebrenica, and that from this intent to kill the further inference could be drawn that Krstić shared the genocidal intent to destroy a substantial part of the targeted group, the Bosnian Muslims of Srebrenica.[581]

---

579 Krstić was convicted of aiding and abetting the genocide of Bosnian Muslims in Srebrenica and sentenced to 35 years' imprisonment (*Krstic, Appeal Judgment).*

580 *Krstić, Appeal Judgment*, paras. 15 - 17 and 23.

581 *Krstić, Appeal Judgment*, para. 21.

Cultural genocide and ethnic cleansing

Genocide is concerned with acts seeking the physical or biological destruction of a human group and not with attacks upon a groups cultural or sociological characteristics, even where the aim of the later is to remove the distinct cultural identity of the group.[582] In other words, the crime of genocide, as understood through the Genocide Convention and under customary international law, does not include cultural genocide, but is limited to acts which concern physical and biological destruction.[583] Evidence of attacks on cultural and religious property or symbols of a group may amount to evidence of an intent to physically destroy a group. [584] Regarding ethnic cleansing, this does not itself constitute genocide, but may also evidence genocide. Thus, the Appeals Chamber in *Krstić*, ruled that whilst the forcible transfer of women and children from Srebrenica did not itself constitute a genocidal act, it could be relied upon as evidence of genocidal intent.[585]

---

582 *Krstić, Appeal Judgment*, para. 25.

583 See the *Prosecutor v. Krstić* (IT-98-33-T), Trial Chamber Judgement, 2 August 2001, analysis at paras. 575 -580.

584 *Ibid.*, at para 580, where the Trial Chamber said that they would take into account as evidence of intent to destroy the group, the deliberate destruction of mosques and houses belonging to members of the group.

585 *Krstić, Appeal Judgment* - see the powerful factual analysis at paras. 24-33, in which the Appeals Chamber also rejected the defence argument that the Trial Chamber had erroneously enlarged the term *"destroy"* to include the geographical displacement of a community.

Protected groups

Four groups are listed as possible victims of the crime of genocide: national, ethnic, racial or religious groups. Other groups, such as, political and social groups are not protected.[586] In *Jean-Paul Akayesu,* the first case at the ICTR to consider the elements of the crime of genocide, the ICTR Trial Chamber defined the groups as follows:

- National group – a group of people who are understood *"to share a legal bond based on common citizenship"*;[587]
- Ethnic group – a group whose members *"share a common language or culture"*;[588]
- Racial group – a group based on *"hereditary physical traits often identified with a geographical region"*;[589]
- Religious group – a group whose members share the same religion, denomination or *"mode of worship"*.[590]

The national, ethnic, racial or religious characteristics must be positively identified, with these groups being identified by their positive

---

586 It is interesting to note that during the drafting process of the Rome Statute, there were some calls to extend the definition of genocide to include political and social groups, namely from Cuba, but these were not acted upon and the definition remained as set out in the Genocide Convention of 1948. For a discussion of the drafting history, see William A. Schabas, *The International Criminal Court, A Commentary on the Rome Statute*, Oxford University Press, 2010 at pp. 120-122 and also at pp.128-129.

587 *Akayesu*, Trial Judgment, para. 512.

588 *Akayesu*, Trial Judgment, para. 513.

589 *Akayesu*, Trial Judgment, para. 514. The Trial Chamber explained that racial group was defined irrespective of linguistic, cultural, national or religious factors.

590 *Akayesu*, Trial Judgment, para. 515.

characteristics of who they are, rather than who they are not.[591] For example, in *Omar Al Bashir, First Arrest Warrant Decision,* the majority of the Pre-Trial Chamber concluded that they had reasonable grounds to believe that the Fur, Masalit and the Zaghawa were distinct ethnic groups, because they had their own language, own tribal customs and own traditional links to its lands.[592]

Contextual element of genocide in the ICCA (Elements of Crimes) Regulations

The elements of five underlying crimes of genocide, as set out in the ICCA (Elements of Crimes) Regulations, also share in common the following contextual element, that:

> *"The conduct took place in the context of a manifest pattern of similar conduct directed against that group or was conduct that could itself effect such destruction".*

The introductory section to the crime of genocide in the Regulations explains that *"[t]he term "in the context of" would include initial acts in an emerging pattern"* and that *"[t]he term "manifest" is an objective qualification".* This contextual element does not appear in either the Genocide Convention, the ICTY or ICTR Statutes, the ICC Statute, or the ICCA. Rather, it appears only in the ICC Elements of Crimes Document and the Regulations. Notably, there has been some debate in the academic literature in relation to the applicability of this element, [593]

---

591 *Omar Al Bashir, First Arrest Warrant Decision',* para. 135 and see the various case law of the ICJ as well as the ICTY and ICTR referred to in that paragraph at footnotes 149-150.

592 *Omar Al Bashir, First Arrest Warrant Decision,* para. 137.

593 In *Omar Al Bashir, First Arrest Warrant Decision,* at para. 125, a majority of the Pre-Trial Chamber noted the controversy about whether the element should be recognised, referring in footnote 143 to the following academic literature: Cryer, R., Friman, H., Robinson, D, and Wilmshurt, E., *An Introduction to International Criminal Law and Procedure,* United Kingdom, Cambridge University Press, 2007, pp. 177-179, and also Schabas, W.A., *Genocide in International Law, The Crimes of Crimes,* 2nd edition, Galway, Cambridge University Press. 2009, pp.245-

and this may provide a fruitful topic for litigation should genocide be tried in the Crown Court.

There is just a single decision from a Pre-Trial Chamber at the ICC considering this contextual element. A majority of the Pre-trial Chamber in *Omar Al Bashir, First Arrest Warrant Decision* observed that the definition in the Genocide Convention does not expressly require any contextual elements,[594] that the Statutes of the ICTY and the ICTR had adopted the same definition as in the Genocide Convention,[595] and that the case law of the ICTY and the ICTR had excluded the definition of genocide as requiring any type of contextual element, such as a genocidal policy or plan.[596] The majority of the Pre-Trial Chamber observed that according to the case law of the ICTY and the ICTR, genocide is committed as soon as the specific intent to target the protected group and destroy it, in whole or in part, materialises, regardless of whether the *"latent threat"* had turned into a *"concrete threat"*.[597] However, the majority of the Pre-Trial Chamber held that according to the contextual element in the Elements of Crimes Document, the crime of genocide is only completed when the *"latent threat"* becomes real.[598] In so finding, the ICC Pre-Trial Chamber took a deliberate and significant departure from the jurisprudence of the ad hoc tribunals.[599]

248, and also Werle, G. *Principles of International Criminal Law, The Netherlands*, TMC Asser Press 2005, pp. 191-194.

594 *Omar Al Bashir, First Arrest Warrant Decision,* para. 117.

595 *Omar Al Bashir, First Arrest Warrant Decision,* para. 118.

596 *Omar Al Bashir, First Arrest Warrant Decision,* para. 119.

597 *Omar Al Bashir, First Arrest Warrant Decision,* para. 120.

598 *Omar Al Bashir, First Arrest Warrant Decision,* para. 124.

599 See for example, *Akayesu,* Trial Judgment, paras. 497, 520 and 523 and *Jelesić* (IT-95-10-T), Trial Judgment 14 December 1999, para. 100, confirmed by the Appeals Chamber in *Jelesić,* Appeal Judgment, 5 July 2001.

Elements of the five categories of conduct

The elements of the five categories of conduct which can be charged as genocide will be set out below as they appear in the ICCA (Elements of Crimes) Regulations. The specific intent element will be noted as '[specific intent element]' which is that: *"[t]he perpetrator intended to destroy, in whole or in part, that national, ethnical, racial or religious group, as such")*. The contextual element will be noted as '[contextual element]' which is that: *"[t]he conduct took place in the context of a manifest pattern of similar conduct directed against that group or was conduct that could itself effect such destruction"*.

Article 6(a) Genocide by killing

1. *The perpetrator killed [footnote] one or more persons.*
2. *Such person or persons belonged to a particular national, ethnical, racial or religious group.*
3. *[specific intent element]*
4. *[contextual element]*

The footnote provides that the term *"killed"* is interchangeable with the term *"caused death"*. The term *"killed"* has been interpreted in the case law of the ad hoc tribunals as being synonymous with homicide.[600]

Article 6(b) Genocide by causing serious bodily or mental harm

1. *The perpetrator caused serious bodily harm or mental harm to one or more persons [footnote]*
2. *Such person or persons belonged to a particular national, ethnical, racial or religious group.*

[600] See for example, *Akayesu* Trial Judgment, 2 September 1998, paras. 500-501.

3. *[specific intent element]*

4. *[contextual element]*

The footnote explains that *"this conduct may include, but not necessarily restricted to, acts of torture, rape, sexual violence or inhuman or degrading treatment"*.[601] The harm caused to members of the group need not be permanent.[602]

Article 6(c) – Genocide by deliberately inflicting conditions of life calculated to bring about physical destruction

1. *The perpetrator inflicted certain conditions of life upon one or more persons.*

2. *Such person or persons belonged to a particular national, ethnical, racial or religious group.*

3. *[specific intent element]*

4. *The conditions of life were calculated to bring about the physical destruction of that group, in whole or in part [footnote].*

5. *[contextual element]*

In the case of *Akayesu*, the Trial Chamber explained that this underlying offence captured the methods of destruction whereby the perpetrator does not immediately kill members of the group, but which, nevertheless, ultimately seek the groups physical destruction.[603] The footnote to the

[601] This reflects paragraph 504 *Akayesu* Trial Judgment, as well as para. 730 where the Trial Chamber underscored the fact that rape and sexual violence constitute genocide, as long as they are committed with the requisite specific intent and at paras. 731-732 found that acts of rape and sexual violence committed against Tutsi women resulted in their physical and psychological destruction, their families and communities and was an integral party of the destruction of the Tutsi group as a whole.

[602] See for example, *Akayesu* Trial Judgment, para. 502.

[603] *Akayesu,* Trial Chamber Judgment, para. 505.

offence in the Regulations provides that "[*t*]*he term "conditions of life" may include, but is not necessarily restricted to, deliberate deprivation of resources indispensable for survival, such as food or medical services, or systematic expulsion from homes*". This reflects the way the offence was interpreted by the ICTR Trial Chamber in *Akayesu*.[604] However, it should be noted that some legal academics have questioned whether the interpretation of the underlying offence in *Akayesu* was overly broad; in that the target of the offence is the destruction of the group and some of the measures referred to in *Akayesu* would not, arguably, result in the groups destruction.[605]

Article 6(d) – Genocide by imposing measures intended to prevent births

1. *The perpetrator imposed certain measures upon one or more persons.*
2. *Such person or persons belonged to a particular national, ethnical, racial or religious group, as such.*
3. *[specific intent requirement]*
4. *The measures imposed were intended to prevent births within that group.*
5. *[contextual element]*

The ICTR Trial Chamber *Akayesu*, held that measures intended to prevent births within the group, included:

- Sexual mutilation,
- Sterilization,
- Forced birth control,

---

604 *Akayesu,* Trial Chamber Judgment, para. 506.

605 See the discussion in Cassese, *International Criminal Law, Cases and Commentary*, Oxford University Press, 2011 ed., pp. 203-204.

- Separation of the sexes,
- Prohibition of marriages,
- Rape, in circumstances where membership of the group is determined by the identity of the father and a woman of the group is deliberately impregnated by a man of another group, with the intent that she give birth to a child who will consequently not belong to her mother's group;
- Also, measures intended to prevent births when the person raped refuses subsequently to procreate.[606]

Article 6(e) – Genocide by forcibly transferring children

1. *The perpetrator forcibly transferred one or more persons [footnote].*
2. *Such person or persons belonged to a particular national, ethnical, racial or religious group, as such.*
3. *[specific intent requirement]*
4. *The transfer was from that group to another group.*
5. *The person or persons were under the age of 18 years.*
6. *The perpetrator knew, or should have known, that the person or persons were under the age of 18 years.*
7. *[contextual element]*

The footnote states that *"[t]he term "forcibly" is not restricted to physical force, but may include threat of force or coercion, such as that caused by fear of violence, duress, detention, psychological oppression or abuse of power,*

606 *Akayesu*, Trial Chamber Judgment, paras. 507 and 508 noting that measures intended to prevent births can be mental as well as physical.

against such person or persons or another person, or by taking advantage of a coercive environment".

CHAPTER SIX

INVESTIGATION, REFERRAL AND PRE-TRIAL

This chapter will focus on the process of referring a case to the war crimes team of the Metropolitan Police Counter Terrorism Command ("SO15"), the initial investigation by SO15, and the steps that will be taken by the Crown Prosecution Service ("CPS"), Special Crime and Counter Terrorism Division ("CTD"), at the pre-trial stage. The chapter includes practical advice for individuals, organizations and legal representatives about the conduct of initial inquiries and investigations and about how to refer a case to SO15. The relevant legal provisions in relation to an application for a private arrest warrant and a private prosecution will also be set out. Finally, the chapter will address the following topics which should be considered at an early stage: immunities, forms of liability, the use of interpreters and requests for assistance from foreign Governments and third parties. Disclosure is an important issue which should be considered at the investigation and pre-trial stage and this is addressed separately in the next chapter.

Referring a case to SO15 and the CPS

SO15, CTD and the War Crimes / Crimes Against Humanity Referral Guidelines

SO15 is responsible for the investigation of alleged war crimes, CAH, genocide and torture. The CTD has responsibility for prosecuting these international crimes. SO15 and CTD have agreed to follow a set of guidelines governing the investigation and prosecution of war crimes, CAH, genocide and torture. These are referred to as the *"War Crimes/ Crimes Against Humanity Referral Guidelines"* and they are available online (hereinafter, referred to as the *"Referral Guidelines"*).[607] The Referral Guidelines will be followed by SO15 and the CTD, whenever a referral is made to SO15 to investigate a suspect.

SO15's scoping exercise

When a referral is made to SO15, the war crimes team conduct a scoping exercise. The purpose of the scoping exercise is to enable the team to make an informed decision about whether to conduct a full investigation. The Referral Guidelines explain precisely what the scoping exercise will involve.[608] The questions that SO15 will consider as part of their scoping exercise include:

(1) Is there a named or identifiable suspect?

(2) If not, is there a realistic prospect of identifying the suspect?

(3) What is the nationality and location of the named and identifiable suspect?

- For ICCA crimes, is the suspect a UK national or resident, present in the UK, or in a country that will provide mutual legal assistance ("MLA");

- For grave breaches of the Geneva Conventions, torture, or hostage taking, are there reasonable grounds to believe that the suspect is present in the UK, or will come to the UK?

(4) Are the victims/ witnesses named or identifiable?

(5) Are there any outstanding investigations at the ICC, or ad hoc tribunals, in relation to any suspect or any witness?

---

[607] https://www.cps.gov.uk/publication/war-crimescrimes-against-humanity-referral-guidelines. The Referral Guidelines were last updated on 30 September 2019.

[608] Referral Guidelines, section A.

(6) Have any complaints been made in any other jurisdiction?

Whilst conducting the scoping exercise, SO15 may refer the case to the Deputy Head of the CTD to obtain advice at an early stage about: (1) jurisdictional issues (i.e. those issues considered in Chapter 1), (2) potential immunities that may apply to the suspect, (3) potential offences disclosed by the evidence available at that stage.[609] A specialist prosecutor will be responsible for providing the early investigative advice. One potential outcome is that the specialist prosecutor may advise SO15 that there are evidential deficiencies in the case that cannot be strengthened by further investigation,[610] which will inform SO15's ultimate decision about whether a safe and proportionate investigation is feasible.[611] The specialist prosecutor should also advise the police and other investigators about possible reasonable lines of inquiry, evidential requirements, pre-charge procedures, disclosure management and the overall investigative strategy, which can include decisions about whether to refine or narrow the scope of the criminal conduct and the number of suspects under investigation.[612] The police are responsible for deciding how to deploy their resources, including the decision whether to start or continue an investigation, as well as the scope of any investigation.[613] An early investigative advice from CTD will therefore inform SO15s decision making about whether to conduct a full investigation and its scope but decisions about the investigation are ultimately taken by SO15.

609 Referral Guidelines, section B.

610 Referral Guidelines, at section B note that this is not to be regarded as a prosecutorial decision.

611 Referral Guidelines, section C.

612 Code for Crown Prosecutors, at 3.2. The Code for Crown Prosecutors can be found at: https://www.cps.gov.uk/publication/code-crown-prosecutors

613 Code for Crown Prosecutors, at 3.2.

SO15's referral to CTD for a prosecution decision

On completion of the investigation, SO15 will submit a file of evidence to the CTD, which will be reviewed by a specialist prosecutor in accordance with the Code for Crown Prosecutors.[614] The *"Full Code Test"* will be applied, which has two stages: (1) the evidential stage and (2) the public interest stage. In relation to the evidential stage, the prosecutor must be satisfied that there is sufficient admissible, reliable and credible evidence in accordance with the rules of the criminal courts of England and Wales, or capable of being put into that format, such that there is a *"realistic prospect of conviction"* for each suspect on each charge. They must consider what the defence case may be and how it is likely to affect the prospects of conviction. The Code for Crown Prosecutors underscores that a case which does not pass the evidential stage must not proceed, no matter how serious or sensitive that case may be.[615] Where the prosecutor is satisfied that there is sufficient evidence to justify a prosecution, the next question is whether a prosecution is in the public interest.[616] However, as noted in the Referral Guidelines, if there is sufficient evidence of war crimes, CAH, genocide, torture, or hostage taking, it is highly likely that a prosecution would be in the public interest.[617] Where the Full Code Test is met, the Attorney General will be asked to consent to the prosecution.[618]

---

614 Referral Guidelines, section D.

615 Code for Crown Prosecutors, para. 4.6. See further para. 4.8, which sets out the questions the specialist prosecutor will consider.

616 The questions that the specialist prosecutor must consider are set out in the Code for Crown Prosecutors. See paras. 4.9 – 4.14 and in particular the questions set out at para. 4.14 a) – g).

617 Referral Guidelines, section D para. 9.

618 Referral Guidelines, section D, para. 10.

How to report or refer a case to SO15

SO15 provides a direct email address where referrals in relation to potential international crimes can be sent.[619] International crimes can be reported on behalf of a victim, for example by their legal representative, or by an NGO. A victim of an international crime can also report the crime directly to the police in the usual way and the report will passed onto SO15 for investigation. There is also a link on the website of the metropolitan police for a victim or witness to report a war crime.[620]

Preparing a dossier to provide to SO15

It is recommended that the legal representatives of a victim, or an NGO representing victims, or any other organisation referring a case to SO15, includes a dossier of relevant material that will assist SO15 in its initial scoping exercise and thus its ultimate decision whether or not to open a full investigation. Whilst what should be included in the dossier will, of course, depend very much on the circumstances of the case, the following types of materials could be included:

- A short summary of the alleged case: what is said to have happened to whom, when and where, and who is said to be responsible;
- A short summary of the involvement of any legal representative, NGO, or other organisation representing victim/s;

---

[619] Referrals can be emailed to: SO15Mailbox.WarCrimesunit@met.pnn.police.uk

[620] See: https://www.met.police.uk/advice/advice-and-information/war-crimes/af/report-a-war-crime/ The online form is currently provided in English, Ukrainian and Russian but it is noted that the report can be made in any language. The following website: https://www.met.police.uk/advice/advice-and-information/war-crimes/what-is-a-war-crime/ also explains that as well as the online form, it is possible to report the crime on 101 or at a local police station.

- Complainant / victim statements or accounts (but note the *"word of warning"* below);

- Statements or accounts from potential witnesses; in particular, eyewitnesses to the alleged crimes (again, note the *"word of warning"* below);

- The names (or other identifying information) of any potential witnesses who have not been spoken to but who may be able to provide relevant information to SO15;

- Relevant information about the potential victims and witnesses, including:[621]

    - their names, and if their names are unavailable whether they are identifiable;

    - any known information which might undermine the credibility of potential victims or witnesses, such as having a criminal record;

- Photographs;

- Video footage;

- Relevant evidence from social media, including for example, Facebook;

- Open source materials which could include:

    - reports or other documents from the United Nations and its mechanisms, including the Special Rapporteurs and the United Nations Human Rights Commission;

---

621 Note the questions in section A, para. 3 of the Referral Guidelines.

  - reports or other documents from NGOs;
  - authoritative publications which refer the history of a relevant conflict or political situation;
  - relevant media publications in relation to alleged crimes or the suspect or suspects;

- A precis including any known details about the suspect, which could include the following information, where it is available:

  - the name of the suspect or suspects;
  - if the name of the suspect is not known, then any relevant information available, for example, a nickname, description of the suspect, whether the suspect held a particular position at, for example, a military base, or detention facility;
  - whether it is thought that the authorities in the country where the crime was committed could assist with identifying the suspect;[622]
  - the nationality of the suspect;
  - the country of residence of the suspect, if known;
  - whether or not the suspect is present in the UK, is a UK resident, visits or is expected to visit the UK;[623]
  - any other relevant information about the suspect, for example, whether they are in the military;

622 It is worth noting the checklist of questions that SO15 will consider in relation to the suspect, at section A, paragraph 1 of the Referral Guidelines.

623 See the questions at section A, para. 2 of the Referral Guidelines.

- A precis about what charges (war crimes, CAH, genocide, torture) any legal representative believes may be applicable (although this is something that SO15 and the CTD will consider, so a dossier could certainly be submitted without a precis of the legal charges);

- A precis referring to any extant relevant domestic or international proceedings (criminal or civil) pertaining to either the suspect, victims or witnesses. This could include:

    - Any relevant criminal or civil complaints made by victims or witnesses;

    - Any known, domestic, or international proceedings in relation to the suspect, which would include any domestic military disciplinary proceedings.[624]

- A summary of any steps taken in relation to disclosure – i.e. recording and retaining any evidence generated during the course of any inquiries or investigation into the case to date;

- Some information about whether it is thought that the authorities where the alleged crimes have been committed are likely to be receptive to, or hostile to an investigation by SO15.

A word of warning in relation to taking witness statements from potential victims and witnesses:

It is strongly recommended that anyone involved in taking accounts or statements from potential victims or witnesses has undergone relevant training and is aware of the fundamental principles, including asking witnesses open questions, which allow them to tell their version of events, and not to ask leading questions, i.e. questions which suggest an answer.

[624] One of the questions that SO15 will consider as part of the scoping exercise is whether there are any outstanding investigations at the ICC, ad hoc tribunals, or in other jurisdictions (Referral Guidelines, section A, paragraphs 4-5).

In terms of taking an initial account from a victim or witness, a good way to do this is by a video recording, but it is of course recognized that in conflict, post-conflict and politically sensitive situations this will not necessarily be possible. It is really important that steps are taken to record and retain any initial statement taken from a victim because a victims first account will be important at the trial.

SO15 will want to conduct their own interviews with victims and witnesses in order to produce witness statements that can be served in the criminal proceedings. It is likely that the police will video-record interviews and they will go into significant detail during the interviews. These video recordings may be played during the trial. It is strongly recommended that any lawyers, or NGOs, involved in taking early accounts from potential victims and witnesses resist the urge to take multiple accounts in a bid to present SO15 with a perfect witness statement. If a witness has produced multiple accounts and statements, the likely outcome is that they will be asked about the various different accounts and statements during cross-examination; with the intended effect of undermining the credibility of the witness by pointing to inconsistencies between the accounts and statements, their final statement and their evidence in court. A prudent representative will therefore minimise the number of accounts and statements taken from any potential victim or witness.

Disclosure and the Referral Guidelines[625]

The police and the CPS have duties under statute and common law in relation to the disclosure of unused material. Unused material is material which may be relevant to the investigation, but which is not relied upon by the prosecution in their case against the accused. The Referral Guidelines explain that it is important that any private individual, lawyer or organization that refers a case to SO15 or CTD records and retains relevant material obtained or generated by them during the course of

[625] Note that the next chapter is dedicated to the topic of disclosure.

their investigation.[626] The importance of this requirement cannot be over-emphasized to those involved in preparing a dossier of evidence to submit to SO15. Furthermore, it is important that representatives start to think about disclosure as soon as they either receive a complaint or start investigating a situation. The obligation is two-fold. First, it is important that any evidence either obtained, or generated, is recorded. Secondly, it is important that such evidence is retained. The Referral Guidelines explain that relevant material is *"any material that appears to have some bearing on any offence under investigation or any person being investigated or on the surrounding circumstances unless it is incapable of having any impact upon the case"*[627] and provides the following examples:

- any rough drafts of statements from victims,
- notes of telephone conversations with witnesses,
- medical notes,
- legal documents,
- e-mails,
- case notes.[628]

The prosecution is under a duty to disclose any unused material that undermines their case, or, assists the defence case. The Referral Guidelines assist by providing the following examples of materials which would fall into this category:

- any information which casts doubt on the reliability of a prosecution witness, or the accuracy of any prosecution evidence,

626 Referral Guidelines, section E.

627 Referral Guidelines, section E, para. 3.

628 Referral Guidelines, section E, para. 4.

- any motives for the making of false allegations by a prosecution witness,
- any material which may have a bearing on the admissibility of any prosecution evidence,
- the fact that a witness has sought, been offered or received a reward,
- any material that might go to the credibility of a prosecution witness,
- information that a person other than the accused was or might have been responsible or which points to another person whether charged or not (including a co-accused) having involvement in the commission of the offence.[629]

In each case the police will appoint a Disclosure Officer who will confirm with the private individual, lawyer or organization that refers a case to SO15, whether they hold such material and whether they are prepared to supply it or to allow the police to inspect it. The guidelines warn that if such material is not provided or disclosed to the Disclosure Officer, that it is likely that a prosecution may fail.[630] This warning is not to be taken lightly. The judge hearing the case may rule that the prosecution is an abuse of process where problems with disclosure mean that it is not possible for the accused to have a fair trial. In this regard, an open and honest dialogue with the Disclosure Office is imperative. Given that international crimes will often arise in the context of a conflict situation, there may be circumstances where potentially relevant documents have been destroyed. For example, where the offices of an NGO have been targeted during the conflict. What's important here is to explain the situation to SO15. Someone from the NGO may be able to provide a

629 Referral Guidelines, section E, para. 6.

630 Referral Guidelines, section E, paras. 7-8.

witness statement explaining what happened. The prosecution, defence and the judge can then assess how the fairness of the trial may be affected.

SO15's decision about whether or not to investigate a case

Where SO15 decides to take on an investigation, they will inform the private individual, lawyer or organization that has made the referral. From that point all investigative decisions, including the decision about whether or not to arrest a suspect will be made by SO15, and decisions about the prosecution of the case will be made independently by the CTD. It is important that the private individual, lawyers and organizations involved stop any independent investigations at this stage. Where SO15 have made the decision not to undertake a full investigation, this will also be communicated by SO15, along with the reasons for that decision, and where evidence has been submitted SO15 will respond in writing.[631] If the individual, lawyer or organization disagree with the decision, they can write to SO15 and request that SO15 reconsider their decision not to proceed to a full investigation.

Challenging a CPS decision not to prosecute

There is some scope to challenge a CPS decision not to prosecute. The Victims' Right to Review (VRR) scheme, which was launched in 2013, gives victims the right to request a review of a CPS decision not to prosecute, as well as a CPS decision to terminate criminal proceedings. Guidance about the VRR is available online (Victims' Right to Review Scheme, Legal Guidance (hereafter, "*VRR Guidance*").[632] Notably, the VRR scheme enables a right to request a review under the scheme where the CPS makes a final decision not to bring proceedings at the pre-charge stage.[633] However, this does not include a decision by the police (SO15)

631 Referral Guidelines, section C.

632 See: https://www.cps.gov.uk/legal-guidance/victims-right-review-scheme (last updated on 27 May 2021).

633 VRR Guidance, para. 18.

not to investigate, or not to investigate a case further when they have consulted the CPS but the CPS have not made a final decision to charge,[634] which would include a situation where SO15 have requested an early investigative advice from the CPS and SO15 have decided not to further investigate after the initial scoping exercise. Here, the recourse for review is to request SO15 to review their decision.[635]

The VRR defines a victim as *"a person who has suffered harm, including physical, mental or emotional harm or emotional loss which was directly caused by criminal conduct"* and includes close relatives of a person whose death was directly caused by criminal conduct.[636] Where an NGO or a legal representative wants to submit a request for a review on behalf of a victim (and they do not fall within the definition of a victim) written confirmation that they have the authority of the victim to act on their behalf must be provided.[637] Victims will be notified of the prosecution decision not to bring proceedings and a request for a review should ordinarily be made within 10 working days of receipt of the notification of the decision, but a request can be made up to three months later, after which the request is unlikely to be accepted unless there are exceptional circumstances.[638]

The outcome of the VRR is either a new decision, in which the old decision is overturned, or to uphold the previous decision.[639] The VRR Guidance gives some examples of circumstances where the CPS will overturn a decision not to prosecute, which includes cases which are stopped so that further anticipated evidence can be collected and

---

634 VRR Guidance, para. 19. Para. 19 sets out 11 circumstances in which the VRR is not available.

635 VRR Guidance, para. 19 (iii).

636 VRR Guidance, para. 16.

637 VRR Guidance, para. 16.

638 VRR Guidance, para. 30.

639 VRR Guidance, para. 12. Para. 31 indicates that the usual timeframe for a response from the CPS will be 30 days but that it may be longer in more complex cases.

prepared and cases which are not prosecuted because of a lack of evidence but where more significant evidence is discovered later.[640] These sort of reasons maybe particularly relevant in the context of referrals of international crimes, where new evidence may come to light over time. Following the VRR process, there is no further scope for any review by the CPS and any further challenge would need to be made by judicial review.[641]

Private Prosecutions and Private Arrest Warrants

A private prosecution may be brought in relation to international crimes. A private prosecution enables criminal proceedings to be conducted from arrest through to trial, and in the event of a conviction, sentencing, without the involvement of either SO15 or the CPS. The right to bring a private prosecution is preserved by section 6(1) of the Prosecution of Offences Act ("POA") 1985, but with the notable limitations that:

(1) the Director of Public Prosecutions (DPP) has the power under section 6(2) POA to take over prosecutions; which could result either in the CPS continuing, or stopping the proceedings where the Full Code Test is not met,[642] and;

(2) in the case of torture, grave breaches of the Geneva Conventions and hostage taking, the private prosecutor must seek the consent of the DPP before the commencement of proceedings.[643]

---

640 VRR Guidance, para. 10. There is also a specific CPS policy document about reconsidering a prosecution available at: https://www.cps.gov.uk/legal-guidance/reconsidering-prosecution-decision (last updated 26 February 2021).

641 VRR Guidance, para. 47.

642 Note that there is CPS guidance about private prosecutions: https://www.cps.gov.uk/legal-guidance/private-prosecutions (last updated October 2019).

643 Section 153 Police and Social Responsibility Act 2011, amended section 1 of the Magistrates' Court Act 1980 by inserting a new subsection (4A), requiring consent of the DPP to be sought in relation to offences under the GCA 1957 (grave-

A private prosecutor can apply to a District Judge sitting at Westminster Magistrates' Court to issue an arrest warrant. Where torture under section 134 CJA 1988, hostage-taking, or grave breaches under GCA 1957 are alleged, the consent of the DPP is required before an arrest warrant can be issued and a District Judge will only hear such an application if there is a recent consent from the DPP.

The CPS website has some helpful guidance: *"War Crimes / Crimes Against Humanity: Guidance for making an application for DPP consent for an application for a private arrest warrant in accordance with section 1(4A) of the Magistrates' Court Act 1980" ("Private Arrest Warrant Guidance on DPP Consent").*[644] The guidance explains that an application for the consent of the DPP should only be applied for when there is a reasonable belief that a suspect will be entering the jurisdiction within 14 days of the application and that it is essential that there is sufficient time for the request to be read and reviewed.[645] The guidance explains to whom the application should be made and the procedure that will be followed.[646] The guidance also sets out what the application should contain, which is the same sort of information and evidence that would be advisable for a legal representative, or NGO representing a victim/s to provide when referring a case to SO15.[647]

breaches), section 1 of the Taking of Hostages Act 1982 (hostage-taking) and section 134 CJA 1988 (torture).

644 https://www.cps.gov.uk/publication/war-crimescrimes-against-humanity-guidance-making-application-dpp-consent-application last updated in April 2016.

645 Private Arrest Warrant Guidance on DPP Consent, section 5.

646 Private Arrest Warrant Guidance on DPP Consent, especially at sections 6 – 27.

647 See the list at section 7 of the Private Arrest Warrant Guidance on DPP Consent.

Immunities

As noted above, whilst conducting the scoping exercise SO15 may refer the case to the CTD to obtain advice at an early stage about issues including potential immunities that may apply to the suspect.[648] Thus, potential immunities will be an issue that SO15 and the CPS should be alive to early in the proceedings. It is also important that practitioners defending in a case involving allegations of international crimes consider whether any potential immunities to prosecution may apply to the suspect / defendant and where appropriate raise the issue with SO15 and CPS, and challenge the decision to investigate, or prosecute, or seek to litigate the issue during a preparatory hearing in the Crown Court.[649] Issues regarding immunities have arisen in a number of potential and actual domestic prosecutions in relation to international crimes, as well as extradition cases in relation to requests concerning international crimes.

Immunity *ratione personae* (personal immunity) means that serving Heads of State and foreign ministers have immunity from civil and criminal proceedings whilst in office. It covers both the official and personal conduct of an active Head of State and foreign minister, while they hold office.[650] Immunity *ratione materiae* (functional immunity) – refers to immunity in relation to official conduct carried out whilst performing functions on behalf of the State.[651] Notably, the Referral Guidelines state that issues of immunity do not preclude investigations against persons still in office, irrespective of their function, but that this may be a factor that SO15 take into account when considering whether it is proportionate to conduct an effective investigation.[652] Some

648 Referral Guidelines, section B.

649 Preparatory hearings are discussed in the final chapter.

650 See for example, Lord Browne-Wilkinson in *Pinochet* (No. 3) at p.201G- 202A.

651 See for example, Lord Browne-Wilkinson in *Pinochet* (No. 3) at p.202B-E.

652 Referral Guidelines, section C, para. 2.

examples are provided below of cases in which issues in relation to immunities have arisen in practice.

R. v Bow Street Metropolitan Stipendiary Magistrate, ex parte Pinochet Ugarte (No.3) [2000] 1 AC 147 ("Pinochet (No.3)")

The seminal case in relation to Senator Augusto Pinochet arose in the context of extradition proceedings. Senator Pinochet, a former head of State of Chile, was on a visit to London when he was arrested under a provisional warrant issued by a stipendiary magistrate in extradition proceedings, following the issue of an international arrest warrant by a criminal court in Madrid. The Spanish request for his extradition concerned charges that during his period in office between 1973 and 1990, he ordered officials to commit acts of torture, hostage taking and enforced disappearances. The conduct alleged related primarily to crimes in Chile but would be heard in the Spanish Court on the basis of universal jurisdiction. The litigation gave raise to arguments in relation to the *"dual criminality"* requirement under extradition law.[653] The law lords ruled by a majority, that Senator Pinochet's extradition could not be ordered in relation to the majority of the allegations of torture because they occurred before torture became a crime of universal jurisdiction in the UK (i.e. when section 134 of the CJA 1988 entered into force, giving effect to the UK's obligations under the Convention against Torture (UNCAT)). However, there were some allegations of torture which occurred after section 134 CJA entered into force and therefore did meet the *"dual criminality"* requirement. In relation to these allegations the law lords had to consider whether Senator Pinochet enjoyed immunity from the extradition proceedings.[654] The House of Lords, by a 6-1 majority ruled that immunity *ratione*

[653] The *"dual criminality"* requirement means that the conduct alleged in the extradition request must also have been a crime in the UK at the time the conduct occurred.

[654] Lord Browne-Wilkinson at p.196H – 197A, referring also to Lord Hope at pp.235F-240E, with p240C-E referring to the charges which were ultimately relevant to the question of immunity. Note that the law lords did not reach a unanimous judgment on this point with Lord Millet dissenting, who would have

materiae in relation to acts performed as a head of state could not prevent his extradition in relation to the remaining crimes of torture and conspiracy to torture.[655] A former head of state would usually have immunity from criminal jurisdiction in the UK for acts done in their official capacity as a head of state, pursuant to section 20 of the State Immunity Act 1978 when read with article 39(2) of schedule 1 to the Diplomatic Privileges Act 1964.[656] However, the law lords ruled that the effect of UNCAT was that all the state parties had agreed that there should be universal jurisdiction to punish a *"public official"* who committed torture, in light of which the State Parties could not have intended that an immunity for former heads of state for official acts of torture would survive their ratification of the Convention. Since Chile, Spain and the UK had all ratified the Convention by 8 December 1988, Senator Pinochet could have no immunity in relation to allegations of torture after that date (Lord Browne Wilkinson, Lord Hope, Lord Saville and Lord Hutton).[657] Notably, Lord Millet and Lord Philips went even further than the other law lords. They took the view that the systematic use of torture was an international crime for which there could be no immunity even before UNCAT came into effect and that there was no immunity under customary international law for such torture.[658]

allowed the appeal in relation to all of the torture and conspiracy to torture charges, including those pre-dating the CJA (p.279C).

655 Lord Goff dissenting at p.213D on the basis that had UNCAT intended to exclude state immunity it would have said so expressly and pp.213E-223B.

656 See for example Lord Browne-Wilkinson at p.202H-F.

657 See for example Lord Browne-Wilkinson at pp.204G-205G, Lord Hope at p.248D-F and the reasoning in the preceding paragraphs.

658 See for example Lord Millet at p.275C-F and 276D-E, 277B 279B-C.

R v Lama (Kumar) [2014] EWCA Crim 1729

Kumar Lama, a Colonel in the Nepalese Army was charged with torture under section 134 CJA 1988.[659] The defence raised issues in relation to potential immunities during a preparatory hearing in the Crown Court and Court of Appeal. Lama sought to rely upon immunity *ratione materiae* (immunity in relation to official conduct carried out whilst performing functions on behalf of the State). He argued that the allegations concerned his *"official conduct"* in his role as a Colonel in the Nepalese army.[660] The Court of Appeal dismissed his argument, applying the "*ratio decidendi*" of *Pinochet (No.3)* that *"as between States party to the Convention against Torture, the Convention excludes the operation of immunity ratione materiae"*.[661] As both the UK and Nepal were States Parties to the Convention, Lama could not rely upon *ratione materiae*. Additionally, the Court of Appeal rejected a further argument that the scope of the *"non-immunity"* under the Convention only related to allegations of widespread and systematic torture.[662]

Lama also claimed he had been entitled to immunity *ratione personae* and ought not to have been arrested because at the time of his arrest he had been a Senior Military Liaison Officer with the UN Mission in South Sudan, which carried the status of an *"expert on mission"* with the UN.[663] The Court of Appeal ruled that Lama could not rely on immunity *ratione personae* because any immunity had been waived by

659 See chapter 1 for a short summary of the allegations. The facts alleged by the complainants are set out in detail in paras 5–15 of the Court of Appeal Judgment in *Lama*.

660 *R v Lama (Kumar)* [2014] EWCA Crim 1729, at para. 4, sets out in short form the arguments made by the defence in the interlocutory appeal to the court of appeal.

661 *Ibid.* paras. 30 and 39.

662 *Ibid.* paras. 40 – 49.

663 *Ibid.* paras. 76 – 101. His status as an *"expert on mission"* arose as a result of a UN *"Status of Forces Agreement"* governing the Nepalese involvement in the mission in South Sudan.

the UN.[664] The Under Secretary-General for Legal Affairs and Legal Counsel to the UN had waived his immunity from personal arrest or detention, after being informed by the UK authorities that Lama had been arrested on allegations of torture.[665]

FF v DPP [2014] EWHC 3419 (Admin)

FF v DPP [2014] EWHC 3419 (Admin) concerned a judicial review of a decision taken by the CPS CTD about potential immunities pertaining to Prince Nasser bin Hamad Al Khalifa of Bahrain. The European Centre for Constitutional and Human Rights had submitted a dossier to SO15 about allegations made by *FF*, a refugee from Bahrain who said he was tortured by the Prince during protests in Bahrain in 2011. The judicial review ultimately settled. The CPS agreed that the Prince was not entitled to immunity from prosecution, which was contrary to its initial decision that he might have been entitled to immunity.[666] So the Divisional Court ordered that the original decision would be quashed and declared that on the evidence the Prince of Bahrain was not entitled to immunity.[667]

664 *Ibid.* para. 100.

665 The details about the waiver are set out at paras 21-22 of the Court of Appeal Judgment in *Lama*.

666 *FF v DPP* [2014] EWHC 3419 (Admin), para. 4.

667 Ibid. para 5. In settling the case, the CPS emphasised that the ultimate decision on whether to investigate the case on the basis of the dossier fell to SO15 and that in its view the case was *"academic"* because SO15 had made the decision not to proceed to a full investigation (para 4).

Forms of Liability

As with any domestic criminal offence, consideration will need to be given about the form of liability with which to charge a suspect. The relevant legislative provisions in relation to liability for the international crimes is set out below. However, as the ordinary principles of the criminal law of England and Wales apply in relation to an individual's responsibility for international crimes,[668] only command and superior responsibility, which is a novel concept in domestic law introduced by the ICCA will be addressed in detail.

Direct / Primary / Principal Liability

A defendant can be charged with an international crime as a direct perpetrator where they are the person who directly committed the substantive offence. [669] Where more than one person was involved in carrying out the substantive offence, there will be several co-perpetrators each of whom may be charged.

Secondary / Accessorial liability

A defendant can be charged with an international crime where they are not the direct perpetrator of the offence but where they are responsible as an accessory to the international crime. In relation to crimes under the ICCA, section 52 provides expressly that it is an offence for a person to engage in conduct ancillary to war crimes, CAH and genocide under the

---

668 These principles are set out in practitioners and academic books in relation to the criminal law of England and Wales, so will not be recited in this book.

669 Under the ICCA section 51(1) provides that it is an offence for a person to *"commit"* genocide, a CAH or a war crime; section 1(1) GCA 1957 states that it is an offence for a person to *"commit"* a grave breach; and, section 134(1) of the CJA 1988 states that liability will attach where a public official or person acting in an official capacity *"commits"* the offence of torture. Notably, under section 134 CJA 1998, liability as a direct perpetrator attaches both to public officials or persons acting in an official capacity who commit torture (section 134(1)) and persons who commit torture at their behest (section 134(2)).

ICCA. Section 55 ICCA sets out that an *"ancillary offence"* under the law of England and Wales refers to:

(a) aiding, abetting, counselling or procuring the commission of an offence,[670]

(b) inciting a person to commit an offence,

(c) attempting or conspiring to commit an offence,[671] or

(d) assisting an offender or concealing the commission of an offence.[672]

Section 55 ICCA includes the forms of secondary liability in Article 25.3 of the Rome Statute. However, as expressly noted in the footnotes to section 55, they are defined in terms of the principles of secondary liability under the law of England and Wales, and not the law applicable at the ICC.

In relation to the GCA 1957, section 1(1) expressly refers not only to a person who *"commits"* a grave breach, but also to the liability of any person who *"aids, abets or procures the commission by any other person of a grave breach"*. Notably, the grave breach provisions in the Geneva Conventions refer to the obligation of each state party to bring to trial

---

670 ICCA, section 55(2) explains that aiding, abetting, counselling or procuring is conduct that in relation to an indictable offence would be punishable under section 8 of the Accessories and Abettors Act 1861.

671 ICCA, section 55(4)(a) explains that the reference to an attempt is to conduct amounting to an offence under section 1 of the Criminal Attempts Act 1981 and that (b) that the reference to a conspiracy is to conduct amounting to an offence of conspiracy under section 1 of the Criminal Law Act 1977.

672 ICCA, section 55(5)(a) explains that the reference to assisting an offender is to conduct that in relation to a relevant offence would amount to an offence under section 4(1) of the Criminal Law Act 1967 and (b) that the reference to concealing an offence is to conduct that in relation to a relevant offence would amount to an offence under section 5(1) of the Criminal Law Act 1967.

both persons who have *"committed"* and who have *"ordered to be committed, such grave breaches"*.[673]

Section 134 CJA 1988 does not expressly state that liability for the offence of torture includes secondary liability. However, the ordinary principles of secondary liability under the law of England and Wales will apply, consistent with the UK's IL obligations under UNCAT.[674] Notably, Faryadi Zardad, was convicted of conspiracy to torture under section 134 CJA 1988.[675] Conspiracy to commit torture, can be charged pursuant to section 1 of the Criminal Law Act 1977.

Joint criminal enterprise

Joint criminal enterprise has featured in numerous international trials, including at the ICC as well as the ad hoc international criminal tribunals. It is of note that Article 25(3)(d) of the Rome Statute, which sets out the liability in relation to a person acting with a common purpose was not incorporated into the ICCA. As such, the rather complex and divergent international case law in relation to joint criminal enterprise liability will not be relevant to a domestic criminal trial. However, it could be relevant in other areas of domestic law, such as in immigration law in relation to exclusion from refuges status.[676]

Command and superior responsibility

The doctrine of command and superior responsibility was introduced into domestic law for the first time by the ICCA.[677] In a nutshell, it is a

---

673 See for example, GCA, Schedule 1, Article 49.

674 Cross-reference the section on "*Secondary liability*" in the chapter on Torture.

675 *R v Faryadi Sarwar Zardad* [2007] EWCA Crim 279 para. 1.

676 See *R (JS (Sri Lanka)) v. Secretary of State for the Home Department [2015] UKSC 15*, see Lord Brown at p. 225C – 226D and 233B – 234A and *KM v. Secretary of State for the Home Department* [2022] UKUT 00125 (IAC), para. 38. Both decisions relate to exclusion from the Refugee Convention under Article 1F(a) of the Convention (see discussion of *KM* in the CAH Chapter).

677 As explained in the Explanatory Note to the ICCA at paragraph 104, it was introduced to enable the investigation and prosecution of cases before domestic

particular form of criminal culpability which holds superiors responsible for the crimes of their subordinates.[678] Section 65 ICCA provides for the individual criminal responsibility of military commanders and other superiors for war crimes, CAH and genocide. Thus, a defendant can be charged either with command responsibility in a military context, or superior responsibility in a civilian context. Section 65 is based upon the corresponding provision in Article 28 of the Rome Statute. Section 65(4) states that a person responsible under section 65 is to be regarded as aiding, abetting, counselling or procuring the commission of the offence. There is no equivalent provision in relation to the GCA 1957 or the CJA 1988.[679]

In relation to military commanders, section 65(2) ICCA states as follows:

> *65(2) A military commander, or a person effectively acting as a military commander, is responsible for offences committed by forces under his effective command and control, or (as the case may be) his effective authority and control, as a result of his failure to exercise control properly over such forces where –*
>
> *(a) he either knew, or owing to the circumstances at the time, should have known that the forces were committing or about to commit such offences, and*

---

courts in all the circumstances where the ICC may find a case on the basis of command or superior responsibility.

678 *Bemba*, Trial Judgment, para. 171. See also para. 173, in which the Trial Chamber explain that Article 28 of the Rome Statute provides for a distinct form of liability, which is different from that of a person who *"commits"* a crime within the jurisdiction of the Court.

679 There is no corresponding provision in relation to torture under section 134 CJA 1988, thus a commander would have to be charged under another form of accessorial liability. Likewise, there is no corresponding provision in the GCA 1957. Notably, Additional Protocol I to the Geneva Conventions 1977 contains Articles 86(2) and 87, which provides for the criminal and disciplinary responsibility of commanders and superiors for the conduct of their subordinates. However, this is not directly incorporated into domestic law.

> (b) *he failed to take all necessary and reasonable measures within his power to prevent or repress their commission or to submit the matter to the competent authorities for investigation and prosecution.*

In relation to superiors in a civilian context, section 65(3) ICCA provides that:

> *65(3) With respect to superior and subordinate relationships not described in subsection (2), a superior is responsible for offences committed by subordinates under his effective authority and control, as a result of his failure to exercise control properly over such subordinates where-*
>
> (a) *he either knew, or consciously disregarded information which clearly indicated, that the subordinates were committing or about to commit such offences,*
>
> (b) *the offences concerned activities that were within his effective responsibility and control, and*
>
> (c) *he failed to take all necessary and reasonable measures within his power to prevent or repress their commission or to submit the matter to the competent authorities for investigation and prosecution.*

As with other interpretative provisions under the ICCA, section 65(5) directs that in interpreting and applying section 65 the court *"shall"* take into account any relevant judgment or decision of the ICC, and that *"account may also be taken of any other relevant international jurisprudence"*. At the ICC, the most significant case so far in relation to command responsibility is *Jean-Pierre Bemba.* Bemba was convicted of war crimes and CAH on the basis of command responsibility by Trial Chamber II,[680] but his conviction was overturned, by a majority, on

[680] *Bemba,* Trial Judgment. Trial Chamber II found that he was responsible as a military commander with effective control over the *Mouvement de libération du Congo* ("MLC") troops who had committed murder, rape and pillage.

appeal.[681] In addition to ICC jurisprudence, there is a wealth of other international jurisprudence, which reflects the long history of the doctrine of command responsibility in IHL. Case law from the ad hoc tribunals, in particular the ICTY, is instructive, such as the legally significant case of *Prosecutor v. Delalić et al.,* in which the Trial Chamber conducted the first elucidation of the concept of command responsibility since the Second World War.[682]

There are three key elements to command/ superior responsibility:

(1) The existence of a superior relationship with the subordinate and one where the superior has effective command or control over the subordinate;

(2) The mental element – knowledge or reason to know by the commander of the offence having taken place, or being about to take place – or - in the case of a civilian superior, knowledge, or conscious disregard of information, which clearly indicated that subordinates were committing, or about to commit offences;

(3) Failure to prevent or punish – a failure to take necessary or reasonable measures to intervene in some manner by, either preventing the crime, punishing those who committed the crime, or submitting the matter for investigation or prosecution, depending on the circumstances.[683]

---

681 *Bemba,* Appeal Judgment. Note that in addition to the majority judgment, there were two dissenting opinions and three separate opinions.

682 *Prosecutor v. Delalić, Mucić, Delić and Landzo,* Trial Judgment, 16 November 1998 ("*Delalić et al.,* Trial Judgment") paras. 330-382.

683 Trial Chamber II in *Bemba,* at para. 170 of the Trial Judgment, set out the necessary elements that must be fulfilled for an accused to be convicted as a military commander, or person effectively acting as a military commander, which also includes that crimes within the jurisdiction of the ICC must have been convicted as a result of the failure of the accused to exercise control properly over the forces.

(1) The superior/ subordinate relationship and the notion of "effective control":

In order to prove that an individual is responsible under this form of liability the prosecution must prove the existence of a superior-subordinate relationship. Responsibility applies to persons in *"de jure"* and *"de facto"* positions. *"De jure"* refers to persons who are recognized by law as holding a position of authority. *"De facto"* refers to persons who as a matter of fact exercise a position of authority.[684] Where command responsibility applies, the prosecution must prove that the accused was a military commander in the armed forces of a state, or in non-governmental irregular armed forces,[685] or was a *"person effectively acting as a military commander"* (as in the *Bemba* case).[686] Command responsibility applies not only to immediate commanders of forces who have committed crimes but also to commanders at the highest level.[687]

The prosecution must prove that the accused had *"effective command"* and *"control"*, or *"effective authority"* and *"control"* over their subordinates. This requirement was considered by the Trial Chamber in *Bemba*, which considered that *"effective control"* requires that a commander / superior have the material ability to prevent, or repress the commission of crimes, or to submit the matter to the competent authorities.[688] It is important to establish the culpable subordinates (principal perpetrators) within the group,[689] although it is not necessary to identify them by name and it is sufficient to identify them by group or unit in relation to a particular

684 *Delalić et al.,* Trial Judgment, para. 348.

685 *Bemba,* Trial Judgment, para. 176.

686 *Bemba,* Trial Judgment, para. 177.

687 *Bemba,* Trial Judgment, para. 179, referring to the ICTY, *Delalić et al.* (IT-96-21-A), 20 February 2001, Appeals Judgment ("*Delalić et al.* Appeal Judgment") paras. 252 and 303.

688 *Bemba* Trial Judgment, paras. 180-190, especially at para.183.

689 In *Prosecutor v Orić* (T-03-68-A) Appeal Judgment, 3 July 2008, the ICTY Appeals Chamber held that a failure to identify any culpable subordinate resulted in a reversal of the Appellant's conviction for command responsibility.

crime scene.[690] Establishing effective control is not a matter of substantive law but of evidence. The evidence must establish beyond reasonable doubt that sufficient control or authority existed to have enabled a superior to prevent, punish, or initiate an investigation.[691]

(2) The mental element – knew or should have known

Having established effective control, the offence is not one of strict liability. A commander must have known (actual knowledge), or, should have known (constructive knowledge) that their forces were committing, or were about to commit the relevant offences. A civilian superior must have known (actual knowledge) or have consciously disregarded information which clearly indicated that their subordinates were committing or about to commit relevant crimes. It is important to note that the mental element is different for civilian superiors and military superiors. A civilian superior is liable only if he *"consciously disregarded information which clearly indicated that subordinates were committing or about to commit such crimes"*. Further of note, is that a charge of command or superior responsibility does not preclude additional charges in relation to other forms of liability under the Act. For example, a commander could also be charged for ordering those under their command to commit ICCA offences.[692]

Actual knowledge must be proved through direct or circumstantial evidence. This may include direct evidence, such as statements made by the defendant about the crimes, or circumstantial evidence, for example, the number, type and scope of illegal acts, the geographical location of

690 *Bemba*, Trial Judgment, para.186.

691 *Bemba*, Trial Judgment, paras. 188-190. Note that the Trial Chamber listed a number of factors that could indicate effective control at para. 188, as well as some factors which may indicate a lack of effective control at para. 190. See also, for example: *Prosecutor v Kordić & Čerkez*

(IT-95-14/2-A) Appeal Judgment, 17 December 2004, at para. 834.

692 ICCA, section 65(6). See also, *Bemba*, Trial Judgment, para. 174.

the acts and the location of the superior at the relevant time.[693] In relation to constructive knowledge, the key element to prove is that the commander was in possession of information that put them on notice that the offence was taking place, or that it might take place. The Trial Chamber in *Bemba* stated that where knowledge is inferred it must be the only reasonable conclusion based on the evidence.[694] There is considerable case law from the ICTY about this, which focuses on the requirement that the commander must have been provided with sufficiently alarming information to put them on notice of the risk that crimes might take place and justifying further inquiry.[695] The Trial Chamber in *Bemba* also stated that the accused must have knowledge of the relevant contextual elements of the crimes alleged.[696]

(3) Failure to Prevent or Punish

The failure to prevent or punish refers to the omission to act when there is a responsibility to do so.[697] Historically, there could be said to be two distinct obligations: (1) to prevent and (2) to punish. Thus, a commander cannot discharge their duty solely by punishing a subordinate, if they knew the act was going to happen and did nothing to prevent it.[698] Notably, under the ICC regime there now appear to be three distinct duties: (1) to prevent, (2) to repress, (3) to investigate and prosecute.[699] The focus of the inquiry should be on the power that the commander or

---

693 *Bemba* Trial Judgment, para. 191.

694 *Bemba*, Trial Judgment, para. 192.

695 See for example, the *Prosecutor v Strugar* (IT-01-42-A) Appeal Judgment, 17 July 2008, para. 308. At the ICC, see the *Bemba*, Trial Judgment, para. 193, where the Trial Chamber expressed themselves differently but listed similar factors that could be relevant to proving constructive knowledge, referring to the ICTY caselaw.

696 *Bemba*, Trial Judgment, para. 195.

697 *Prosecutor v. Seffer Halilović* (IT-01-48-T) Trial Judgment, 16 November 2005, para 54.

698 *Bemba*, Trial Judgment, para. 201.

699 See the discussion in *Bemba*, Trial Judgment, para. 201 and at paras. 202 – 204 (duty to prevent) and paras. 205 – 209 (failure to repress or submit). Note also, in particular, *Bemba*, Appeal Judgment, para. 10.

superior has over their subordinates, in other words, their material ability to act, rather than legal capacity to do so.[700] The duty of the commander or superior is to take all necessary and reasonable measures in discharging their responsibility.[701] Necessary measures are those appropriate for the superior to discharge their obligations, showing that they genuinely tried to prevent and punish. Reasonable measures are measures reasonably falling within the material power of the superior and will be case specific depending on the superior.[702] Thus an assessment is required of what measures were at the commander / superiors' disposal in all the circumstances (including the operational realities on the ground) at the relevant time.[703] What is clear from the case law is that the superior is not expected to achieve the impossible but only what they can feasibly do with the power and resources at their disposal to prevent or punish international crimes.[704]

Causation

Pre-Trial and Trial Chambers in *Bemba* ruled that whilst *"but for"* causation between the commander / superior's omission and the commission of the crime/s by the subordinate/s was not required,[705] a nexus between the omission and the commission of the crimes must be established.[706] Notably, the issue of causation has also been considered at the ICTY. In *Blaškić* the Appeal Chamber of the ICTY held that

700 *Bemba*, Trial Judgment, para. 199, *Bemba*, Appeal Judgment, paras. 5 and 167.

701 *Bemba*, Appeal Judgment, para. 6.

702 *Bemba*, Trial Judgment, paras. 197-199, *Bemba*, Appeal Judgment, paras. 7 – 9 and see paras.169- 170.

703 *Bemba*, Appeal Judgment, para. 168 and 170.

704 *Bemba*, Trial Judgment, para. 200. *Bemba*, Appeal Judgment, paras. 5 and 167.

705 *Bemba*, Trial Judgment, para. 211.

706 *Bemba*, Trial Judgment, paras. 213 and 210 – 213 generally.

causation was not an element of command / superior responsibility under customary IL.[707]

Interpreters

An important practical issue to think about at the pre-trial stage is the number of interpreters that will be needed during the lifetime of the proceedings. Interpreters may be needed for the following tasks during the investigation stage:

- Assisting SO15 officers during the interview of potential victims and witnesses,
- Assisting SO15 officers with the translation of any relevant documentary evidence,
- To assist the defendant during interview by SO15 officers,
- To assist the defence representatives in taking instructions from their client,
- To assist the defence representatives in speaking to potential witnesses,
- To assist the defence representatives with the translation of any relevant documentary evidence.

At the pre-trial phase, SO15 and the CPS should develop a coordinated strategy in relation to the requirements for interpreters and translators, as depending on the languages or dialects in question, there may be a limited pool of qualified, willing and able

[707] *Prosecutor v. Blaškić* (IT-95-14-A) Appeal Judgment, 29 July 2004, at para. 77 and see the analysis at paras. 73-77, noting at para. 76 a passage from the *Delalić et al.*, Trial Judgment at para. 398.

interpreters.[708] It is better if interpreters used during the investigation phase are not also used during the trial, in case there are disputes about what the victim / witness / defendant has said to them.[709] However, where the pool of potential interpreters is small options may be limited. In the case of Colonel Kumar Lama, an initial trial at the Central Criminal Court had to be aborted because of problems that arose with the quality and very limited pool of Nepalese interpreters.[710]

In terms of who bears the responsibility for the provision of interpreters:

708 There are national guidelines in relation to the standard of interpreters. The National Agreement on for the Use of Interpreters, Translators and Language Professionals in Investigations and Proceedings within the Criminal Justice System, as revised 2007" (the "National Agreement") is a policy guidance document, which provides guidance about best practice. It is available on the website of the National Register of Public Service Interpreters (NRPSI) at: https://www.nrpsi.org.uk/news-posts/National-Agreement-on-Arrangements-for-the-use-of-Interpreters-in-the-CJS-Revised-2007.html When this link was last visited (14.11.22), the NRPSI indicated that the National Agreement had been revised in 2022 but a link to the new National Agreement had not yet provided on the NRPSI website. The National Agreement explains that it is essential that interpreters used in criminal proceedings should be competent to meet the ECHR obligations and to that end the standard requirement is that every interpreter working in courts and police stations should be registered with one of the recommended registers, i.e. the National Register of Public Service Interpreters (NRPSI) at full or interim status (paragraph 3.3.1), although the guidance specifically acknowledges that there will be circumstances when it will be necessary to depart from that standard requirement (paragraph 3.4).

709 For example, para. 4.41 of the National Agreement, *ibid.* explains that it is important that as far as possible the interpreter who is booked for court is not the same one who interpreted at the police station, either for the police, or for the defendant's solicitors.

710 See further the discussion in the final chapter under the sub-heading, *"Interpreters"*.

- SO15 will organize interpreters to interview the victim/s and witnesses during the investigation;[711]

- It is the responsibility of SO15 to ensure that an interpreter, is present during the interview of the defendant;[712]

- It is the defendant's representatives' responsibility to find interpreters for use both with the defendant when taking instructions and if needed for the purposes of defence investigations, including for defence witnesses who will give evidence in court;[713]

- It is the CPS's responsibility to organize interpreters for the victim/s and witnesses during the trial;[714]

- It is the courts responsibility to appoint an interpreter for the defendant to use during court proceedings and at any trial (if needed).[715]

---

711 Para. 4.41 of the National Agreement provides that the appointment and payment of interpreters for suspects and witnesses during investigations is the responsibility of the police or other investigating agency.

712 Ibid., and note also 4.4.1, regarding the responsibility of the police or other investigating agency to provide an interpreter at court, where there is a court hearing within two working days of charge.

713 Para. 4.7 of the National Agreement. Note paragraphs 4.7.2 and 4.7.3 regarding the different provisions for payment of defence witnesses pre-trial (defence representatives responsible) and trial (court responsible).

714 Para. 4.6 of the National Agreement, which notes, however, that in practice the police will often book interpreters.

715 Para. 4.5 of the National Agreement.

Requesting assistance from foreign Governments, international courts and tribunals and other international organisations

At the investigation and pre-trial stages, it may be appropriate to request assistance from various third parties located overseas. This could involve requesting the assistance of foreign Governments. Here the CPS will draft an International Letter of Request (ILOR). Where crimes have already been the subject of investigation by an international court or tribunal, it is appropriate to contact the relevant court or tribunal for assistance; although, a good deal of information is publicly available on the websites of the respective courts and tribunals. As regards contacting other relevant organisations based overseas, see the next chapter on *Disclosure*.

CHAPTER SEVEN

DISCLOSURE

Disclosure should be considered at an early stage in proceedings and must be kept under review throughout the course of the trial.[716] This Chapter will begin with an overview of the most relevant legislation.[717] The Chapter will address some of the practical steps that can be taken by the Disclosure Officer, in conjunction with the prosecution team to ensure that the prosecutions' disclosure obligations are met. The Chapter will then consider how those defending can and should contribute to process of disclosure and how challenges can be made in relation to any shortcomings in the disclosure process.

The legal framework

Criminal Procedure and Investigations Act 1996 (the "CPIA") and the CPIA Code of Practice

The starting point in relation to criminal investigations is the *Criminal Procedure and Investigations Act 1996* ("the CPIA")[718] and the *CPIA Code of Practice.*[719] The CPIA aims to ensure that criminal investigations are conducted in a fair, objective and thorough manner. The CPIA requires

---

716 See for example the Attorney General's Guidelines on Disclosure (reference below) at para. 136.

717 This is not an exhaustive analysis but a review of the most relevant legislation. There are also important cases to be aware of and a criminal practitioners' books should be consulted for a more exhaustive analysis of disclosure obligations in proceedings before the Crown Court.

718 CPIA 1996 is available at: https://www.legislation.gov.uk/ukpga/1996/25/contents

719 CPIA Code of Practice 1996 is available at: https://www.gov.uk/government/publications/criminal-procedure-and-investigations-act-code-of-practice

prosecutors to disclose material which might reasonably be considered capable of undermining the case for the prosecution against the accused, or of assisting the case for the accused.[720] The *CPIA Code of Practice* sets out that a fair investigation involves pursuit of material following all reasonable lines of enquiry, whether they point towards, or away from the suspect.[721] What is *"reasonable"* will depend on the context of the case and a fair investigation does not mean an endless investigation.[722]

The Attorney-General's Guidelines on Disclosure of unused material in criminal cases and the Disclosure Management Document

The CPIA and the Code of Practice is supplemented by a number of important guidance documents. One of these is the *Attorney-General's Guidelines on Disclosure.*[723] The *Attorney-General's Guidelines* state that the Crown's approach to disclosure should be outlined in a *"Disclosure Management Document"* ("DMD").[724] The DMD is a *"living document"*, which should be amended in light of developments in the case and kept up to date as the case progresses. Its purpose is to assist the court in case management and to enable the defence to engage at an early stage in the proceedings, with the prosecution's approach to disclosure.[725] It may include detail relating to third party and foreign material, including steps taken to obtain such material.

In relation to *"international matters"*, the *Attorney General's Guidelines* explain that the obligations under the *CPIA Code* to pursue all reasonable

[720] CPIA, section 3.

[721] CPIA Code of Practice, para. 3.6

[722] CPIA Code of Practice, para. 3.6. See also, the Attorney General's Guideline's on Disclosure, at para. 17.

[723] The Attorney General's Guideline's on Disclosure are available at: https://www.gov.uk/government/publications/attorney-generals-guidelines-on-disclosure (references below are to the 2022, revised guidelines).

[724] Attorney General's Guidelines on Disclosure, para. 97 and see also 96. The guidelines helpfully set out what should be included in the Disclosure Management Document at para. 95.

[725] Attorney General's Guidelines on Disclosure, paras. 93- 94.

lines of enquiry apply to material held overseas.[726] Where it appears that there is relevant material, the prosecutor must take *"reasonable steps"* to obtain it, either informally, or making use of the powers contained in the Crime (International Co-operation) Act 2003 and any international conventions.[727] The *Attorney General's Guidelines* notes that there may be situations where a foreign state or a foreign court refuses to make material available to the investigator or prosecutor, and explains that for that reason there is no *"absolute duty"* to disclose relevant material held overseas by entities not subject to the jurisdiction of the courts in England and Wales.[728] Prosecutors have a margin of consideration as to what steps are appropriate in the particular case, but prosecutors must be alive to their duties and there may be some circumstances where these duties cannot be met. Whether the prosecutor has taken reasonable steps is for the court to determine in each case if the matter is raised.[729] Regarding materials held by a foreign state, the *Attorney General's Guidelines* state that the DMD must record and explain the situation i.e. in as far it is permitted by the foreign state, the document should set out what steps have been taken to obtain materials and the results of enquiries.[730]

Crown Prosecution Service Legal Guidance, Chapter 35: International Disclosure Issues

Another important document is the CPS guidance on *"International Disclosure Issues"*.[731] This guidance recalls the obligation set out in the *CPIA* and the *Attorney General's Guidelines* to take *"reasonable steps"* to

---

726 Attorney General's Guidelines on Disclosure, para. 46.

727 Attorney General's Guidelines on Disclosure, para. 47. The Crime (International Co-operation) Act 2033 is available at: https://www.legislation.gov.uk/ukpga/2003/32/contents?view=plain, see in particular, Chapter 2 on the *"Mutual provision of evidence"*.

728 Attorney General's Guidelines on Disclosure, paras. 48 - 49.

729 Attorney General's Guidelines on Disclosure, para. 50.

730 Attorney General's Guidelines on Disclosure, para. 53 - 54.

731 The CPS guidance can be found at: https://www.cps.gov.uk/legal-guidance/disclosure-manual-chapter-35-international-disclosure-issues

obtain relevant unused material and that the approach to disclosure in the international context is consistent with disclosure principles generally. However, it is important to note that the witness summons procedure cannot apply to third parties outside the UK. Thus, whereas the Crown can apply to a judge for a witness summons in order to force an uncooperative UK based third party to produce material or information,[732] there is no such procedure available in relation to overseas material; which patently is not subject to the jurisdiction of the UK courts.[733] The CPS guidance highlights that in some countries the CPS has a Liaison Prosecutor, who can be contacted to assist and provide guidance. It also highlights that in many countries, material which is provided or generated may be given with an expectation of confidentiality by the overseas authority. In these circumstances, prosecutors need to assess the material in accordance with the CPIA and consider whether it meets the test of being sensitive material. There is specific guidance on sensitive material and it is beyond the scope of this Chapter to go into the detail of that topic, save to say that sensitive material is any material the disclosure of which would give rise to a real risk of prejudice to an important public interest and that this applies to both materials received from overseas and unused material generated as part of international enquiries.[734]

War Crimes / Crimes against Humanity Referral Guidelines

These important guidelines are referred to in the previous Chapter and there is a sub-heading in that chapter in relation to disclosure.

---

732 Section 2 of the Criminal Procedure (Attendance of Witnesses) Act 1965 / Section 97 of the Magistrates Courts Act 1980.

733 Section 3(5) of the Crime (International Co-operation) Act 2003 provides that any process served on a person outside the UK cannot impose any obligation upon the recipient to comply.

734 There is for example, a sub-heading, in the CPS guidance on *"Sensitive Material"*.

Practical considerations for the Disclosure Officer and the CPS

Obtaining relevant materials from third parties:

In proceedings before the Crown Court involving international crimes there may be a

significant number of third parties who could be in possession of material relevant to the case, which could potentially be subject to disclosure. This could include, for example:

- Any organization, or NGO involved in taking initial complaints from the victims/ witnesses e.g. this could be an organization involved with taking statements from refugees;
- Any organization, or NGO which makes a referral to SO15;
- Any solicitor instructed to act on behalf of a potential victim in the proceedings;
- Domestic or international NGOs who have had contact with any potential victims, witnesses, or suspects;
- Domestic or international NGOs, with information potentially relevant to the alleged crimes e.g. which has conducted activities in relevant locations at relevant times;
- UK agencies, such as the UKBA and the FCO;
- Government agencies in the country where the alleged crimes took place;
- Government agencies in other countries relevant to potential victims, witnesses, or suspects, for example, in countries that they currently reside in, or that are otherwise relevant to the case;

- International courts or tribunals, who have, or are investigating crimes in the relevant country and the relevant time.

It is important that the Disclosure Officer writes to any relevant third parties, outlining the disclosure obligations under the CPIA regime, and asking whether they possess relevant material, giving examples of such material, and asking whether they are prepared to supply these documents, or, to allow the Disclosure Officer to inspect them. Early and effective communication with third parties about their disclosure obligations is important.

Effective communication with third parties

It is important to identify who is the most appropriate person (or people) to communicate with about disclosure at the third-party organization. This should be the head of the organization, and / or, the person who has ready access to all of the material, and / or, someone who is specifically designated with that role by the organization. In the case of overseas bodies it might be tempting to communicate with an English speaker for the sake of ease but care should be taken to ensure that the head of the organization is also aware, and that the English speaker has access to all of the material, or, has been specifically designated with that role by the head of the organization. Communication to non-English speaking third parties, should be conducted in the person's first language in order to minimize the likelihood of misunderstanding. Confirmation of receipt of the correspondence by the third-party organization should be sought and chased at an early stage, if not received.

Potential difficulties in obtaining evidence from third parties:

Potential difficulties that may arise in obtaining materials from the third parties in the case, include:

- A lack of response by third parties to requests from the Disclosure Officer;

- Responses by third parties that are so slow that they have a damaging effect on the progress of the criminal proceedings;

- Inadequate responses from the third parties to the Disclosure Officer, which cause the prosecution to have to make repeated enquiries, with a knock-on effect on the progress of the criminal proceedings.

Some third parties may, of course, be unwilling to engage with the Disclosure officer and the criminal proceedings.[735] In such circumstances, it is nevertheless important to contact the third party and notify the court and defence and to set out the situation in the DMD. In the case of UK based third parties, an option available to the prosecution is to apply for a witness summons. However, in the case of third parties, outside the UK, for the reasons discussed above, applying for a third-party summons is not a tool in the prosecution's armory. The only recourse is repeated requests, which will result in a delay to the completion of the disclosure exercise, and / or concessions by the prosecution that there may be relevant material that it had not been able to examine.

Foreign Governments

In addition to the third-party requests, the prosecution may also send International Letters of Request (ILORs) to the foreign Governments to request their assistance in relation to disclosure, as well as in relation to furthering any investigation.[736] ILORs may be sent to the Government of the country where the crime/s are alleged to have occurred. ILORs may also be sent to other relevant Governments. For example, this could be the Government of a country where the victims, witnesses, or suspects live, or have lived. It could include, for example, a request for any

[735] One example could be the International Committee of the Red Cross, who historically seek to remain neutral.

[736] Note the CPS guidance on international enquiries, which includes a section on drafting an ILOR. Found at: https://www.cps.gov.uk/legal-guidance/international-enquiries

antecedents. It may be prudent for the Crown to send a ILOR, even in circumstances where the relevant Governments are unsympathetic to the proceedings, because the prosecutions legal obligation is to take all *"reasonable steps"* to obtain assistance from the relevant Governments, and further it may be that a change in Government during the course of the proceedings could result in a different response to an ILOR that may have initially seemed futile.

Where a foreign Government is actively hostile to the proceedings, this will inevitably hinder the extent to which investigations can be made because SO15, the prosecution team and / the defence representatives will be unable to travel to the country to conduct their investigations. Indeed, an attempt to do so, without the approval of the foreign Government could result in allegations of espionage with ramifications for the individuals involved. In such circumstances, it may be possible to progress investigations, for example, by arranging for witnesses to be interviewed in a third state but there will of course be inevitable limitations as compared to a situation where the foreign state is willing to assist in the investigation of the case.

Impact of difficulties in fulfilling disclosure duties:

If the prosecution cannot fulfil their disclosure obligations, the CPS can ultimately make a decision not to proceed with the case, or alternatively, the judge can rule that the case should not proceed to trial (see, abuse of process applications (below)). Further, a conviction may be overturned on appeal, if the Court of Appeal do not agree with decisions made by the trial judge in relation to disclosure.

Defending and disclosure

Defence representatives should participate in the disclosure process at an early stage in the proceedings and are actively encouraged to do so in the relevant guidelines.[737] The defence should be kept informed of steps

737 See for example the Attorney General's Guidelines, para. 82.

taken in relation to disclosure, including for example the results of requests for third party disclosure.[738] One of the purposes of the DMD is to assist the defence in engaging from an early stage with the prosecution's proposed approach to disclosure.[739] Thus, if the prosecution has not served a DMD, this is something defence representatives should raise with the prosecution and the court.

The Attorney General's Guidelines describe the Defence Case Statement ("DCS") as *"an integral part of the statutory disclosure regime"*.[740] The DCS should set out the defence case in terms which help to focus the attention of the prosecution on the relevant issues in order to identify materials which may meet the test for disclosure. The DCS provides an opportunity to request that the Disclosure Officer contact third parties who may hold relevant materials, which might either support the defence case, or undermine the prosecution case. So, if the prosecution does not appear to have requested material from a third party which may help the accused this should be set out in the DCS. After a DCS has been provided, the Disclosure Officer must look again at material that has been retained and draw the attention of the prosecutor to any material which might reasonably be considered capable of undermining the case for the prosecution against the accused, or of assisting the case for the accused and he must reveal it in accordance with CPIA Code.[741]

Where defence representatives form the view that there are problems with disclosure, there are two principle routes that can be taken:

First, where a DCS has been served and the prosecution has considered whether any further prosecution material should be disclosed, the defence can make specific requests for disclosure under section 8 CPIA.[742] An

---

738 Attorney General's Guidelines, para. 54.

739 Attorney General's Guidelines, para. 94.

740 Attorney General's Guidelines, para. 123 and see further paras. 124 – 128.

741 CPIA Code, para. 8.3.

742 CPIA, section 8 in conjunction with section 7A(5). Note that the Attorney General's Guidelines at paragraph 131 emphasise that a section 8 application can only be made where an *"adequate"* Defence Case Statement has been provided.

application under section 8 CPIA should be made in writing and needs to describe the material which is subject to the application. It should explain why there is reasonable cause to believe that the prosecution has the material and why it meets the test for disclosure.[743] The prosecution will then review the section 8 application and come to a decision about whether any of the items referred to in the application meet the test for disclosure, which may require the prosecutor to inspect the items or copies of them.[744] If agreement cannot be reached then the judge will hear legal argument about it and make a ruling in relation to disclosure. This may involve the judge inspecting the items, or copies of them.

Secondly, an application for abuse of process can be made, inviting the judge to stay the proceedings on the basis that: (a) it would be impossible for the defendant to have a fair trial and/ or (b) a stay is necessary to protect the integrity of the criminal justice system. The applicable law is set out in the practitioners' books.[745] An abuse of process application may be made where there are significant concerns about the disclosure exercise. For example, where potentially exculpatory evidence from abroad has not been provided by third parties, or where there are issues in relation to the destruction of evidence. There is a high bar to reach in persuading the judge to stay proceedings and the judge would ultimately have to come to the view that the trial process could not remedy the potential risk of unfairness to the accused.[746]

[743] Attorney General's Guidelines, para. 123.

[744] Attorney General's Guidelines, para. 124.

[745] See for example, *Archbold Criminal Pleading, Evidence and Practice* 2023 ed. 4-75 onwards.

[746] See *Archbold Criminal Pleading, Evidence and Practice* 2023 ed. 4, 4-77 referring to *R (Ebrahim) v. Feltham Magistrates' Court; Mouat v DPP* [2001] EWHC Admin 130; [2001] 2 Cr.App.R 23, as well as other authorities.

CHAPTER EIGHT

THE TRIAL

Chapter six focussed on the investigatory and pre-trial stage of the proceedings. This Chapter will focus on the trial process, starting with the preparatory hearing and concluding with sentencing. The cases in which international crimes have been tried at the Crown Court to date, have been heard by juries who have reached a verdict on the facts[747] and have been directed on the applicable law by the presiding Crown Court judge.[748] A trial involving international crimes at the Crown Court operates in the same way as any other serious criminal trial and is governed by domestic rules of criminal procedure and evidence. It is important that anyone involved in representing and advising individuals charged with international crimes understands the rules of procedure and evidence applicable to Crown Court proceedings. Procedure in the Crown Court is, of course, very different to practice and procedure before international courts and tribunals, which have their own procedural rules and in which cases are heard by panels of judges.

Preparatory hearings

A preparatory hearing will almost certainly be held in the Crown Court in relation to a trial for international crimes. Section 29 of the Criminal Procedure and Investigations Act 1996 ("CPIA") enables a Crown Court judge to order a preparatory hearing in complex, serious and potentially

[747] The trial of Kumar Lama at the Central Criminal Court involved allegations arising from the civil war in Nepal. The jury were unable to reach a decision in relation to the allegations made by Janak Raut (the first of the two complainants in the case) but the CPS did not seek a re-trial.

[748] It is now regular practice in the Crown Court for the judge to provide the jury with a *"Route to Verdict"*, setting out the questions that must be addressed and answered by the jury in order to decide the case on the facts and according to the law.

lengthy cases, where there are likely to be substantial benefits from such a hearing. Section 30 CPIA states that where a judge orders a preparatory hearing, the trial shall start with that hearing and that arraignment (the process whereby the defendant enters their plea) shall take place at the start of the hearing, unless it had already taken place.

During a preparatory hearing the judge can make rulings on any question relating to the admissibility of evidence, or any other question relating to the case.[749] The judge may also order the prosecution to provide the court and the defence with a written case statement addressing: the principal facts of the case for the prosecution, the witnesses who will speak to those facts, any exhibits relevant to those facts and any proposition of law on which the prosecutor proposes to rely.[750] The defence then has an opportunity to address any of the matters raised by the prosecution in the written case statement.[751]

The preparatory hearing provides an opportunity for the defence to make initial legal challenges in relation to potentially determinative issues relating to the jurisdiction of the Crown Court to hear the case against the accused. The CPIA provides that an appeal lies to the Court of Appeal from any ruling of a judge in relation to any question relating to the admissibility of evidence, or any other question relating to the case,[752] either with leave of the judge, or with leave of the Court of Appeal, and that a further appeal may be made to the Supreme Court.[753]

There have been three cases under section 134 CJA 1998 in the Crown Court to date. Two have resulted in appellate litigation about jurisdictional issues during the course of preparatory hearings.

---

749 CPIA, section 31(3).

750 CPIA, sections 4-5.

751 CPIA, section 6.

752 CPIA, section 31(3).

753 CPIA, section 36.

R v. Kumar Lama

R v. Lama (Kumar) [2017] Q.B. 1171

Kumar Lama was a Colonel in the Nepalese army. He was charged with torture under section 134 CJA. Two complainants alleged that they had been tortured by or at the direction of Kumar Lama at an army barracks in Nepal. During the course of a preparatory hearing the defence raised several legal challenges in relation to the Crown Court's jurisdiction to hear the case. The Crown Court judge dismissed the following arguments:

(1) that Colonel Lama was entitled to immunity *ratione materiae* in respect of his *"official conduct"* as a Colonel in the Nepalese army;

(2) that at the time of his arrest, Colonel Lama was entitled to immunity *ratione personae* because he was a Senior Military Liaison Officer with the United Nations Mission in Southern Sudan, which carried the status of an *"expert on mission"* with the UN;

(3) that the rule of double jeopardy / *autrefois convict* precluded Colonel Lama's prosecution because it was argued that he had already been convicted and punished under Nepalese criminal law for the alleged torture of the first complainant, Janak Raut.[754]

The Court of Appeal dismissed all three legal challenges,[755] after which the proceedings returned to the Crown Court and the case proceeded to trial.

[754] *R v. Lama (Kumar)* [2017] Q.B. 1171, at 1178 D-F. Note that (1) and (2) are referred to in chapter six in relation to immunities.

[755] R v. Lama (Kumar) [2017] Q.B. 1171, at 1220 C.

R v Agnes Taylor

R v. TRA [2019] UKSC 51.

The case against Agnes Taylor related to allegations under section 134 CJA said to have arisen during the first Liberian civil war. The prosecution case was that Agnes Taylor had been responsible for certain crimes committed by the rebel group, the National Patriotic Front of Liberia ("NPFL") at the beginning of the war. During the course of a preparatory hearing an important jurisdictional issue arose, which was litigated all the way up to the Supreme Court (this is addressed in detail in the chapter on *Torture*). In a nutshell, the Supreme Court ruled that pursuant to section 134 CJA a *"person acting in an official capacity"* was not limited to persons acting on behalf of a government and could include persons acting on behalf of groups exercising governmental functions;[756] which could include a rebel group seeking to overthrow a government, in circumstances where they exercised governmental functions and authority. However, when the case returned to the Crown Court, the judge ultimately ruled that the trial could not go ahead. There was a lack of sufficient evidence to put before the jury in support of the legal requirement that at the time and location of each alleged offence, the NPFL forces were exercising the functions of government, rather than merely the functions of a rebel group, whose authority and influence could not yet be characterised as *"governmental"*.[757]

It is important to note that during the preparatory hearing there are restrictions on making any report of the proceedings. However, the judge (Crown Court/ Court of Appeal/ Supreme Court) may direct that reporting restrictions do not apply to any specified extent during the preparatory hearing stage. In practice this permits some limited details

---

[756] *R v. TRA* [2019] UKSC 51.

[757] There are a number of media reports about this hearing. See for example: https://www.bbc.co.uk/news/uk-50685426

about the charges against the accused to be reported by the press.[758] Indeed, this is what happened in the case against Agnes Taylor, where the Crown Court judge permitted the press to report some short summaries about the crimes that had been alleged in the indictment.[759]

Interpreters

The likely need for a pool of interpreters during the lifetime of the case is addressed in the chapter six. During the trial itself the defendant may need, or choose, to have an interpreter. The Court has a legal obligation to provide an interpreter for the defendant during the trial.[760] The prosecution witnesses are likely to require an interpreter and where there are a number of prosecution witnesses, all of whom require an interpreter, it is best if there are several interpreters who can be rotated during the witnesses evidence. The CPS has the legal obligation of ensuring that interpreters are booked for the trial.[761] Defence representatives must book interpreters for any defence witnesses called during the trial.[762] It is important to ensure that any interpreters who are involved in the trial have the adequate level of skill and ability and knowledge of the language in question, including any relevant dialects.[763] In the case in relation to Colonel Kumar Lama, an initial trial had to be abandoned during the course of one of the complainant's evidence because of problems with the

---

758 CPIA, section 37.

759 See for example, the link to the BBC report, *ibid.*, which summarised some of the charges against Agnes Taylor pursuant to a reporting restrictions order made by the Crown Court judge.

760 National Agreement on the Use of Interpreters, Translators and Language Professionals in Investigations and Proceedings within the Criminal Justice System, as revised 2007 (the "National Agreement") at para. 4.5.

761 National Agreement, para. 4.6.

762 National Agreement, para. 4.7. Note that para. 4.7.3 provides that the Court is responsible for the payment of interpreting of interpreting for defence witnesses at court.

763 See, the details set out about the provisions in the National Agreement in the footnotes to the previous Chapter, in the section about interpreters.

interpreter who had been booked and difficulties obtaining a suitable replacement, owing to the small number of interpreters with the requisite UK qualification.[764] Thus, this is a very important practical consideration, which the parties in conjunction with the court should turn their minds to early in the proceedings.

Special measures

In trials before international courts and tribunals *"protective measures"* may be granted to witnesses and victims who are at risk by virtue of giving evidence in the proceedings. Protective measures may be granted both in and beyond the courtroom.[765] The latter can extend to security arrangements, such as moving the witness and their family either temporarily, or as a last resort by permanently relocating a witness and their family. The former can include measures that apply while the witness gives their evidence in the courtroom, such as the use of a pseudonym, or face / voice distortion. Proceedings may also be conducted in private, or closed sessions, where necessary to protect the witness' identity, or that of other individuals who are at risk as a result of the witness' evidence.

In proceedings before the Crown Court similar measures to the courtroom *"protective measures"* are available under the under the Youth Justice and Criminal Evidence Act 1999 ("YJCEA") and are referred to as *"special measures"*.[766] Special measures under the YJCEA are available

764 For reports about this, see: https://www.bbc.co.uk/news/uk-england-sussex-31932371 and https://www.reuters.com/article/uk-britain-nepal-torture/london-court-delays-torture-trial-of-nepali-army-officer-idUKKBN0ME1CV20150318

765 See for example the following page of the ICC website which provides information about witnesses in trials before the ICC: https://www.icc-cpi.int/about/witnesses

766 The YJCEA is available at: https://www.legislation.gov.uk/ukpga/1999/23/contents. A useful guide to special measures is available on the CPS website at: https://www.cps.gov.uk/legal-guidance/special-measures . Section 57, ICCA expressly extends the protections offered under the YJCEA to proceedings under the ICCA, as well as protections

to prosecution and defence witnesses, but not to the defendant. An application has to be made for special measures and granting special measures is at the discretion of the trial judge. Special measures are available for vulnerable or intimidated witnesses which are defined in sections 16 and 17 YJCEA, respectively. The special measures available to vulnerable and intimidated witnesses include: the use of screens to shield the witness from the defendant,[767] the use of a live link[768] which enables the witness to give evidence during the trial from outside the courtroom, giving evidence in private,[769] the removal of wigs and gowns,[770] giving evidence-in-chief through a visual recorded interview,[771] and pre-trial visual recorded cross-examination or re-examination,[772] examination of the witness through an intermediary,[773] and giving evidence with the use of certain aids to communication.[774] A combination of special measures may be granted. The purpose of special measures is to help witnesses to give their best evidence and in considering an application for special measures the judge is required to consider whether the special measures will *"maximise the quality of the evidence"*.[775] In practice, it may be that evidence of a medical professional would assist in an application for special measures, which could specifically address issues such as post-traumatic stress disorder and

---

under the Sexual Offences (Amendment) Act 1976 and 1992 and the Sexual Offences (Protected Material) Act 1997.

Section 23 YJCEA.

768 Section 24 YJCEA.

769 Section 25 YJCEA.

770 Section 26, YJCEA.

771 Section 27, YJCEA and see also section 103 of the Coroners and Justice Act 2009.

772 Section 28, YJCEA.

773 Section 29, YJCEA.

774 Section 30, YJCEA.

775 Section 19, YJCEA and see also the Criminal Procedure Rules 18.8-18.13, 18.23-18.26 and 22.7).

whether and how any special measures available under the YJCEA could help the witness to give their best evidence at trial.

Attendance at court and remote attendance

An important consideration in cases involving international crimes is whether witnesses, be they prosecution or defence, will give evidence in the court room, or via live link from another country. [776] That could be their country or residence, or a third country; if it is not safe or not possible for them to give evidence from their country of residence. Where is it anticipated that evidence will be given via live link, an application will need to the made to the trial judge.[777]

Practical considerations in relation to live link evidence from abroad include:

- Where will the witness be physically located when they give their evidence? For example, arrangements may be made for the witness to give evidence from a courtroom in the witnesses' country of residence. If it is not possible, or safe for the witness to give evidence in their country of residence, is it possible to arrange for them to give evidence from an embassy in a third country?

- What time the evidence will be heard. Given that there will be a time difference between the trial day at the Crown Court and the time in the country the witness is in, is it necessary to request that the Court sit *"Maxwell hours"*?

---

[776] See section 32 of the Criminal Justice Act 1988.

[777] The application should be made pursuant to the CPRs 18.3-18.24. The link to the application form to apply for a witness to give evidence by live link is available at: https://www.gov.uk/government/publications/application-for-a-witness-to-give-evidence-by-live-link

- Ensuring that the technology for the remote link is reliable – a test should be run before the witness gives evidence.

- Who will administer the oath?[778] Will this be done by a legal official sitting with the witness abroad, or by the judges' clerk in the Crown Court?

- Is a request for mutual legal assistance ("MLA") necessary to facilitate the logistics of where, when and how the witness will provide their evidence to the Court?

Admissions (agreed facts)

As in any criminal trial in the Crown Court, a series of admissions can be agreed between the prosecution and the defence and can be read to the jury during the trial.[779] The use of admissions during a trial involving international crimes may be a particularly helpful way of setting out for the jury important background facts about the country where the alleged offence occurred (including about its history, people and geography) and the historical development of any conflict situation (including, for example, about its duration, geographical focus and the warring parties).

Witnesses

In a trial involving international crimes the following types of witnesses are likely to give evidence as part of the prosecution case:

- Crime-base witnesses – these are witnesses who give evidence about the underlying offence/s that is/are alleged to have taken place and will usually either be victims, or, eyewitnesses to the crimes.

---

[778] Note section 32(3) of the Criminal Justice Act 1988, which refers to the oath.

[779] See section 10, Criminal Justice Act 1967.

- Witnesses who provide contextual evidence – these are witnesses who give evidence about the conflict, or the contextual circumstances of the alleged crimes. This type of evidence could include about the timing, whereabouts and activities of warring factions. Such witnesses could be introduced from a variety of witnesses, including for example: local or international journalists, or staff from NGOs who were on the ground in country at the time of the alleged crimes or relevant events.

- Insider-witnesses – these are witnesses who have a direct connection with the defendant. These witnesses will be most relevant where the defendant is not alleged to have directly participated in alleged offence, but where secondary liability is in play i.e. where the defendant is alleged to have engaged in conduct ancillary to torture, war crimes, CAH, or genocide, including command / superior responsibility. For example, the defendant could be a military commander and the insider witness a soldier under their command who committed the offence in question,[780] or a soldier who was present when the defendant gave the order for the crime to be committed.

- Expert witnesses – expert witnesses may be called about a variety of topics: from medical issues, to forensics issues, to ballistics, issues about the history and development of the conflict, as well as about the history, geography and demographics of the country.

Witness familiarisation versus witness coaching

In proceedings at the Crown Court, familiarising a lay witness before giving evidence during the trial is permitted, but witness training, or coaching is strictly prohibited. In the context of proceedings before

780 In the international context, courts and tribunals have sometimes relied on, so called *"iron letters"* to promise that an insider witness will not be prosecuted before the court or tribunal itself after giving evidence about crimes under the court or tribunal's jurisdiction, that they committed at the behest of the accused. The issue is yet to be fully explored in the domestic context.

international courts and tribunals, lawyers sometimes conduct extensive meetings with witnesses about their evidence and in preparation for giving evidence at trial. This does not happen in preparation for a criminal trial in England and Wales, no matter how serious. The witnesses' evidence will have been taken by police officers, usually by way of a video recorded interview and put into a statement, which the witness will have had an opportunity to check and amend. If the prosecution lawyers want the witness to clarify any issues or to address further issues, they will advise the police to take a further statement, or to conduct an additional vide-recorded interview. In preparation for the trial, prosecution counsel will meet with witnesses but any discussion will be comparatively limited and is guided by relevant criminal practice directions and protocol.[781]

Expert witnesses

It is important to ensure that expert witnesses are familiar with their duties to the court. This should be set out in their witness statement along with a statement of truth. Although an expert is instructed by a party to the proceedings, the expert must help the court to achieve the overriding objective to deal with cases justly, by providing an opinion which is objective and unbiased and within their area of expertise.[782] Part 19 is the relevant part of the Criminal Procedure Rules in relation to expert evidence.

The use of expert witnesses to provide evidence about the historical and political context in which international crimes charged in a trial before the Crown Court was specifically considered and encouraged by the Court of Appeal in the case against *Anthony Sawoniuk*.[783]

---

[781] Regarding the rationale behind the distinction in domestic law between witness training or coaching and witness familiarisation, see *Archbold Criminal Pleading, Evidence and Practice* 2023 ed. 8-222.

[782] CPR 2020, as amended October 2021, Part 19.2 titled, *"Expert's duty to the court"*.

[783] *R. v Sawoniuk* [2000] 2 Cr. App. R 220 ("*Sawoniuk*").

R. v Sawoniuk [2000] 2 Cr. App. R 220

Anthony *Sawoniuk* had been convicted by a jury at the Central Criminal Court of two charges of murder under the War Crimes Act 1991. Specifically, he was convicted of the murders in 1942 of two Jewish females, who eye-witnesses said he had shot and killed during a search and kill operation carried out by the local police in Domachevo, Belorussia, which at that time was a town under German occupation.[784] Expert evidence had been called at the trial to describe Nazi policy towards the Jews and about how that policy was carried out in Domachevo.[785]

In addressing challenges made by the defence to the admission of evidence, including the expert evidence, Lord Bingham C.J., delivering the judgment of the Court of Appeal, emphasised that *"criminal charges cannot be fairly judged in a factual vacuum"* and that *"in order to make a rational assessment of evidence directly relating to a charge it may often be necessary for a jury to receive evidence describing, perhaps in some detail, the context and circumstances in which the offences are said to have been committed".*[786] Lord Bingham C.J. quoted from an earlier judgment of the Court of Appeal:

> *"Where it is necessary to place before the jury evidence of part of a continual background of history relevant to the offence charged in the indictment and without the totality of which the account placed before the jury would be incomplete or incomprehensible, then the fact that the whole account involves including evidence establishing the commission of an offence with which the accused is not charged is not of itself ground for excluding the evidence".*[787]

---

784 *Sawoniuk,* p.220.

785 See *Sawoniuk,* p.225 for a description of the expert evidence that was called at the trial.

786 *Sawoniuk,* p.234.

787 *Sawoniuk,* p.234.

In relation to the appeal on *Sawoniuk,* Lord Bingham C.J. explained that:

> *"This approach seems to us of particular significance in an exceptional case such as the present in which a London jury was asked to assess the significance of evidence relating to events in a country quite unlike our own, taking place a very long time ago in the extraordinary conditions prevailing in 1941 to 1942".*[788]

Sawoniuk therefore provides good authority to support the use of expert evidence to establish facts about the conflict, including the relevant historical and political situation in which the international crimes are alleged to have taken place.

Bad character evidence

It is important to be aware that evidence, not only of a defendant's *"bad character"* but also a prosecution or defence witnesses' *"bad character"* may be introduced during the trial. *"Bad character evidence"* is widely defined, as *"evidence of, or a disposition towards, misconduct on his part, other than evidence which (a) has to do with the alleged facts of the offence with which the defendant is charged, or (b) is evidence of misconduct in connection with the investigation or prosecution of that offence".*[789] There are specific rules of procedure governing the timing and content of applications to introduce evidence of bad character,[790] as well as the body of caselaw in relation to such applications. Legal representatives should make potential witnesses aware that they may be asked about past misconduct at the trial, should the judge decide to admit such evidence.

---

[788] *Sawoniuk,* p.234 – 235.

[789] Section 98 of the Criminal Justice Act 2003.

[790] Criminal Procedure Rules 2020, as amended October 2021, Part 21.

Hearsay

Hearsay evidence given by a witness is generally not admissible in a Crown Court trial. However, there are exceptions to this general rule. Section 114 of the Criminal Justice Act 2003 provides various *"gateways"* for the admissibility of hearsay evidence. Where a party wants to introduce hearsay evidence they will need to make an application to do so pursuant to the Criminal Procedure Rules.[791] The application may be agreed or contested by the opposing party. Section 114 sets out the test that the judge must apply to determine whether or not to admit hearsay evidence.[792] As with bad character evidence, there are specific rules of procedure governing the timing and content of applications to introduce the hearsay evidence, as well as a body of caselaw in relation to such applications.

Prior statements

Where witnesses have given statements and / or evidence before other courts, tribunals, or truth commissions, such statements and/ or testimony may be put to the witness during the trial at the Crown Court. Specifically, if the witness has made any prior inconsistent statement before another court, tribunal or truth commission, they may be cross-examined about this by counsel at the trial. Witnesses can also be cross-examined not only on prior statements given in legal proceedings but in relation to previous statements made in other contexts. An example arises in the case of *Zardad.*

---

[791] CPR 2020, as amended October 2021, Part 20.

[792] Criminal Justice Act 2003, section 114.

R v Faryadi Sawar Zardad [2007] EWCA Crim 279.

In *Zardad*, the prosecution called evidence from a journalist called Stefan Smith. Mr Smith gave evidence that he had seen the defendant present at a checkpoint where the alleged crimes were said to have taken place. Mr Smith said that he had been on a bus which was stopped at the checkpoint, that he was made to get off the bus along with women and children, but that the men on the bus had to remain and that soldiers went into the bus and fired into it with Kalashnikovs. Mr Smith had made a statement to another well-known journalist, Mr Sandy Gall, some eight months after the event and at trial Mr Smith was cross-examined about inconsistencies between his accounts. The sole ground of appeal concerned a direction that the trial judge had given about how the jury should approach the previous inconsistent statement.[793]

The defendant's case

A defendant in proceedings before the Crown Court must provide a *"defence case statement"* (or *"defence statement"*) where the prosecutor has provided, or, purported to provide initial disclosure.[794] The defence case statement should set out:

- The nature of the defence, including any particular defences upon which the defendant proposes to rely;
- Set out the matters of fact with which the defendant takes issues with the prosecution;

[793] *R v Faryadi Sawar Zardad* [2007] EWCA Crim 279.

[794] CPIA, section 5.

- Set out the matters of fact on which the defendant intends to rely in support of their defence;

- Indicate any points of law (including points about the admissibility of evidence, or abuse of process) which they intend to raise, as well as any case law relied upon in support;[795]

- Where a defence of alibi is raised there are particular statutory provisions that apply in relation to providing details of the alibi.[796]

The defendant can elect whether or not to give evidence. However, even where the defendant does not give evidence, they must provide a defence statement, explaining that they call upon the prosecution to prove the case and do not advance a positive case.[797]

If the defence wish to call witnesses they need to give notification of their intention to call defence witnesses,[798] and if they intend to rely on any expert witnesses notification must be provided of the of names of expert/s instructed.[799]

In view of the requirements for the defence case statement, where legal issues are to be raised during a preparatory hearing these should initially be set out in the deference case statement.

Any particular defences that the defendant relies on should also be set out in the defence case statement. There is no appellate caselaw in relation to any particular defences in the context of a trial for international crimes

---

795 CPIA, section 6A (1). There are time limits in relation to the provision of the defence statements, as well as procedural rules and there is body of practice and procedure, which can be found in the relevant criminal practitioners' handbooks.

796 CPIA, section 6A (2).

797 See *Archbold Criminal Pleading, Evidence and Practice* 2023ed. 12-65.

798 CPIA, section 6C.

799 CPIA, section 6D.

before the Crown Court. However, given that there are differences between defences potentially available in international proceedings before the ICC and in proceedings for international crimes before the Crown Court this is an area in which there may be litigation in the future. Notably, before the ICC defences such as duress[800] and superior orders[801] are potentially available, but duress is not available as a defence under domestic criminal law[802] and the ICCA is silent in relation to any defence of superior orders, which may be available under customary international law in relation to war crimes.[803] Additionally, the scope of self-defence as a defence to international crimes may also prove different under ICL and domestic law.[804] Further, there may be a defence under domestic law in relation to certain reprisals based on a potential customary international law defence.[805]

Adverse inferences may be drawn against a defendant where at trial they put forward a defence that they have not referred to in their defence statement, or, is different to any defence referred to in the defence

---

800 ICC Statute, Article 31(d).

801 ICC Statute, Article 33.

802 At least in respect of crimes involving murder in view of *R. v Howe* [1987] A.C. 417.

803 See Robert Cryer and Olympia Bekou, *"International Crimes and ICC Cooperation in England and Wales"*, , Journal of International Criminal Justice 5 (2007) 441-459 at 447 and 449 and Robert Cryer, *"Implementation of the International Criminal Court Statute in England and Wales"*, I.C.L.Q., 733-747 at 740-741. Also, cross-reference chapter 2 in relation to Torture, noting that under UNCAT Article 2(3) there is no defence of superior orders in relation to a crime of torture.

804 Note that self-defence is referred to in the ICC Statute in Article 31(c) but as the general law of England and Wales, rather than the general part of ICC law governs defences, the scope may be different. See Dr Kate Grady, *"International crimes in the courts of England and Wales"*, Crim. L.R. 693, at 703 and Robert Cryer, *"Implementation of the International Criminal Court Statute in England and Wales"*, I.C.L.Q., 733-747 at 740.

805 See Robert Cryer, *"Implementation of the International Criminal Court Statute in England and Wales"*, I.C.L.Q., 733-747 at 741-742, giving the example of a defendant potentially seeking to use such a defence in relation to a charge of intentionally directing attacks against a civilian population or civilian objects (contrary to ICC Statute Article 8(2)(b)(i) and (ii)).

statement.[806] Adverse inferences may also be drawn where at trial the defendant relies on a matter (or matters) which should have been included in the defence statement but was not, or relies on an alibi who was not previously notified in the defence statement.[807]

Beyond the trial – sentencing and appellate proceedings

Sentencing

The potential sentences that may be imposed by a judge in relation to the different international crimes are set out in the relevant legislation: the ICCA, the GCA 1957 and the CJA 1988.

The sentencing provisions under the ICCA are somewhat convoluted.[808] In summary:

(1) For all ICCA offences committed after 1 September 2001, section 53(6) ICCA provides that the maximum sentence for genocide, CAH or war crimes is <u>30 years imprisonment</u>.[809]

(2) For an offence of genocide, in as far as it was already a crime under domestic law before 1 September 2001, and for grave breaches of the Geneva Convention, committed after 1 January 1991 and before 1 September 2001, the maximum penalty is <u>14 years imprisonment</u>.[810]

---

806 CPIA, section 11.

807 CPIA, section 11.

808 See section 65B ICCA, *'Modification of penalties: provision supplemental to section 65A'*, which reflects amendments made to the ICCA by the Coroners and Justice Act 2009.

809 This is the maximum offence whether the conviction is for committing the substantive offence, or for conduct ancillary to the commission of the offence.

810 ICCA, section 65B. The Explanatory Note to the Coroners and Justice Act, paragraph 401 explains that *"for domestic genocide and grave breaches of the Geneva Conventions…both of which were already offences in domestic law in 1991, a*

(3) For CAH and war crimes (not including grave breaches of the Geneva Conventions) committed on or after 1 January 1991 but before 1 September 2001 and in relation to which it can be established that the crimes existed in international law at the time of their commission, the maximum offence is 30 years imprisonment.[811]

(4) However, where a defendant is convicted of any offence (genocide, CAH or war crimes) involving murder,[812] they shall be dealt with as they would be for a domestic murder conviction, meaning that the judge will impose a mandatory life sentence.

The sentencing provisions under the ICCA are similar to those set out in the GCA 1957. Under that Act, a person convicted of a grave breach of the Geneva Conventions faces a maximum sentence of 30 years imprisonment, where the offence was committed on or after 1 September 2001, but where the offence was committed prior to that date, the maximum sentence would be 14 years imprisonment.[813] As under the ICCA, where a person is convicted for an offence involving murder they

maximum penalty of 14 years' imprisonment applies instead of 30 years' (other than where murder is involved). This provision ensures that a higher penalty cannot be imposed for such offences than existed in domestic law at the time of their commission and consequently ensures compliance with Article 7 of the ECHR". See: https://www.legislation.gov.uk/ukpga/2009/25/notes/division/5/1/2/3/1 The use of "domestic genocide" should be noted because the Genocide Act 1969 (repealed as a result of the enactment of the ICCA) created the offence of genocide when committed in England and Wales, rather than an extraterritorial offence – note the reference to the Genocide Act 1969 in the first Chapter. Presumably therefore this means that for an extra-territorial offence of genocide committed between 1 January 1991 and before 1 September 2001, the maximum sentence would be 30 years imprisonment, rather than 14 years.

811 Section 65B *'Modification of penalties: provision supplemental to section 65A'.*

812 ICCA section 53(5), this includes a conviction for conduct ancillary to the commission of an offence of murder.

813 GCA 1957 1A(6) as amended by the ICCA, Part 5 section 70(2).

shall be dealt with as they would be for a domestic murder conviction, so a life sentence will be imposed.[814]

In relation to a conviction for torture under section 134 of the CJA 1988 the defendant will be liable to a sentence of life imprisonment.[815]

In relation to the two cases before the Crown Court that have thus far resulted in convictions, the following sentences were imposed:

- Faryadi Zardad, 20 years imprisonment for conspiracy to torture (under section 134 the CJA 1988) and conspiracy to take hostages;[816]

- Anthony Sawoniuk, life imprisonment for two counts of murder under the WCA 1991.[817]

Given that there have only been two convictions in the Crown Court to date, and as yet no cases at all under the ICCA, the sentencing authorities specific to international crimes in the Crown Court are nascent. However, in future cases it is likely that the trial judge may be assisted both by relevant domestic cases and international case law.

The sentencing hearing provides an opportunity for both the defendant (through their advocate) and the victims of their crimes (through victim personal statements) to make representations to the judge. The role of victims in a Crown Court trial is much more limited than the role of victims in proceedings before the ICC. It is only at the sentencing stage that victim personal statements may be heard from the victims of the international crimes, providing an opportunity for them to explain how they have been affected by the crimes. Victim personal statements will usually be read out during the sentencing hearing and the judge will take

---

814 GCA 1957 1A(5).

815 CJA 1998 section 134(6).

816 *R. v. Faryadi Sarwar Zardad* [2007] EWCA Crim 279.

817 As record in the appeal against conviction in the Court of Appeal judgment: *R v. Anthony Sawoniuk* [2000] 2 Cr.App.R 220.

these statements into account along with all the other evidence when deciding upon the sentence.[818]

Appellate proceedings

As with any other criminal cases before the Crown Court, a convicted defendant can appeal against their conviction and / or their sentence to the Court of Appeal, Criminal Division. Indeed, in the two ICL cases which resulted in convictions in the Crown Court, *Zardad* and *Sawoniuk*, both defendants appealed to the Court of Appeal and both appeals were dismissed.[819]

818 There is guidance online both about making a statement and for police officers, investigators and criminal justice practitioners. See: https://www.gov.uk/government/publications/victim-personal-statement

819 See the references in the footnotes just above.

MORE BOOKS BY LAW BRIEF PUBLISHING

A selection of our other titles available now:-

'A Practical Guide to Parental Alienation in Private and Public Law Children Cases' by Sam King QC & Frankie Shama
'Contested Heritage – Removing Art from Land and Historic Buildings' by Richard Harwood QC, Catherine Dobson, David Sawtell
'The Limits of Separate Legal Personality: When Those Running a Company Can Be Held Personally Liable for Losses Caused to Third Parties Outside of the Company' by Dr Mike Wilkinson
'A Practical Guide to Transgender Law' by Robin Moira White & Nicola Newbegin
'Artificial Intelligence – The Practical Legal Issues (2nd Edition)' by John Buyers
'A Practical Guide to Residential Freehold Conveyancing' by Lorraine Richardson
'A Practical Guide to Pensions on Divorce for Lawyers' by Bryan Scant
'A Practical Guide to Challenging Sham Marriage Allegations in Immigration Law' by Priya Solanki
'A Practical Guide to Legal Rights in Scotland' by Sarah-Jane Macdonald
'A Practical Guide to New Build Conveyancing' by Paul Sams & Rebecca East
'A Practical Guide to Defending Barristers in Disciplinary Cases' by Marc Beaumont
'A Practical Guide to Inherited Wealth on Divorce' by Hayley Trim
'A Practical Guide to Practice Direction 12J and Domestic Abuse in Private Law Children Proceedings' by Rebecca Cross & Malvika Jaganmohan
'A Practical Guide to Confiscation and Restraint' by Narita Bahra QC, John Carl Townsend, David Winch
'A Practical Guide to the Law of Forests in Scotland' by Philip Buchan
'A Practical Guide to Health and Medical Cases in Immigration Law' by Rebecca Chapman & Miranda Butler
'A Practical Guide to Bad Character Evidence for Criminal Practitioners by Aparna Rao
'A Practical Guide to Extradition Law post-Brexit' by Myles Grandison et al

'A Practical Guide to Hoarding and Mental Health for Housing Lawyers' by Rachel Coyle
'A Practical Guide to Psychiatric Claims in Personal Injury – 2nd Edition' by Liam Ryan
'Stephens on Contractual Indemnities' by Richard Stephens
'A Practical Guide to the EU Succession Regulation' by Richard Frimston
'A Practical Guide to Solicitor and Client Costs – 2nd Edition' by Robin Dunne
'Constructive Dismissal – Practice Pointers and Principles' by Benjimin Burgher
'A Practical Guide to Religion and Belief Discrimination Claims in the Workplace' by Kashif Ali
'A Practical Guide to the Law of Medical Treatment Decisions' by Ben Troke
'Fundamental Dishonesty and QOCS in Personal Injury Proceedings: Law and Practice' by Jake Rowley
'A Practical Guide to the Law in Relation to School Exclusions' by Charlotte Hadfield & Alice de Coverley
'A Practical Guide to Divorce for the Silver Separators' by Karin Walker
'The Right to be Forgotten – The Law and Practical Issues' by Melissa Stock
'A Practical Guide to Planning Law and Rights of Way in National Parks, the Broads and AONBs' by James Maurici QC, James Neill et al
'A Practical Guide to Election Law' by Tom Tabori
'A Practical Guide to the Law in Relation to Surrogacy' by Andrew Powell
'A Practical Guide to Claims Arising from Fatal Accidents – 2nd Edition' by James Patience
'A Practical Guide to the Ownership of Employee Inventions – From Entitlement to Compensation' by James Tumbridge & Ashley Roughton
'A Practical Guide to Asbestos Claims' by Jonathan Owen & Gareth McAloon
'A Practical Guide to Stamp Duty Land Tax in England and Northern Ireland' by Suzanne O'Hara
'A Practical Guide to the Law of Farming Partnerships' by Philip Whitcomb
'Covid-19, Homeworking and the Law – The Essential Guide to Employment and GDPR Issues' by Forbes Solicitors
'Covid-19 and Criminal Law – The Essential Guide' by Ramya Nagesh
'Covid-19 and Family Law in England and Wales – The Essential Guide' by Safda Mahmood

'A Practical Guide to the Law of Unlawful Eviction and Harassment – 2nd Edition' by Stephanie Lovegrove
'Covid-19, Brexit and the Law of Commercial Leases – The Essential Guide' by Mark Shelton
'A Practical Guide to Costs in Personal Injury Claims – 2nd Edition' by Matthew Hoe
'A Practical Guide to the General Data Protection Regulation (GDPR) – 2nd Edition' by Keith Markham
'Ellis on Credit Hire – Sixth Edition' by Aidan Ellis & Tim Kevan
'A Practical Guide to Working with Litigants in Person and McKenzie Friends in Family Cases' by Stuart Barlow
'Protecting Unregistered Brands: A Practical Guide to the Law of Passing Off' by Lorna Brazell
'A Practical Guide to Secondary Liability and Joint Enterprise Post-Jogee' by Joanne Cecil & James Mehigan
'A Practical Guide to the Pre-Action RTA Claims Protocol for Personal Injury Lawyers' by Antonia Ford
'A Practical Guide to Neighbour Disputes and the Law' by Alexander Walsh
'A Practical Guide to Forfeiture of Leases' by Mark Shelton
'A Practical Guide to Coercive Control for Legal Practitioners and Victims' by Rachel Horman
'A Practical Guide to Rights Over Airspace and Subsoil' by Daniel Gatty
'Tackling Disclosure in the Criminal Courts – A Practitioner's Guide' by Narita Bahra QC & Don Ramble
'A Practical Guide to the Law of Driverless Cars – Second Edition' by Alex Glassbrook, Emma Northey & Scarlett Milligan
'A Practical Guide to TOLATA Claims' by Greg Williams
'A Practical Guide to Elderly Law – 2nd Edition' by Justin Patten
'A Practical Guide to Responding to Housing Disrepair and Unfitness Claims' by Iain Wightwick
'A Practical Guide to the Construction and Rectification of Wills and Trust Instruments' by Edward Hewitt
'A Practical Guide to the Law of Bullying and Harassment in the Workplace' by Philip Hyland
'How to Be a Freelance Solicitor: A Practical Guide to the SRA-Regulated Freelance Solicitor Model' by Paul Bennett

'A Practical Guide to Prison Injury Claims' by Malcolm Johnson
'A Practical Guide to the Small Claims Track - 2nd Edition' by Dominic Bright
'A Practical Guide to Advising Clients at the Police Station' by Colin Stephen McKeown-Beaumont
'A Practical Guide to Antisocial Behaviour Injunctions' by Iain Wightwick
'Practical Mediation: A Guide for Mediators, Advocates, Advisers, Lawyers, and Students in Civil, Commercial, Business, Property, Workplace, and Employment Cases' by Jonathan Dingle with John Sephton
'The Mini-Pupillage Workbook' by David Boyle
'A Practical Guide to Crofting Law' by Brian Inkster
'A Practical Guide to Spousal Maintenance' by Liz Cowell
'A Practical Guide to the Law of Domain Names and Cybersquatting' by Andrew Clemson
'A Practical Guide to the Law of Gender Pay Gap Reporting' by Harini Iyengar
'A Practical Guide to the Rights of Grandparents in Children Proceedings' by Stuart Barlow
'NHS Whistleblowing and the Law' by Joseph England
'Employment Law and the Gig Economy' by Nigel Mackay & Annie Powell
'A Practical Guide to Noise Induced Hearing Loss (NIHL) Claims' by Andrew Mckie, Ian Skeate, Gareth McAloon
'An Introduction to Beauty Negligence Claims – A Practical Guide for the Personal Injury Practitioner' by Greg Almond
'Intercompany Agreements for Transfer Pricing Compliance' by Paul Sutton
'Zen and the Art of Mediation' by Martin Plowman
'A Practical Guide to the SRA Principles, Individual and Law Firm Codes of Conduct 2019 – What Every Law Firm Needs to Know' by Paul Bennett
'A Practical Guide to Adoption for Family Lawyers' by Graham Pegg
'A Practical Guide to Industrial Disease Claims' by Andrew Mckie & Ian Skeate
'A Practical Guide to Redundancy' by Philip Hyland
'A Practical Guide to Vicarious Liability' by Mariel Irvine
'A Practical Guide to Applications for Landlord's Consent and Variation of Leases' by Mark Shelton
'A Practical Guide to Relief from Sanctions Post-Mitchell and Denton' by Peter Causton

'A Practical Guide to Equity Release for Advisors' by Paul Sams
'A Practical Guide to Financial Services Claims' by Chris Hegarty
'The Law of Houses in Multiple Occupation: A Practical Guide to HMO Proceedings' by Julian Hunt
'Occupiers, Highways and Defective Premises Claims: A Practical Guide Post-Jackson – 2nd Edition' by Andrew Mckie
'A Practical Guide to Financial Ombudsman Service Claims' by Adam Temple & Robert Scrivenor
'A Practical Guide to Advising Schools on Employment Law' by Jonathan Holden
'A Practical Guide to Running Housing Disrepair and Cavity Wall Claims: 2nd Edition' by Andrew Mckie & Ian Skeate
'A Practical Guide to Holiday Sickness Claims – 2nd Edition' by Andrew Mckie & Ian Skeate
'Arguments and Tactics for Personal Injury and Clinical Negligence Claims' by Dorian Williams
'A Practical Guide to Drone Law' by Rufus Ballaster, Andrew Firman, Eleanor Clot
'A Practical Guide to Compliance for Personal Injury Firms Working With Claims Management Companies' by Paul Bennett
'RTA Allegations of Fraud in a Post-Jackson Era: The Handbook – 2nd Edition' by Andrew Mckie
'RTA Personal Injury Claims: A Practical Guide Post-Jackson' by Andrew Mckie
'On Experts: CPR35 for Lawyers and Experts' by David Boyle
'An Introduction to Personal Injury Law' by David Boyle

These books and more are available to order online direct from the publisher at www.lawbriefpublishing.com, where you can also read free sample chapters. For any queries, contact us on 0844 587 2383 or mail@lawbriefpublishing.com.

Our books are also usually in stock at www.amazon.co.uk with free next day delivery for Prime members, and at good legal bookshops such as Wildy & Sons.

We are regularly launching new books in our series of practical day-to-day practitioners' guides. Visit our website and join our free newsletter to be kept informed and to receive special offers, free chapters, etc.

You can also follow us on Twitter at www.twitter.com/lawbriefpub.

www.ingramcontent.com/pod-product-compliance
Lightning Source LLC
LaVergne TN
LVHW052305200926
848481LV00002B/468

* 9 7 8 1 9 1 4 6 0 8 3 4 6 *